THE
MARRIAGE SABBATICAL

THE
MARRIAGE
SABBATICAL

*The Journey That
Brings You Home*

CHERYL JARVIS

PERSEUS PUBLISHING

Cambridge, Massachusetts

Many of the designations used by manufacturers and sellers to distinguish their
products are claimed as trademarks. Where those designations appear in this
book and Perseus Publishing was aware of a trademark claim, the designations
have been printed in initial capital letters.

A CIP catalog record for this book is available from the Library of Congress.
ISBN: 0-7382-0339-4

Perseus Publishing is a member of the Perseus Books Group.

Text design by Heather Hutchison
Set in 11-point Electra by the Perseus Books Group

1 2 3 4 5 6 7 8 9 10—03 02 01
First printing, January 2001

Perseus Publishing books are available at special discounts for bulk purchases in
the United States by corporations, institutions, and other organizations. For
more information, please contact the Special Markets Department at Harper-
Collins Publishers, 10 East 53rd Street, New York, NY 10022, or call
1–212–207–7528.

Find us on the World Wide Web at http://www.perseuspublishing.com

It may be as important to give a place to the individual soul life of one's spouse as to foster closeness and togetherness.

—THOMAS MOORE,
SoulMates

The sign of a good marriage is that everything is debatable and challenged.

—CAROLYN HEILBRUN,
Writing a Woman's Life

Contents

1

INTRODUCTION

I'm sitting at the dining-room table making phone calls, struggling to get a job in a city where creative opportunities are limited. The right side of my neck aches from my prolonged, hunched-over position. A pain shoots its way down my arm. I'm longing for a shoulder rub when the phone rings. It's the senior producer of the television show I worked on before it moved east. The producer who replaced me isn't working out, he says, and her successor can't start for a few months. Will I come to Connecticut to fill in?

By the time I'm off the phone, I've forgotten the pain. I start to feel light-headed as I think about how luxurious it would be to focus on the job without feeling pulled in all directions. Before, when I was at work, I was thinking of home; when I was at home, I was thinking of work, my loyalties divided always. Rushing in late to the office, after negotiating breakfasts and schedules and last-minute school projects, racing out early for baseball games, tennis matches, music lessons, I always had the nagging feeling that the single producers on staff were putting in longer hours, achieving more. I think of the shows I could create if I weren't constantly worrying about who or what I was neglecting. My thoughts meander to living alone for three months, to having Sundays just for me. I fantasize about long walks in the New England countryside. Guilty pleasure suffuses my body like an endorphin high.

At dinner I barely touch my food as I talk excitedly about my opportunity. My husband says little; after years of practicing psychotherapy, he is well trained to listen, well trained not to react. The boys, ten and fourteen, ask a few questions: When would you leave? How long would you be gone? Later that evening, I'm reading in bed, psychologically already airborne, when my younger son walks in, closes the door behind him, and sits on the edge of the bed. "I don't want you to go," he says. "School will be starting then. What if I have a problem? I need you when school starts. You can go another time. Please don't go now." Later, my older son comes in, closes the door, and sits at the same spot on the edge of the bed. Same plea, different reason.

Feelings whirl through me: sureness that I won't accept the offer; dejection, now that my chance to live and work alone for a few months has vanished; elation that my sons need me. But something significant has happened. I have admitted to myself how much I long to go.

I was thirty-eight then. Over the next ten years, I celebrated my twenty-fifth wedding anniversary, sent two boys to college at opposite ends of the country, and navigated through five different jobs. Every time I saw single co-workers take off for Chicago or Los Angeles or New York, I felt a pang for the path not taken. Many of them, I knew, looked at married colleagues and longed for a couple's steady intimacy the way I looked at them and longed for their freedom. Is it just human nature that after fulfilling our desire for one, we yearn for the other? Or is it that we really crave both at once? Each time I helped one of our sons pack—for Outward Bound, for a summer in Oregon, for a semester in Spain—I envied his going away on an adventure by himself. I'd take him to the airport, feeling his life widening, mine narrowing, a sense of time and opportunity slipping away. Somewhere in the goodbyes, amid smiles and hugs and admonitions to call/be careful/stay safe, I'd utter what had become my standard line: "In my next life."

The year I turned forty-eight, something clicked. What next life?

This book was born out of conflict—between loving my husband yet wanting to leave him. No, *needing* to leave him. It wasn't frustration over traditional gender roles. He has been doing the laundry since I spilled bleach on his favorite tennis shirt the first year we were married. It wasn't irritation over masculine deficiencies as depicted in women's magazines. I'm the one who scrambles at the last minute for his birthday gift, I'm the one who drops my clothes all over the bedroom floor, I'm the one who spends hours zapping the remote. He was a feminist when we met, and we had a peer marriage before sociologist Pepper Schwartz coined the phrase. We lead independent lives. We have what some people call "a long leash."

Feeling free at home, however, was not enough. I needed to go away, alone. Not for a week—I'd done that often. Just for a little while. But the yearning felt unnatural, and guilt invaded my body like the arthritis I've developed from years of overexercise. As the guilt deepened, anger flashed: Where was it written that I couldn't take a solo adventure, that because I was married I couldn't take time off, time away, time alone? What did one have to do with the other? And where were these emotions coming from?

I had no answers to these questions because I didn't know any married women who had done what I wanted to do. For the first seventeen years of my marriage I didn't imagine it. Once I imagined it, I couldn't voice it. Growing older, however, meant I came increasingly to believe that if I felt something strongly, there must be other women who felt the same way. I wrote this book to find these women, women who had successfully left home to pursue a dream, women in good marriages who could explain the journey and support me along the way. I wrote this book because I needed answers to my questions. Subconsciously, I needed permission to leave.

I began by confiding my thoughts hesitantly to an older friend, who told me her story. She led me to other women, who told me theirs. And then I came to realize what was missing from our culture: a new narrative for marriage. And when I found the narrative, I discovered the grace within the tension: a way to reconcile my desires for both commitment and freedom, a way to honor both my marriage and myself. Rooted in language that goes back two thousand years, the narrative is contemporary, the model ancient.

The Bible tells us that after God created the heavens and the earth, "he rested on the seventh day from all his work which he had done." And then he blessed the day. Honoring the Sabbath (from *shabbat*, to rest) became one of the Ten Commandments and a distinguishing feature of the Jewish faith. Today, most religions of the world honor periods of rest. The ancient Hebrews extended the principle to agriculture: According to Mosaic law, the land and vineyards were to lie fallow every seventh year "as a Sabbath to the Lord." The belief was that fields could be grazed for only so long without losing nutrients. They needed replenishing. The Hebrews called the respite a "sabbatical year."

Modern interpretations give the word a deeper dimension. Theologians have defined the Sabbath as spirit in the form of time, a day of re-creation or reconnection. One Jewish scholar believes it is intended to be an invigorating experience, focused on human fulfillment. With its theological underpinnings, the concept spread to the secular world: If God needed to rest from the work of creation, then surely mortal men and women needed to rest, too. In 1880, Harvard University became the first American institution to grant sabbaticals to its faculty. While today the practice is most widespread in the teaching profession, sabbaticals can be found in journalism, medicine, law, government, and business. The connotation has remained essentially the same over the last hundred years: time off from daily routines to develop intellectually, focus creatively, renew physically. The parameters, however, have changed considerably. Sabbaticals today are accelerated, shortened, and variable. One college offers them after just three years; another offers faculty development leaves over six-week short terms. Some companies require that sabbaticals be spent on social service. Others urge employees to go after a dream. A paid sabbatical in business typically lasts four to six weeks.

Yet in marriage—one of the world's oldest institutions, one of life's greatest challenges, a relationship which can be as emotionally intense as any job, which even conventional wisdom calls *hard work*—there is no development leave, no ritual rest. It may not be coincidence that in biblical times the land was to lie fallow every seventh year and that the average length of marriage at the time of divorce in this country is 7.4 years, making "the seven-year itch" more than a catchphrase. What would happen if we looked to nature and let our marriages rest for a while in order to regenerate? What would happen if we took time out for an invigorating experience, focused on human fulfillment?

Sabbaticals have actually been taking place in marriage under other guises for centuries. In the Middle Ages, wealthy married women who wanted time alone retreated to convents. In Victorian times, the treatment for hysteria, a psychiatric condition characterized in part by excessive anxiety, was a sea voyage, a long journey, a move from town to country—anything to stimulate the nervous system. Among the prescribed treatments for neurasthenia, a mental disorder characterized by inexplicable exhaustion and irritability, was separation from family and familiar surroundings. Water-cure establishments, sanitariums, and other retreats proliferated during this era.

No wonder these illnesses were considered predominantly female. No wonder they were overdiagnosed. No wonder they were found only in the middle and upper classes, those who could afford a retreat or sea voyage. No wonder these "treatments" usually brought relief. Getting sick was one of the few acceptable ways women could get time for themselves.

Today, many marriages have built-in separations from commuter jobs, travel-dependent professions, military service, and company relocations. When a man gets transferred and his wife waits a year to join him because she's putting the house on the market or when a man takes a few months to follow his wife, who has moved to a new position in another city, whether they are conscious of it or not, the relationship is getting a rest.

But what about couples whose jobs don't provide such opportunities for renewal? What makes a sabbatical an idea worth examining today is our longer life expectancy and its corollary, a longer marriage expectancy. At the turn of the century, few people lived to see all their children grown. Most were dead by fifty. Today at fifty, we have another thirty years to go. At the same time that we're looking at a longer and healthier life span than any other time in history, we're having fewer children and, therefore, spending fewer years raising all of them. We're also living in a society that's changing faster than we are. A world in which people can, or must, reinvent their lives at forty, fifty, and sixty is a world in which marriage for life becomes an increasing challenge. With the rise in gender equality has come another cultural shift: a revolution in marital expectations. How many of us enter marriage expecting our spouse to be our lover, best friend, parenting partner, recreational companion, and spiritual soul mate? That's a lot of psychic weight to place on one relationship—given that nearly half of all couples divorce, more weight than it apparently can bear. A time when many are wondering how to make their marriages thrive over a long stretch of years is a time to examine sabbaticals in marriage not as pathology but as promise.

A marriage sabbatical is as relevant for men as it is for women. The more men I talked with, the more I struggled with focusing only on women's journeys. But while the emotions are universal, cultural realities and expectations are not. Four specific realities make taking a sabbatical a bigger issue for women than for men.

Marriage disproportionately benefits men. Pioneer marital researcher Jessie Bernard said it in 1972, and both male and female researchers say it today. Married women suffer more depression than married men—twice the rate, in fact, over the last three decades. When compared to their single counterparts, married women have more stress, less sense of mastery, and lower self-esteem. Married men, on the other hand, are healthier and happier and live longer than single men. A study led by social psychologist Marjorie Fiske Lowenthal found early warning signs: Newlywed women think about death more often than the middle-aged and the elderly, while newlywed men think about it the least. The Victorians anticipated that women's health would decline after they married, and it was this belief, historians say, that fueled the rise of sanitariums and water-cure retreats. What was assumed in the nineteenth century, researchers proved in the twentieth: Marriage carries greater health hazards for women than for men.

A sabbatical is a greater issue for women because it is harder for women to leave. In spite of men's increasing involvement in family life, women still outnumber men in all caregiving roles. Studies overwhelmingly show that in families of two working parents, women still put in longer hours with children and household tasks. When a child of two working parents gets sick, it is still the mother who most often stays home. Women spend significantly more time than men taking care of elderly relatives, and this time is destined to increase. An American working woman today can expect to spend more years caring for an aging parent than she will for a dependent child. And as women themselves grow older, they are more likely to take care of their husbands than their husbands are to take care of them.

Sabbaticals are also a bigger issue for women because of psychological gender differences. As behavioral psychologist Carol Gilligan theorized in her groundbreaking work *In a Different Voice,* women are conditioned to be more relational than men and while men develop their identity through separation and autonomy, women develop their identity through relationship with others. Because women are raised to invest more in relationship, because their sense of self is organized around affiliation, it is psychologically more difficult for them to move away from the relationships in their lives.

Swiss psychiatrist Carl Jung proposed a different theory of psychological development, but equally relevant. Historically, our culture has suppressed what we once called "male" characteristics (power and independence) in women and "female" characteristics (emotional expressiveness and nurturing) in men. The task of the second half of life, said Jung, is to claim our contrasexual energies—in other words, to find our missing selves. To fulfill this task, "to become whole," men who need to discover their "feminine" side are pulled inward, toward home and family life, while women who need to develop their "masculine" traits are pulled outward, away from home and family life. Although increasing numbers of women find personal power in their twenties and thirties, those who spend the first half of their adult life raising children often don't discover this power until their middle and later years.

And finally, sabbaticals are a bigger issue for women because women have fewer role models. In the classroom, we grew up on male archetypes. *The Odyssey* was the world's first story that combined wanderlust with married love, but it was the Greek hero Odysseus who traveled the world while his wife Penelope stayed at home. His ten-year sea voyage after the Trojan War was a journey of self-discovery; her ten-year wait, a model of virtue. Homer wrote his epic prose poem more than 2,700 years ago, yet the marital myth of men's mobility and women's rootedness still predominates on the screen. Whether the Knights of the Round Table ride into forests to search for the Holy Grail, soldiers cross continents to fight for a cause, or adventurers dare oceans, mountains, and skies just for the challenge, our cinematic history is filled with images of men leaving and returning home.

When women leave home, however, the movies tell a different story. In *Fatal Attraction*, when the wife leaves *for the weekend*, all hell breaks loose. Her husband commits adultery with a woman so deranged that she stalks him, terrorizes his family, and finally ends up dead in their bathtub, murdered by the wife whose absence started it all. In *Thelma and Louise*, Thelma leaves her husband to go on a two-day road trip and ends up driving off the edge of the Grand Canyon. If women who leave home aren't punished, it's a sure thing they're not coming back. When the heroine of *Shirley Valentine* leaves her house in London for an island in Greece, she stays in Greece. Why wouldn't she? Her marriage is stifling, her husband both tyrant and bore. When Billy Crystal leaves home in *City Slickers*, however, he leaves a likable and sympathetic wife and two engaging children. He not only returns, he comes back with new energy for life, for love, for work. Why hasn't a movie been made about a married woman who leaves home and returns a stronger person to a loving family? The problem with these stereotyped images is that they shape our perceptions, and then they shape our lives.

Many of us grew up seeing our fathers go off—on hunting, fishing, golfing trips—but how many of us over forty have memories of our mothers leaving home for anything but a visit to relatives or a stay in the hospital? How many of us had a mother who went off for herself alone? Men have always had permission to leave, but of women's leaving we have two dominant images: Edna walking into the ocean in Kate Chopin's *The Awakening*, and Nora walking out the door in Ibsen's *A Doll's House*. A self submerged or a relationship severed. Either way, sinking or bailing, a permanent disconnect.

There is no paradigm for a married woman's leaving home *for a while* for personal growth. There is no paradigm for a married woman's returning at all, much less fulfilled, energized, maybe newly in love with her husband. If women lack role models, if women are suffering in marriage, if women are increasingly the ones choosing to dismantle in court what they once yearned to wreathe in ceremony, then it's women who need to write a new script.

Who are the women whose voices appear on these pages? When interviewed, the youngest was twenty-nine, the oldest seventy-four, married or in a committed relationship from five years to more than fifty. At the time of their sabbaticals, they ranged in age from twenty-eight to sixty-four. The women come from twenty-two states, the District of Columbia, Canada, and New Zealand, from towns of 500 to cities of 5 million. They represent diverse cultures and backgrounds, but they are all middle- and upper-class women with educations and professions. They are not a cross-section or a representative sample of married women who have left home. This book is not the result of clinical research or a sociological study. Many names came to me by word of mouth. I asked each woman if she knew of other married women "who left home to pursue their own growth and returned," and many did. I sent out inquiries over the Internet. I placed ads in regional newspapers.

This book is based on interviews with fifty-five women. I interviewed some women either before or during their journeys, then again after they arrived home. The majority, however, were looking back on their experiences with some distance and perspective. Real names are used for those whose experiences were already in print. I changed all other women's names to protect their privacy but kept their professions because the nature of their sabbaticals was often linked to their work. To give a broader dimension to women's experiences, I talked with thirty husbands and twenty children. For psychological insights, I interviewed twenty-four professionals, including marriage counselors and researchers, psychologists, psychiatrists, psychoanalysts, and Jungian analysts. I didn't want academic answers. All were clinicians, the majority married ten years or longer. A number of them had taken sabbaticals themselves.

This book is not a marriage manual or how-to guide. It is not an analysis of a sociological trend or a simplistic endorsement. It is an exploration of married women leaving home—their reasons, their anxieties, their experiences—and the impact of these experiences on them, their husbands, and their marriages. The more I delved into the topic, the less I wanted to include my own story. Other women had greater obstacles to overcome and more dramatic stories to tell. While it was fascinating to interview others, it was painful to look at my own life, the mistakes I made, the fears and insecurities I harbored. I wasn't prepared to recognize other women's land mines as my own. I included my story, in the end, because it is from the heart of these emotions that the book was written.

How do I define sabbatical? I use the term the same way it is used in professional life: a personal time-out from daily routines for creative, professional, or spiritual growth, for study, reflection, or renewal. It is not a prolonged visit with friends or an emergency leave to care for an ailing parent. It is not summers with the children at the lake, with husbands arriving on the weekend. The sabbaticals—in this book—are solo journeys in which women voluntarily leave all that is familiar and comfortable and safe to venture into the unknown.

What time frame constitutes a sabbatical in marriage? The more I tried to contain the duration, the more elastic it became. It's whatever a woman needs to re-create her life or fulfill a dream, which means it's different for each woman. What's important about the duration is less the time spent, more the stretch and the effect. A five-week leave for one woman can be a more difficult and transformative act than a five-month leave for another. In this book, four sabbaticals lasted more than a year. Six extended over several years, when women went out of town for graduate school, which meant several leaves of four months each. The rest ranged from one to nine months. The average time away was four months, the typical length of a sabbatical in academia today. But more than half of the women's journeys lasted between one month and three, a duration likelier to be found in the business world.

Some women readily admitted they had taken a sabbatical; others had never used the word but thought it appropriate. One woman was amused by the term. And one woman bristled: I was not *leaving* my husband, she said. No woman I interviewed was *leaving* her husband, any more than professors on sabbatical are *leaving* the universities where they teach. While they were away, women telephoned, e-mailed, wrote letters, sent gifts, arranged visits. They were not leaving emotionally. They were leaving physically. Whether or not they were looking for a rest from the relationship, they got one.

Twelve years after the dream arose like a genie from a burnished lamp—elusive yet powerfully seductive—I decided to leave for three months to begin writing this book, three months to live and work alone. One thought predominated: What happens when a married woman takes some time and space away?

A sabbatical is biblical, historical, archetypal. A time to lie fallow. It may be an atypical narrative for marriage, but it is one narrative, and it needs to be told.

2

MOTIVATIONS

I mean to lead a simple life, to choose a simple shell I can carry easily—like a hermit crab. But I do not. I find that my frame of life does not foster simplicity. My husband and five children must make their way in the world. The life I have chosen as wife and mother entrains a whole caravan of complications. . . .

This is not the life of simplicity but the life of multiplicity that the wise men warn us of. It leads not to unification but fragmentation. It does not bring grace; it destroys the soul. . . .

All her instinct as a woman—the eternal nourisher of children, of men, of society—demands that she give. Her time, her energy, her creativeness drain out into these channels if there is any chance, any leak. . . . Eternally, woman spills herself away in driblets to the thirsty, seldom being allowed the time, the quiet, the peace, to let the pitcher fill up to the brim.

—ANNE MORROW LINDBERGH,
Gift from the Sea

*I*t's 1996. The boys are gone, and I have turned the younger one's room into my office. There I am drawn to the warm southern exposure, the familiarity of my papers strewn everywhere, piles on the bed, the floor, the desk. Mostly, I'm drawn to the stillness. The only sound is the muted hum of the computer. I've dreamed of a room like this for years but never imagined how comforting it would feel to walk in each day.

"Mom!" It's an e-mail from my younger son. "I need a few things. Could you send me my new Nike T-shirt and look for another one that's gray with the sleeves cut off. Also *Walden*—it's on one of the shelves in my room—it's a required book for a class."

"Mom!" It's the instantly recognizable voice of my older son on the phone.

"I'm on deadline, honey. Can I call you back this evening?"

"It'll just take a minute. I need to talk to you about something."

He is charming, and insistent. Thirty minutes later, I'm still listening.

On the answering machine is a message from my mother: "I left the house in a hurry today and can't remember if I left the stove on. Could you check it for me?" Other days, she leaves other messages: "Can you help me coordinate my clothes for my trip?" "Can you take me to the airport?" I am one of three, but the only daughter. I am the one who spends the morning in the emergency room when my mother breaks her wrist. I am the one who cancels the university class I teach to be with my mother before her emergency hip operation. I love my mother, so I cannot leave her alone and frightened.

When days like these stretch into weeks, then months, I can't help but wonder why the main characteristic of my life is adapting to others. Years of conditioning, I guess, years of being the good daughter/wife/mom, years of saying yes. Years of fulfilling my children's every need, of being the soft touch. Of course I'm the one they call. Like the woman with multiple personalities in Nicole Hollander's comic strip *Sylvia*, my waitress persona is never far from the surface. Sure, I'll pick you up at the airport, send you the package, buy your favorite shampoo since you can't find it on campus. Like a puppet pulled by increasingly fragile strings, I feel as though the ground beneath me is no longer solid. As long as I am in my house, even in my office, it's impossible not to be a mother and a daughter.

It's impossible not to be a wife, either, but the marital pulls are both more subtle and insidious because they come mostly from within. What I do because I am married: I remain in a city I'd like to leave because my husband cannot transfer his psychology practice. I sit down to a regular meal almost every night when sometimes I'd rather skip dinner, just microwave a bag of popcorn or eat a candy bar. When I rent a video, I often select a techno-thriller I know he'll enjoy rather than a foreign film I know I'll enjoy. He doesn't ask me to do these things and probably wouldn't care if I didn't. But our relationship is fraught with my "shoulds," which have been there so long they've carved grooves in my mind. I do these things without thinking, but I also do them because I love him, because I feel that not to do them would be rude and thoughtless. Marriage is about consideration and compromise—not once in a while but every day, every day for ten or sixteen or twenty-eight years.

Some days I don't want to compromise. I don't want to adapt to someone else's schedule, to listen, soothe, advise, to be mindful of what everyone else needs or wants. I want to escape all my roles for a while. Just once, I want the days phone-call free.

When I told a New York writer the subject of this book, she said, "I call that running away from home." That's what Anne Morrow Lindbergh, writer, wife of the acclaimed aviator, and mother of five called her solo trips to a Florida beach house. "I have run away," she wrote in her slim memoir, *Gift from the Sea*. "I have shed the shell of my life." But if women who leave home are running away, what are they running from? For most women I interviewed, it isn't a difficult relationship, but, as with Lindbergh, a fragmented life, a life where dreams get lost in the day-to-day of earning a living, running a household, being a wife, a mother, a daughter-in-law, a sister, a neighbor, a friend. It's a life at odds with what they yearn for: dedicated work time, time to immerse themselves wholly and fully, without demands, responsibilities, distractions, noise. Some women are so socialized into caretaking that unless they leave, they cannot separate from it. They not only can't break the pattern, they don't even have the psychic space to figure out what the pattern is.

Immersion

When Melissa graduated from law school, she gave herself a day and a half to bask in her achievement. Then she had to focus on the federal bar exam in the midst of a family move. Her husband had just taken a position in another city, so Melissa began looking for a prep course even as she was unpacking. When she discovered no course was offered in the smaller town where they'd relocated, she tried to commute to the nearest big city. Awakening in the dark, however, left her too sleep-deprived to concentrate during the day, and the long hours on the road sapped the energy she needed to study at night. She bought the course on tape to learn the material at home, but her life at home was one of distraction, peaking during the less-structured summer months. Home was where others' needs came before her own, where interacting with her husband, tending to her children, driving to baseball games, shopping for groceries, doing laundry, coping with stereos blaring, phones ringing, dogs barking left her asking, "Where am I going to find twelve hours a day to study?"

Melissa had always tried to fit the demands of her work around the needs of her family, and though it had never been easy, it was easier when the demands came from teaching school than when they came from studying law. "I made it through law school studying after everyone else went to bed, drinking coffee all night long," she said. "It almost killed me."

The night before one critical exam, Melissa had just settled in to study when a close friend called in crisis. Melissa explained her situation and offered her time the following night, but reason could neither defuse the panic nor stop the tears. So with her insides churning, Melissa stayed on the phone and listened. She listened as she stared at the thick legal texts, the course notebooks, the stacks of papers surrounding her on three sides. She listened as she watched the clock and battled fatigue. When after three hours she finally said goodnight to a calmed and grateful friend, she felt so drained she couldn't imagine getting through her test the next day.

Melissa got through it the same way she always did, studying after everyone else's needs had been met, drinking coffee all night long. When she passed the test, she gave more credit to luck than scholarship. She couldn't rely on luck this time around because federal exams have different rules, no makeup tests, no second chances. "This time, I knew I had to leave and be alone to accomplish my goal," she said. With the audio course and a few clothes, Melissa left home for two months to study in a furnished apartment.

When a woman has difficulty denying access to others and consoles a friend the night before a crucial exam, some would say: Get into therapy, join a support group for codependents, sign up for assertiveness training, just say no. The problem with these responses is that adult personality doesn't change over a six-month therapy or an eight-week workshop, and it definitely doesn't change overnight. Most psychologists, in fact, think personality is pretty well set by the age of six. Melissa grew up the only child of two loving and attentive parents. When she graduated from college, she chose teaching over law because it was a better fit with her vision of family life, where she could be home with her children after school and over the summers. When Melissa's mother was dying, she took a semester's leave from teaching to care for her; when Melissa's father could no longer live by himself, she moved him to her home for his last two years. When Melissa had a bedroom to spare, she and her husband volunteered as emergency foster parents, then adopted one of the children they housed. When for years a woman has emotionally invested in the well-being of others and physically responded to their needs, she doesn't change that behavior or turn off that emotion like a light switch. And when her home is the environment infused with the emotion and fused to the behavior, *then when she is in that home she can feel a psychic demand even if someone isn't knocking on her door.*

Context is powerful. What Melissa experienced, modern science has proven: Our environment influences our thoughts and actions as much as our genes do. When the issue is habitual devotion—whether to behavior or person or drug—studies reveal that the physical environment of the devotion signifies. Findings worldwide show that after a year most drug addicts who don't relapse have moved to a different city, an environment not necessarily drug-free but free of their associations with drug use. New widows move past depression more quickly if they change their surroundings so that they no longer associate their homes with loss. To change habitual behavior, researchers say, disconnect from the environment that triggers it, separate from the associations that strengthen it. In other words, to change habitual behavior, change the scene.

Women like Melissa, determined to achieve but conditioned to nurture, sometimes gravitate to this geographic solution. They get out of the house, out of the neighborhood, out of town altogether. Some women leave for an educational program or degree because it isn't offered in the city where they live, but others leave in spite of a program nearby. When I asked why, I heard: Because at home I couldn't have said no to seeing friends, attending family gatherings, baby-sitting for nieces and nephews and grandchildren, visiting friends in the hospital and mothers of friends in the hospital, taking my in-laws to the grocery store, my sister to the airport, my aunt to the doctor. Because at home I could not have extracted, extricated, distanced myself from others' needs. Because at home it would have taken so much longer. *Because I wanted to immerse myself.*

Men throughout history have more easily defined separateness, more easily claimed it. It's always women, we hear, who long for rooms of their own. But what happens when the longing is all there is, when women suffering from what researchers call "role overload" and "role conflict" are unable to take time and space for themselves? Dreams are abandoned, personal achievement sacrificed. Feminist theologian Valerie Saiving wrote that since women's temptations are not the same as men's, neither are their sins. Her thesis, proposed in an essay in *Womanspirit Rising*, was that our concept of sin is based on men's character and that women's real sins are underdevelopment of the self, lack of focus, diffuseness, distractibility.

Distractions can be self-made, but if attention is a pathway in the psyche, motherhood sears the synapses. When a mother is always on call, her time evolves from soothing a crying infant to reading with a restless toddler, from listening for two hours to a distraught teenager to spending a night in the hospital with a frightened young adult. A mother's needs can change over the years, as Melissa's did, but her children's expectations of her don't change accordingly. They still want her attention, and they want it now. Their interruptions, day after day, year after year, and her responses to them, day after day, year after year, rearrange her mental wiring. Concentration fades and flickers while distractibility steadily gains power.

The day arrives when her children are out of the house, her juggling days supposedly over, and she can concentrate at home uninterrupted. Instead, she can find herself darting from project to project, desk to desk, working frantically but ineffectively, physically racing but mentally spinning, because a twenty-year pattern of fragmentation does not disappear as easily and inevitably as the children do. *Because diffuseness has become habitual.* Just when she finally has the luxury of working deeply, she discovers she has lost the ability. Fortunately, the loss isn't permanent because concentration is a learned skill. And if context had the power to set the behavior, then context has the power to reset it.

Interestingly, 100 years ago married women left home to focus on their work. They were rare, perhaps, but they were also among the most accomplished and influential women of their time. Writer Charlotte Perkins Gilman was a leading feminist in the decades preceding World War I. In her second marriage, which lasted thirty years, Gilman toured three months on the lecture circuit and spent nine months at home with her husband. Carrie Chapman Catt, president of the National Women's Suffrage Association for more than twenty years, reportedly drew up a prenuptial contract with her second husband that stipulated she would be guaranteed freedom from the responsibilities of marriage for three months a year so she could concentrate on politics. Her marriage to

George Catt lasted fifteen years, until his death. Birth-control pioneer Margaret Sanger left her longtime husband Noah for weeks or months at a time to promote her cause. In the second half of her life, Elizabeth Cady Stanton, a leading activist for working-class, antislavery, and feminist causes, spent more time on the road on lecture tours than at home with her husband. She was married for nearly half a century.

In the years since these women worked so hard for equality, the modern women's movement has opened professions, increased earning power, and redefined gender roles. For women not raised by feminist mothers, however, it has also brought higher standards. Many women over forty are locked in an ongoing struggle between the caretaking messages of their mothers' generation and the achievement messages of feminism. As sociologist Arlie Hochschild noted in *The Second Shift*, many women today remain unliberated from traditional roles and responsibilities. They can be high achievers, high earners, professionals, feminists—yet when they walk through their front doors at night, with the same reflexes they use to slip into sweatpants, they slide into gender roles. Caretaking as a role, however, is rarely compensated, seldom praised, often not even acknowledged. And when culturally devalued, it becomes more than a physical load. Sitting in therapists' offices across the country are professional women who feel more responsible at home, more responsible for the children, more responsible for family connections, emotionally more burdened.

No matter whether there is a personality or genetic component to women's caretaking drives, who can deny the heavy cultural pressures women still suffer? While we are told we can and should be anything we want, we are bombarded with traditional caretaking messages in magazines seductively greeting us in grocery store checkout lines, everything from "Comfort Food To Wow Your Guests" to "28 Little Ways To Make Your Husband Feel Special," the latter a 1998 article in *Redbook* that suggests "washing, folding, and neatly arranging all his boxers in his dresser." The fact that *Redbook* is addressed to some 10 million "young married women and moms" suggests that younger generations will not remain immune to the conflict.

Martha Stewart is the media icon of these mixed messages and escalating standards. A billionaire business tycoon selling domestic perfection, she gives home entertaining the sizzle of a hot career, marketing the position of "hostess" as a glamour job and "pleasing the multitudes" as a mission statement. When she urges her mostly female audience of millions to transform their homes into a tropical garden for a luau or host a picnic in a pumpkin patch, she elevates caretaking to an art form. Feeding others is always a generous act and a joyous one, too, if it comes from a woman's own desires, but if it's a have-to instead of a want-to, it drains body and soul. I recently counted on a magazine stand sixty-two publications specializing in glorified images of home and hearth. But home can be a hassle as well as a haven for women who go from a shift in the workplace to a shift at home. And when the daily "commute" is a stroll down the hall, how do you focus on self in surroundings saturated with cues to focus on others? Happily married women don't need to leave home to go after a dream, argue some therapists. *Some* women don't, that's true. They can pen song lyrics in a doctor's office, compose poetry in a diner. They can study while waiting in line or watching TV, in bookstore or bathtub, on bleacher or bus. They can produce bestsellers on a kitchen table littered with Legos and crumbs. What works for *some* women, however, does not work for *all* women. For those who cannot concentrate in compressed time or chaotic space, who need large blocks of solitude, phones unplugged and doors shut, "at home" can't solve the problem because "at home" *is* the problem.

Activist and author Letty Cottin Pogrebin told me she could not have completed her third book, *Growing Up Free*, without leaving home. She spent eight years working on it, during which time she was an editor at *Ms.*, a wife, and a mother of three. Not that she was less motivated to write when she was at home, but at home her writing came *after* her husband, her children, her job. "Creaking under the weight," she said, she left for seven immersive weeks at a writer's colony. So dramatic was the difference in her productivity that she chose to finish her next three books the same way. Devoted to her husband of thirty-five years, a man she calls "my oasis," she summarized the conflict: "He is a wonderful distraction, but he is still a distraction."

Identity

Some women's days amount to such a conglomeration of tasks, their lives so lost in details, that they hardly know who they are anymore, much less who they aspire to be. They know they are someone's wife, someone's mother, someone's daughter, someone's colleague, but who are they without the labels of their lives?

The search for self is an ageless and mythic theme. Embedded in stone at Delphi more than two millennia ago was the oracle's admonition: Know Thyself. To lead a conscious life we need to integrate who we are with who we have been and who we will be. The search leads us to psychotherapy and mysticism, philosophy and poetry, travel and study and art. It compels us to revisit childhood homes and research ancestral roots, to write journals and essays, screenplays and memoirs. We search identity in culture and class, family and profession, religion and race and gender, in our physical selves and our spiritual selves.

Psychiatrist Erik Erikson studied identity in our psychological development, which he outlined in "Eight Ages of Man," a concept which has influenced most contemporary research on identity formation. Erikson defined each stage by a central conflict we need to confront and resolve for healthy functioning. In the pivotal fifth stage, the conflict is role confusion; the challenge, integration of identities. The wider the range of those identities, he said, the more necessary and problematic the challenge will be. Carl Jung believed the task of the second half of life was to discover who we are in our deepest self, the self that exists apart from longtime roles.

In 1968, I was a junior in college. Sitting in my dorm room one afternoon was Judy Woodruff, who had graduated the year before. A friend of my roommate's, she had come to visit from the Atlanta television station where she hoped to be a reporter. My roommate and I talked about what we were going to do when we graduated. I decided I'd go to Atlanta to work in television like Woodruff.

The following fall, I had a blind date with a graduate student. Jim was broad-shouldered and blond, tall and good-looking. We had been dating a few weeks when I caught a cold. He came by my dorm to leave an envelope with a note and vitamin C pills. A few weeks later, I invited him to a party where he was charming and funny, as comfortable talking to people he had never met as I was quiet and self-conscious talking to people I knew. With him at my side I felt smarter, more interesting, more lively. His was the personality I had always longed to have. When my mother asked, "What are his faults?" I answered, "I can't think of any." Simon and Garfunkel were singing "Bridge over Troubled Water," and I had found the man who, when evening falls so hard, would comfort me.

Many women in our graduating class married that summer. We married, too. Jim continued his graduate studies while I worked for the university's news service. I had already made my first compromise, but I didn't know it.

I would have followed him anywhere, but he wanted to go only as far as the closest clay tennis courts. On a hot July day in North Carolina, we were playing our first match in a mixed-doubles tournament. We had drawn the number one seed, the women's state singles champion and her brother, and because of their renown, they drew a crowd, which had gathered on the grass to watch. The humidity oppressed and the sun blinded. Sweat burned my eyes. By the time the match mercifully ended, I felt queasy and faint. I stumbled off the court toward a large trash container and, in full view of the crowd, threw up.

Two days later, Jim came home with an apple-green bikini I had admired in a store window. He apologized for entering us in the tournament, promised he wouldn't sign us up for any more. I loved the bikini. We spent the evening playing tennis.

The questions I ask today with some embarrassment: Why, as a bride, was I playing tennis five, six times a week when I didn't like the game? Why did I so willingly let his interest become mine? He didn't drag me onto the courts, he didn't coerce me. Tennis was important to him and he was important to me, and that's all the motivation I needed. But his life became our life became my life. For twenty years, we played almost every weekend, singles with each other, mixed doubles with friends. We even played—I cringe to write it—in more tournaments. I started out just wanting to please, but it didn't take long for a tacit accommodation to become habit and then ritual. The process is subtle and unconscious, the result entrenched and powerful. Then one day you realize you've lost yourself in the needs and desires of the other.

Here's the irony: After a back injury and a year's hiatus with not one moment of missing the game, I knew my tennis-playing days had ended. "How would you feel," I asked him, "if I didn't play tennis with you anymore?"

And he answered, "No problem. I don't want to play anymore either."

The twentieth century is over, yet women still talk of how easily they can let their partners' lives consume their own. Dalma Heyn's premise in *Marriage Shock: The Transformation of Women into Wives* is that women submerge a vital part of themselves when they marry. I saw my younger self on every page of Heyn's provocative book, a recognition I attributed to marrying before the first issue of *Ms.* hit the stands. What was surprising was that the women she interviewed *more than two decades later* ranged from their twenties to their fifties. The question the author posed was existential: How can women keep both their marriages and themselves? She concluded that to thrive in a marriage for more than a few years women will need to "step outside the structure." One way women have found to do this is to spend time away from their husbands. Some leave every year—for a month or so—to reclaim what they've submerged.

The drive for identity can be acute in women who married young, who became half of a couple before they had a chance to become a whole individual. Zora Neale Hurston explored this theme in her 1937 novel, *Their Eyes Were Watching God*. Hurston's heroine, Janie Crawford, is poor, Southern, and black, only sixteen when she marries. Trying to voice the erosion of her identity to her second husband, she says, "Mah own mind had tuh be squeezed and crowded out to make room for yours in me."

More than sixty years later, the movie *Runaway Bride* portrayed the same theme through a very different heroine. Maggie Carpenter, the title character played by Julia Roberts, is middle-class, Northern, and white, a single twentysomething living at home, managerial by day (running a hardware store) and creative by night (designing light fixtures). Her habit of leaving fiancés at the altar drives the narrative, which centers on the efforts of journalist Ike Graham (Richard Gere) to write her story for a magazine. Ike arrives in town to find Maggie and her current fiancé planning their wedding and honeymoon. The townsfolk want to see if she's going to bolt again; Ike wants to know why she bolts in the first place. After he hears her order an omelet, egg whites only, echoing the exact order of her jock fiancé, he nails her problem with one question to each abandoned groom: How did she like her eggs? Fried, like me, says the rock 'n' roller. Scrambled, with salt, pepper, and dill, same as me, says the priest. Poached, says the entymologist, just like me.

After sixty years of feminism, Maggie remains Janie Crawford's psychic sister, trying to conform to each man's ideal woman. Before Maggie can follow through on a commitment, she samples eight different egg dishes to discover which one *she* prefers. The film's message lies on the kitchen counter: A woman needs to know who she is before she marries. Hurston's novel, unappreciated in its time, has become a literary classic, studied in courses across the country. Garry Marshall's comedy, panned by reviewers, became a box-office hit, enjoyed by millions. The theme endures because the theme still resonates. The rise in the median age when women first marry — 25 today, up from 20.6 in 1970 — is a positive direction for female identity because marrying at a young age, especially when combined with having children at a young age, plugs in the wiring early for being more other-directed than self-directed. And the earlier the wiring is coded, the harder a woman's struggle to change it will be.

The drive for identity also motivates women who married strong, dynamic men. The very qualities that attract a woman to a man — the signs of dominance that anthropologists claim are embedded in evolution — can over the years overshadow her. Anne Morrow Lindbergh, wife of an international hero, found her identity as a writer, not at home in Connecticut, but in Captiva on the west coast of Florida, where she went yearly for decades, usually alone. For most of her marriage to celebrated photographer Alfred Stieglitz, Georgia O'Keeffe spent every summer painting in New Mexico, in part because she needed to create an artistic vision away from the powerful aura of her famous husband and the Manhattan art world over which he reigned. A woman does not need to be married to someone with the stature of Lindbergh or Stieglitz to battle the same problem. A woman married to a brilliant academic can find that when she has a good idea, everyone assumes it is his. A woman married to a dazzling debater or irrepressible raconteur can find that when they're at social gatherings, he's the center of attention.

A woman is vulnerable to loss of self in marriage, even if she doesn't marry young or her husband isn't dynamic. If her nature is to please, if she instinctively places her husband's needs before her own, she is almost guaranteed a lengthy struggle for her identity. Loss of self is insidious because, like heart disease, it invades in silence. If a woman is unaware of what's happening, it's unlikely those she lives with will point it out to her. A man will generally not see his wife's accommodation as a problem when— on the surface anyway—he benefits from it. Children will not detect a mother's loss of self when time lost to her needs is time gained for theirs. Danish philosopher Søren Kierkegaard expressed the problem this way: "The greatest danger, that of losing one's own self, may pass off quietly as if it were nothing; every other loss, that of an arm, a leg, five dollars . . . is sure to be noticed."

Who noticed what I lost playing a sport I didn't like? "I had no idea you didn't like playing tennis," said my younger son, after reading an early draft of this book. Jim seemed a little surprised, too. "There was a time you were playing better than I was," he said. "The summer we won that tournament, we won because of you." How could they have known how I felt about playing when I couldn't admit it to myself? What becomes customary in our lives and our marriages becomes easy not to notice, then not to question. I never thought about the self I submerged until I read Heyn's book. I thought about it again when I heard stories like Sarah's.

In the aftermath of her divorce, Sarah felt older and wiser, surer now of what she wanted in a relationship. And what she wanted was someone exciting, challenging, different. Sarah was attracted immediately to Steve, his expansive personality, his keen intellect. Everything about him exuded energy—his movements, his conversations, his ideas. His life force was so magnetic and Sarah so powerfully drawn to it that she not only married him, she "didn't come up for air for several years." By that time, a pattern had taken hold.

Like most charismatic men, Sarah's husband had big dreams. When those dreams created risk and chaos, Sarah provided the stability and support to nurture them. When those dreams led to entrepreneurial ventures all over the country, Sarah organized the moves and willingly followed. For twelve years, Steve pursued his dreams while Sarah worked at whatever jobs she could find when they moved into town. For twelve years, whenever they walked into a room together, he commanded everyone's attention.

Sarah gained the dynamic husband and exciting marriage she wanted but in the process suffered an unanticipated loss. "My identity got put on the back shelf," she said, "both because of the force of my husband's personality and because I wasn't doing what I needed to promote my own life and work." When her identity suffered, so did her feelings of self-worth.

Sarah understood her problem intellectually but physically was too caught up in the pattern to detach from it. She had self-awareness, but lacked the tools for change. When the company where she was employed closed her division, Sarah saw an opportunity to change the pattern. To create a career that would be integral to who *she* was, that would take her in a direction *she* wanted to go, she landed a scholarship to become certified as a systems engineer. Then she decided to spend three months of her online studies in a scenic coastal town. Since Sarah had no trouble working at home, she didn't need a distraction-free environment. She wasn't looking for immersion; she was looking for wholeness.

"When I'm with my husband, I'm always reacting to him, automatically jumping up to take care of him in some way," she said. "I wanted to learn a way of living where I don't do that, where I don't succumb to his intensity, where I lead my own life, thinking of what I need and want instead of getting so wrapped up in what he needs and wants."

Sarah's struggle—to live *her* life within *their* marriage— has been an essential female struggle for centuries. Some women, in fact, are so convinced that being an autonomous woman and a wife are irreconcilable that they choose to remain single. For those who marry, reconciling the two will continue to be a struggle as long as more than twice as many women as men say they would be willing to move for their future spouses, as long as women are more likely than men to defer to their partners' careers, more likely to choose their work and then cut back on it for the benefit of family life. When accommodation truncates a career, it can also weaken a woman's identity. Sarah understood this dynamic all too well. "I wanted him to start following me around," she said.

The identity we are ultimately in search of is the identity within, defined by inner resources alone. It's tough to achieve, and for those who do, it usually takes a lifetime. Meanwhile, we struggle with the identities we're more familiar with, the ones defined by—and therefore dependent on—externals. These are fluid identities, as anyone who has lost a job knows. A woman who forgoes or cuts back on her career when her children are small, even if by choice, can find her identity shaky, even if once strong. Sarah's problem surfaced not with her first husband but with her second, not when she was in her twenties but her forties.

Certainly, a woman doesn't have to leave her home and husband to strengthen her individuality and *in theory* she shouldn't have to. But *in practice*, in a marriage like Sarah's, "separating physically makes it easier, because it interferes with the old structures and roles," said Bill Bumberry, a St. Louis clinical psychologist who specializes in marriage counseling. "Leaving also makes it clearer to everyone that you need to do this." Leaving vocalizes what was lost in silence. The voice is strong, projecting the importance, the *necessity*, of a woman's selfness. And the voice reverberates, ensuring that others hear what had been so easy to miss.

Adventure

For many women the time-out for themselves has little or nothing to do with the relationship, everything to do with adventure. Brooklyn artist Joan Mister wanted to take a Big Trip based on a big idea and a big number. Her goal was to drive more than 25,000 miles, a greater distance than the earth is round at the equator. Her six-month, cross-country trip, featured in the *New York Times*, meant, on one level, "making a big idea happen," she said, "like Christo's wrapping a building." For Mister, the adventure was a longtime dream rooted in a longtime passion: driving on the open road. She left New York in an eleven-year-old Volvo, 118,000 miles on the dashboard; itineraries, maps, and travel guides piled beside and behind her; and a rambling route to California and back ahead of her. The adventure was part wanderlust, part heroine's journey: to drive a thousand miles a week, along back roads and blue highways, visiting places she'd never seen, talking to people she'd never met, feeling the breadth of the country and the diversity of its people, all the while holding steadfast to an idea of her own creation, directing each moment of each day herself, exploring through the road ahead the woman within.

For several dedicated backpackers the adventure was hiking the length of the Appalachian Trail, which stretches across fourteen states, from Springer Mountain in Georgia to Mount Katahdin in Maine. For a wilderness enthusiast and mountain climber, it was reaching the base camp of Mount Everest. And for a woman who was neither climber nor hiker, the adventure was traveling around the world for six months with $1,500 and a backpack. If adventure was not the primary motive, it often was an underlying one.

"Why didn't you study French or German or nursing in your hometown?" I asked, and women answered, "Because it wouldn't have been an adventure."

Women like these created their experiences. Others recognized opportunity. The catalyst for many women's adventures was simply a notice in a magazine, an announcement in the mail, a random encounter, an unexpected call. Whether course or class, trek or dig, it came without design, revealing a desire that until that moment they didn't know they had, offering an adventure that until that moment they didn't know they wanted.

Adventure arouses curiosity, stirs imagination, evokes mystery, suggests that life can be more than our routines. More than driving car pools and scheduling appointments and racing from home to office to home again, more than returning phone calls while preparing dinner, then throwing in a load of laundry before going to the track, then falling asleep while listening to a "freedom from worry" tape and wondering if this is as good as it gets. Adventure is so far removed from the reality of most women's lives that somewhere along the way we have stopped imagining it for ourselves. If, in addition, we were raised with neither the expectations nor the role models, we can find ourselves living in a culture that fuels the fantasies yet discourages their realization. If a woman has a spirit of adventure within her, however, it's there, behind the shuttered thermal windows and beside the goose-down comforter, in the stack of reading material by her bed, novels and memoirs set in exotic locales, oversized photography books and glossy travel magazines, Post-its highlighting destinations remote and magical, sensual and serene.

Then one day the phone rings with the lure of an adventure, and she feels as if she's been shot out of a cannon. The longer she has spent in cozy domesticity, the greater her feeling of disembodiment. Adrenalin courses through her bloodstream as she feels the exhilaration of movement, beyond, ahead, within. With the thrill of the unexpected and the promise of change she feels younger, more alive. *Yes*, she thinks, *life just got better than this.*

There doesn't have to be anything wrong with a woman's life for her to want to leave her ordinary routines for an extraordinary experience. There doesn't have to be anything wrong with a woman's marriage for her to want to leave her husband for the adventure of her lifetime. As one woman said, "That it meant being away from my husband for three months was only a footnote. It was a challenge to make sure I could live and work on my own again, that I could still grow."

This was the motivation that kept resurfacing in women's conversations: *I wanted to test myself, to prove I could do it. . . . I needed to know I could still take a risk. . . . I needed a way to grow.* The urge to grow is innate. It is a genuine impulse to live an authentic life, to reach our fullest potential. Some therapists say the desire for individual growth is so strong that some women will force a separation to attain it. Chilean poet Pablo Neruda phrased it similarly: *Y no es la adversidad la que separa los seres, sino / el crecimiento*, or "It isn't adversity that separates us / but growing."

To grow we need challenge, and adventure guarantees a challenge. Travel, whether across a historic trail or up a legendary mountain, halfway across the country or halfway around the world, ensures that the challenge will be physical. Newness, of environment or experience or both, crisscrossing the United States in 180 days on a route you've never driven, or studying in a country where you don't speak the language and don't know a soul, ensures that the challenge will be mental. And if the adventure is connected to one's work, teaching a course in Europe or taking a course at Harvard, researching a novel or studying for a degree, then there's a professional challenge, too.

Karen had always been attracted to challenge. She was drawn to it in choosing psychology as a profession, and she was drawn to it in her husband. They were compatible in this way, continually pushing themselves, pursuing degrees, changing jobs, developing businesses. The laid-back atmosphere of the Hawaiian island where they lived mirrored the plateau Karen had reached with her job. Life had become too comfortable, and she was restless. When her company offered her a position at its headquarters on the mainland, she recognized the challenge she needed in a dream she'd long harbored: "to have a big job in a big city."

The opportunity was great, but not the timing. Karen's husband, feeling similarly restless, wanted to move to an even more rural part of the state to start a new business. Conflicting desires were not new; their eight years together had been a marital seesaw, one always giving something up for the other. The last time, Karen's husband had made the sacrifice, and both admitted, he was slow to forgive. "I knew if I made the sacrifice this time, I'd be the resentful one," said Karen. What good would it do, she asked herself, to sacrifice her dreams for his if she resented it for the next two years? What good would it do if her resentment ruined their marriage? Why did it always have to be either/or, with one of them miserable in the process? Why couldn't they have a marriage where, for one brief period, they went in opposite directions but each toward what each wanted?

Karen felt a sense of urgency. "I was afraid if I didn't take this opportunity, I wouldn't get another chance," she said. "I felt I had something important to do as an individual and that our love was strong enough to outlast the divergence of our goals." As a commitment to her marriage, Karen gave herself a time limit of two years and negotiated with the company for a paid weekend trip home each month.

What makes Karen's time away a sabbatical, then, and not simply a commuter marriage? One difference is that a sabbatical begins with a time limit; a commuter marriage typically doesn't. Another is that "commuter" wasn't intended to connote a distance of 4,500 miles. The biggest distinction, though, is in psychological motivation. Karen's language was telling. She didn't say, "I have to go because of my job." She knew she had a choice, and she was choosing—for a limited time—to thrust her energies into her own development. Many commuter marriages *are* determined by the circumstances of a job, but some may have aspects of a sabbatical within them. Some may be sabbaticals in disguise.

The adventure a woman takes is as individual as she is, the challenge she seeks a manifestation of where she is in life and what she needs to grow. For every woman who is married, however, what heightens the adventure is doing it alone, because doing it alone guarantees that psychological and emotional challenges will be added to the mix.

Spiritual Quest

A sabbatical can be an adventure, immersion, and search for self all at the same time. For some women, it can have an even deeper dimension as it takes the form of a spiritual quest. Sue Bender, an artist and therapist in California, went to live in an Amish community over eight summers, an experience she described in the lovely memoir *Plain and Simple*. "I didn't know when I first looked at an Amish quilt and felt my heart pounding," she wrote, "that my soul was starving, that an inner voice was trying to make sense of my life. I didn't know that I was beginning a journey of the spirit."

Before she left the first summer, Bender thought she was drawn to live among the Amish to learn more about their quilts. Much later she understood that the quilts were only symbolic guides, "leading me to what I really needed to learn, to answer a question I hadn't formed yet: 'Is there another way to lead a good life?'" Bender was on a lifelong quest for self-improvement, earning advanced degrees at Harvard and the University of California–Berkeley, continually taking classes afterward. Her search for answers kept leading her back to the question: What really matters?

When the motive is contemplation, a woman's journey becomes a sabbatical in the truest sense of the word. Like the Sabbath, it is a time to step back from routine to examine the deeper meaning of life. For women on journeys of the soul, the time-out is for turning inward, stepping back from a material culture to examine spiritual values, re-examine priorities, deepen faith, honor reflection—critical tasks if we're going to learn from life rather than just react to it. Spiritual growth can be the sole motivation, as it was for Bender, or it can be one layer of many. Joan Mister's cross-country odyssey combined a grand adventure with a soul search. Mister began and ended her journey with overnight stays at a retreat house, and she visited cemeteries, churches, and missions along the way. "I don't think of myself as a religious person," she said, "but in some private part of myself I felt I was doing God's work."

Traditionally, journeys of the spirit have been to sacred sites. In the Middle Ages, English mystic Margery Kempe left her husband of twenty years to travel to Jerusalem; after her eighteen-month pilgrimage in search of spiritual understanding, she returned to domesticity. Contemporary journeys assume contemporary forms. Trying to make sense of life led a striver like Bender, fragmented and tyrannized by to-do lists, to a community of simplicity. Seeking a wider arena for compassion led a nurse to a hospital in Haiti, a teacher to a village in Africa, a journalist to a disaster relief effort in the flood plains. For other women, attending to spiritual growth meant leaving established careers to attend seminary; for a yoga teacher, it meant taking a pilgrimage to India.

In the Hindu religion, spiritual liberation (*moksha*) is considered the supreme aim of human existence and the final stage of an ideal life. Hinduism defines four distinct stages (though in India's patriarchal culture they apply only to men): student, householder, forest dweller, and world renouncer. After fulfilling societal obligations—working, raising children, and retiring to the forest with one's mate to live simply in meditation and quiet—a person may leave home, spouse, and family to live a spiritual life. Women I interviewed, like Margery Kempe, transposed these last two stages. After years spent raising children, they took time off from family obligations to attend to their spiritual growth, then returned home to live with their spouses again.

The search for the spiritual, like the search for adventure, does not require solitude. For thousands of years pilgrims have walked en masse to the great shrines of the world, to Canterbury and Mecca, Rome and Jerusalem, Assisi and Lourdes, to the peaks of Machu Picchu and the valleys of Delphi. Churches and synagogues, monasteries and meditation centers all nurture spiritual life in a communal setting. Spiritual growth does not require distance, either. We can find it in a house of worship in our town or a woodland garden in our yard. We can find it right in our living rooms, in books of philosophy and books of prayer, in spiritual discussion groups and Internet list-serves.

For some women at some time in their lives, however, soul work means time away and alone. What is a desire in the best of times can become a necessity in the worst, and acute loss is often the catalyst for a spiritual journey. It was after his beloved older brother died of lockjaw that Henry David Thoreau retreated to Walden Pond. His experience there shaped his belief that at some point in life *everyone* needs to retreat from the entanglements and expectations of others. It was the only way, he felt, that one could discover or recover oneself. Today, the New England philosopher is revered for his moratorium and its literary legacy.

When Sue Bender left home to live among the Amish, she was "looking to fill an empty space," but what it was empty of she didn't know. Maria, on the other hand, knew exactly what caused her emptiness: the death of her child, the deepest of wounds to the soul. Maria was drawn to leave a world that had become too painful, where she had too many memories and others too many questions. She was drawn toward a world where she wouldn't have to worry about what she said or what others said or how others reacted to what she said. When she left her husband, home, and teaching job to walk the Appalachian Trail, she was "dropping out" but moving forward. As a native New Englander, she grew up listening to stories of the trail, evocative legends of her childhood. As an avid backpacker, she viewed the trek as the ultimate physical challenge. Now, as a mother who had lost a son, she saw it as a pilgrim's journey: on foot, in faith, and with purpose. Carrying a Bible in her backpack, she set out to find in the 2,100 miles of wilderness a sanctuary in which to grieve and a silence in which to pray. In the nature she and her son both loved, she hoped to find regeneration: healing for a stricken heart, direction for a shattered life.

In the classic *She: Understanding Feminine Psychology*, Jungian analyst Robert Johnson wrote that a woman "seems to have to go back to a very still inner center every time something happens to her, and this is a creative act. This 'getting right' is always accomplished in the feminine by being very still."

Sense of Place

When a woman links her life to someone else's, she can be so myopically in love and expansive in her thinking, that she doesn't foresee limitations, that where she ends up living may be determined by where her husband works, transfers, starts a business. Then one day she realizes that the place her life is rooted is not the place that feeds her soul. How then does she separate the landscape from herself?

Sinclair Lewis portrayed this conflict in his 1920 novel *Main Street*. His protagonist, Carol Kennicott, is a young woman yearning for a more conscious life. After marriage to a family doctor, however, she finds herself not in a progressive city where she can develop her interests but in Gopher Prairie, a small Midwestern town full of complacent dullness and petty gossip. Her adversary is her environment, and after envisioning a hundred escapes, she goes to Washington, D.C., for a while "to be quiet and think."

Eighty years after Lewis wrote his best-selling novel, a woman can still struggle with loving a man but not loving the place he inhabits. Maybe it's a conservative city in the Heartland, and she's a developing free spirit. Or the rainy Northwest, and she suffers from seasonal affective disorder. Or a small town in the South, where rural life for him softens a stressful law practice but for her limits career opportunity. Maybe it's a city in northern Alaska, where the winters are long and harsh and the hours of daylight few. She went to Alaska feeling daring and adventuresome, but marriage to a man who lives less than a hundred miles from the Arctic Circle means he runs when it's forty below while she hates the cold and is frightened of the dark.

A woman can respect that her husband needs to live in a particular place, professionally, emotionally, spiritually, and at the same time recognize that by living there with him she is giving up something—professionally, emotionally, spiritually. When the landscape feels like loss, it evolves from a physical place to a psychic one, from geography to symbol. An environment that assaults our sensibilities or thwarts our ambition or depletes our energy, in some way limits our development, makes life feel less than what it could be. After that, it's a short step to feeling that *we* are less than what we could be. Since our surroundings affect how we see ourselves, they can play a powerful role in identity. When that self-image is negative, they can play a powerful role in a marriage. When the environment that buoys his spirit drags hers like undertow, it's easy for a woman to see her husband both as comfort and burden, soul mate and shackle.

What she's looking for is a sense of place, a feeling of home. It's the difference between treading water and floating with the sun on her back. How does a woman live in Alaska and feel the sun on her back? How does she live in a small town and feel the wideness of the world? How does she respect her husband's desires without relinquishing her own?

Debra grew up in a multicultural environment in southern Louisiana and met her husband at a college renowned for its liberalism. From the day they married, she imagined their future in a cosmopolitan area among people who celebrated diversity.

Their future started out that way as the two of them pursued doctorates in another university town. But when Debra dropped out of her program after their third child was born, she knew the next move would be determined by where her husband landed a job. After he came home with the news that he had been offered a teaching position in the Ozarks, she told me, "I can remember almost losing consciousness." She anticipated benign stereotypes; she didn't anticipate the racism, sexism, and classism she found.

Debra and her husband decided he'd keep his position for five years, then they would move. By the time five years had elapsed, however, he had gained seniority, was up for tenure, liked his department, had adapted to life there, was content. Debra had tried to adapt, gave the town her best shot. She taught English as a second language and tutored, became a social activist, raised four children, supported her husband, enjoyed family life, but never stopped wrestling with her environment. She was an intellectual African-American in a city where only 20 percent of the population had attended college and only 2 percent were minorities. She was a woman ideologically "just left of center" in a male bastion of political conservatism and religious fundamentalism, a cultural arts enthusiast in a provincial enclave offering no foreign films, no avant-garde concerts or theater. "Battling life here is exhausting," she said. "If my husband weren't here, I wouldn't be here."

A solution eluded her until the day she met an older woman who had also followed her husband to this particular backwoods. Debra listened as this woman shared her life story, which included her master's degree in modern dance, her years performing with Martha Graham, her inability to teach and perform in this town. After twenty-five years of giving it all up to stay with her husband, he left her. By that time, she had children and grandchildren living nearby and, wanting to stay close to them, found herself tethered to a city she had wanted to escape long ago.

Debra came home from that conversation determined that her life would follow a different course, that marriage to a man she loved would not diminish her development as an individual, that a limiting environment would not limit her. She knew from years of trying to change her environment that her environment wasn't going to change. If she wanted movement in her life, she knew it had to come from her actions, not from her surroundings. And not from her husband. She didn't want to blame him for what her life had become. And she didn't want him to blame her for what his life might become. She didn't want to force a move that he didn't want to make, a move that could jeopardize his career and their finances. She would take responsibility for *her* self-fulfillment; she would not take responsibility for his discontent. She sat down at her desk and applied for a grant to teach overseas during the summer, a practice she has repeated every year since.

"To grow, to develop myself, to become the person I always wanted to be, I have to get out of the Ozarks," she said. "Booker T. Washington said, 'Cast down your bucket where you are.' I try, but by May I'm chomping at the bit. My summers away enable me to live with the compromise I've made."

Pop psychology says that "wherever you go, there you are" and "you're only running away from your problems," but scientific research has proven that where we live and work has a major effect on our lives. For the unconvinced, Winifred Gallagher amassed more than 300 pages of evidence in *The Power of Place*, a formidable rebuttal to the platitudes. Among the scores of studies she detailed was one by Marc Fried that focused on identifying the elements that determine quality of life. Fried's conclusion: The number one predictor of satisfaction was a good marriage; the number two, our immediate surroundings.

Debra's summer landscapes spoke both to her spirit and her intellect; in the Far East, where she usually went, she could use the linguistic skills that had flourished in academia but withered in the Bible Belt. As we scramble to reinvent our careers as quickly as the world around us changes, new working landscapes can lure us away from home. A technical writer from the Midwest with dreams of writing screenplays spent several autumns in Los Angeles, taking classes from industry pros and meeting with agents and producers. "I didn't want to be on my deathbed and not have tried," she said. Georgia O'Keeffe found her ideal canvas and fullest expression as an artist in what she called "the wonderful emptiness" of the Southwest. The beauty of the stark desert landscape nurtured her soul and inspired her imagination, and with each return she absorbed more of its energy. O'Keeffe, too, said if her husband hadn't been in Manhattan, she wouldn't have returned each fall, and when Stieglitz died, she moved to New Mexico permanently. Anne Morrow Lindbergh found renewal in the imagery of Captiva, and as Scott Berg wrote in his fascinating biography of her husband, "for the rest of her life, she would find herself drawn to that region, in search of metaphors."

Breathing Space

For nearly 2 million years of human evolution, couples lived in tribes, where men went off hunting for months at a time. American anthropologist George Murdock conducted an ethnographic survey of 554 of the world's societies and found that in a quarter of them, the husband/father was present only occasionally. Murdock also discovered that in some primitive societies husbands and wives don't eat together. In others, certain taboos demand that husband and wife sleep apart for long periods of time.

During the Renaissance, aristocrats and wealthy couples kept separate retreats and bedchambers. Privacy, highly valued, continued to be a symbol of status in the home in the seventeenth and eighteenth centuries. In the Victorian era, affluent American couples continued the practice of their British ancestors and had separate apartments and private bedrooms. What was most striking about house plans of the post–Civil War era was their design for separation. By the early twentieth century the most striking element of new house plans was their design for togetherness. (Ironically, one of the architects of this new idea about domestic space, which provided no special areas for individual activities, was Frank Lloyd Wright, who left his wife and six children in the home he designed for togetherness to go to Europe with the woman he later married.) With the post–World War II emphasis on marital togetherness, double, queen- and king-size beds became symbols of intimacy. Today we share not only beds and bedrooms and bathrooms, family rooms, living rooms, and kitchens, but also home offices. With more than 30 million people now working at home, and millions more predicted to join them, many couples are spending more time together than they ever anticipated. At the same time, external energies are bombarding us more than at any period in history, stimulation coming at us faster than we can calm it down, technology changing faster than we can figure it out, information accelerating faster than we can take it in. We can absorb only so much of the world's—and each other's—energies before we need to empty ourselves of them in order to discover and strengthen our own.

So it's not surprising that when a 1996 study commissioned by *Redbook* asked married women, "What do you dream about?" half answered, "More time alone." In my conversations with women, I found the yearning for time alone expressed by those who had *never* had that luxury, who married right out of college or married later but always had roommates, women who grew up with more siblings than space, women who in fifty years had never slept alone in a bed. And I found the yearning expressed by those who, until marriage, *always* had it, who grew up as only children, or had siblings but always their own bedrooms, or had been on their own for many years.

Amelia Earhart had been on her own for many years and was intimately aware of her need for solitude when publisher George Putnam proposed. Initially she said no because she "didn't want *anything*, all the time." He persevered and she changed her mind, but right before the ceremony she handed him a letter, which read in part: "I may have to keep some place where I can go to be myself now and then, for I cannot guarantee to endure at all times the confinements of even an attractive cage." Her primary place alone was the sky, but she also spent one month a year—without her husband—at Purdue University as a visiting professor, aeronautical advisor, and women's career counselor.

Women whose work keeps them grounded on land, married to men whose work keeps them grounded at home, can find themselves living with another human being most every day of every month of every year. When it's not the relationship that compresses but its physical circumstances, a woman can adore her husband yet still feel euphoric when he leaves the house. She can say she'd marry him all over again yet still envy women whose husbands travel in their work. She can be blissfully married yet long for time alone. It's not a repudiation of her partner but a time-out for herself, not a desire to *be* free but to *feel* free. What's more unnatural: living apart for thirty, sixty, or ninety days, or living continuously together for more than 9,000 days? It's not surprising that marriage counselors talk of clients who said they might not have divorced if their spouses had traveled in their work.

Breathing space is a powerful need. It can be a thinking space or a feeling space, a physical place or a mental place, a conscious motive interspersed among many or unconscious motive realized in retrospect, but whatever its characteristics, it's that space that is clearly our own, where we don't have to consider anything but what's going on inside our own heads. It's a room emptied of clutter so that calm and clarity can flourish, allowing us to restore equilibrium or gather energy, birth an idea or nurture thought. In ancient Greek, the word for "breath," *anapnoi*, means both life and soul, while the Hebrew *ruah* signifies both breath and spirit. In the Eskimo language, the same word means "to breathe" and "to make a poem." Breathing space is where we exhale stress and inhale inspiration, the air we need to shape a career, compose a life, make a poem, remake a marriage.

One day, I run into an old acquaintance, a lawyer I had met twenty years ago when we lived in the same apartment complex and our children were babies. The only news I'd had of him since came from a newspaper item revealing that in one week he had won two major medical malpractice cases, setting him up for life.

"Still married?" I ask.

He smiles. "Yes."

"What do you attribute it to?"

He smiles again. "Inertia."

We laugh, but I wonder.

How many couples find their marriages rooted in habit, sliding toward entropy? For all the media blitz on the culture of divorce, the reality is that half of all couples in this country remain together until one partner dies. That's plenty of time for routines to grow stale, for energy to ebb. The problem is that many of us don't have role models for long *and* satisfying marriages, and the culture we live in doesn't do much to provide them. Almost half of all paperback novels are romances that end with the promise of a marriage beginning. From thirty-second commercial come-ons to two-hour cinematic seductions, our visual culture exudes images of Romeo-Juliet passions. But these images are at odds with the ebb and flow of real relationships. The reality is more akin to the image of the distressed woman on the postcard exclaiming, "When I said 'till death do us part,' I never dreamt I'd live this long!" John Updike explored this territory eloquently in his short story "Transaction": "In life there are four forces: love, habit, time and boredom. Love and habit at short range are immensely powerful, but time, lacking a minus charge, accumulates inexorably, and with its brother boredom levels all." What happens when there aren't surprises anymore? What happens when your partner doesn't need surprises, but you're bored?

"Do you want to go to a movie tonight?"

"I've got a lot of work to do, I can go either way. How about you?"

"I've got a lot of work, too. I can go either way. What are you interested in seeing?"

"I haven't looked at the listings yet. What do you want to see?"

We replay this dialogue three out of four weekends a year, our version of the diner scene in the 1950s film classic *Marty*. "What do you feel like doing tonight, Marty? I don't know. What do you feel like doing tonight?" What happened to the spontaneity, the energy, the fun? Why are we so exhausted by Saturday night that we can't come up with a creative way of spending the evening? When I asked Jim these questions, he said, "We're worn out. We've had some rough years—lots of caretaking, unexpected financial expenses. We work all the time." Agreeing on the answer doesn't solve the problem. Almost every Saturday night, we go to the movies.

I love the movies, actually. I like to see them the way they were meant to be seen—on a huge screen in a darkened theater. As the lights dim, I automatically reach for his hand, lean into his body. The familiarity and reassurance of this ritual reminds me of what I love about marriage. I can't think of anyone else I'd rather see a movie with. As the film starts to roll, vivid images transport me to another time and place. I become absorbed in the story, fall under the spell of Hollywood magic. Then invariably, two out of four weekends a month, I see projected on the screen magnified images of lust—graphic, urgent, intense—in the middle of the day, in the middle of the office, on an elevator going down, on a ship going under. Suddenly, I'm back in my own world wondering: Is he thinking what I'm thinking? Where's our lust?

It's Sunday morning, just the two of us, one of my favorite times to be together. It's the only morning we can sit and talk for hours. We discuss projects we're working on, brainstorm ideas, talk about the morning headlines, the state of the world, the state of our families. I love having his attention all to myself. This morning, however, other thoughts preoccupy me.

"If we're going to spend the second half of our lives together, you're going to have to come out of your cave," I say.

He looks up from the sports pages.

"Do I live in a cave?" he asks, smiling.

"Yes. You're always in your room, with your computer and your stereo. I want us to climb mountains, take swing classes, go dancing."

This last comment is ludicrous. He hates to dance.

He smiles again. "I didn't realize our life was that dull."

"Well, it is."

The next day, he calls from work.

"There's an art fair this weekend that's supposed to be really good. Why don't we go? Afterwards we can go to dinner, someplace new, maybe eat outdoors."

"Great. Sounds fun."

It is fun.

The next weekend:

"Do you want to go to a movie tonight?"

"I don't know. Do you want to go to a movie tonight?"

"Maybe. What do you want to see?"

"Haven't looked at the listings yet. What do you want to see?"

If marital ruts are inevitable, and therapists say they are, how do we dig our way out of them? How do we move back and forth from routine to rapture? What does it take to change the dynamics of a marriage? It takes someone noticing, it takes concern, and then it takes serious effort. As Ursula K. Le Guin wrote in *The Lathe of Heaven*, "Love doesn't just sit there, like a stone, it has to be made, like bread; remade all the time, made new." Ruts indicate that it's time to add sustenance, shape a new pattern, raise the temperature, remake love, *take action*. Therapists agree that as the guardians of intimacy, women more likely notice the rut, women more likely confront their partners about it, and women more likely expend energy to dig out.

But it's not work some women can do in their spare time or in the midst of the marriage. Time is too limited or attention too scattered, and the patterns too long-standing. To gain perspective, they need to move out of the routine of the relationship, and they need more than a weekend to do it. To wonder about a marriage, to re-design it, takes time. A marriage of quality takes time, and some women don't want any other kind. They refuse to settle into a marriage of convenience, a relationship without surprises. They know what they want, but this time they're not looking for answers from their husbands. They're looking for answers within.

Couples begin with a psychological contract as well as a legal one. The psychological contract contains the expectations that we bring to a marriage and the norms that develop as the marriage evolves. The expectations originate in the home we grew up in and the marriage that was modeled there. Usually we slide into these expectations and roles, often unconsciously patterning them after our parents. For many couples—maybe most—the psychological contract is unwritten, its clauses undiscussed. How many couples create psychological contracts when they marry, put them in writing like Amelia Earhart? How many create new contracts as years progress?

In Celtic tradition, as late as the twelfth century, Irish couples could decide on February 1, the feast of Imbolc, to part ways if their relationship no longer satisfied. The implication in the seasonal rite is that as time passes, individuals grow and change, and as they change they need to reevaluate their marriages. The Celts believed marriages should be renewed yearly, like license plates. Some therapists think that couples naturally renegotiate their relationships every seven years, unconsciously following the ancient Hebrews' agricultural practice. And some believe couples remap the marital terrain with life passages: when children arrive, leave, return, for example, or when couples begin and end careers.

To borrow Jung's metaphor, we cannot live in the afternoon of life according to the program of life's morning. We cannot assume that the marriage we had when we were twenty-five is the marriage that will work for us at forty or fifty. Throughout our lives we disengage — from cities and schools, jobs and friends. Why should it be any different to disengage from one marriage to turn it into another? While some couples become more physically enmeshed over time, others find the desire for breathing space intensifies as the years together increase. In a 1996 cross-cultural study of couples married for decades, researchers discovered that many of the American spouses were actively negotiating separateness from each other, both psychologically and physically. Many of the couples found bliss through a separate, distinct self, which meant separate computers, separate cars, separate interests, and separate spaces within the house. Berit Ingersoll-Dayton, one of the researchers, relayed the study's conclusion: "We discovered that happy, long-married couples enjoyed their times together more when they allowed each other distance. They saw time apart as a way of enhancing intimacy."

Anne Morrow Lindbergh compared the middle years of marriage to the oyster shell, heavily encrusted with accumulations and firmly embedded on its rock. The middle years of marriage should be a time for shedding shells, she wrote, for a loosening from the rock. Some people aren't convinced that a loosening is all a woman wants. They think a sabbatical is just a separation in cultural camouflage. What's the difference between the two? A sabbatical is a move toward self; a separation is a flight from the other. A sabbatical is planned. It says "I care about you." A separation can be impulsive; it says "Maybe I don't." A sabbatical has a return date, which says "I'll be back." A separation is usually open-ended, which says "Maybe I won't." The difference? Intention.

Catherine Gray, a psychologist in Washington, D.C., has been recommending sabbaticals to couples who come to her for marriage counseling. She is, to the best of my knowledge, the only professional to have researched the subject. She described the difference this way: "A sabbatical implies growth. A separation implies rupture. In a sabbatical the partners can grow without jeopardizing the relationship and, in fact, can enrich it. A year after the divorce, a lot of people wish they hadn't. But so much animosity has occurred that they cannot go back. I'm convinced a lot of people divorce when all they needed was a meaningful break."

The Midlife Collision

The motivations for a sabbatical parallel the needs of midlife, which explains why most of the women I interviewed were in their forties and fifties the first time they left. Many, in fact, left the year they turned forty or fifty. Physician and analyst Jean Shinoda Bolen said that it is during major life transitions that we most need time out from our routines. In her memoir *Crossing to Avalon*, she used the medical metaphor "diastole," the time when the heart relaxes and fills. "For the heart to work and provide sustenance to the whole body," she wrote, "it must relax and fill. And so must we."

From the growing body of research on midlife issues, we know that this developmental stage of adulthood is an emotional threshold that begins with an awareness of loss and a sense that time is limited. It's a period of psychological upheaval, when old identities are lost and new ones are born, when we raise questions, seek answers, fill the empty spaces. It's a time of transition signaling the end of one life structure and the beginning of another, a time to move out of roles and into the self, a time to re-evaluate our lives and then renew them, to keep learning, change careers, make a difference. In her seminal works on life passages, journalist Gail Sheehy identified the essential tasks of the middle years: Individuals must recreate their lives or they stagnate. Couples must renegotiate their contracts. Women must transcend dependency through self-declaration.

The midlife task for married women is illuminated in the fairy tale "The Wife Who Became King," one of a number of tales that psychiatrist Allen Chinen gathered from around the world and analyzed in *Once Upon a Midlife*. This particular tale comes from China and begins with a man and woman who fall in love and marry. Instead of living happily ever after, however, the wife is kidnapped by an evil king, imprisoned in his palace, and pressured to become one of his concubines. Her freedom and identity at stake, she disguises herself as a man and, using her intellect, resourcefulness, and determination, flees the palace, successfully eluding a host of attackers on her way home. She reunites with her husband, who helped her escape by following her instructions, which included wearing her clothes to impersonate a woman and give credibility to her disguise. The wife ends up becoming king herself, but after the coronation, she reveals her true identity, whereupon her husband is crowned king; she, queen and equal partner. The tale's message is that at midlife married women need to reclaim their power, with spouses reversing roles. As Chinen points out, what's interesting about this tale, besides the fact that its feminist message comes from a patriarchal culture, is that the wife overthrows societal oppression and claims her unrealized power *while* remaining a loving partner to her husband. Unlike the resolution of many feminist stories, she doesn't forgo marriage for autonomy; she integrates the two.

Whatever the shape or source of the research, those who have studied midlife say it brings a second surge of identity issues. Jung said if we look at what we envy, we'll know what we have neglected in our lives.

It's the summer of 1994, and I am nestled in my well-worn sofa, sipping jasmine tea and feeling a rush of nostalgia as I open my college's twenty-fifth reunion yearbook. Each reminiscence takes me further back to the dramatic spires of the Gothic architecture, the delicate fragrance of the magnolia trees, the brilliant fuchsias and golds of the gardens. I sink into the pillows, finding the entries as seductive as a good novel. Then, like a driver cruising the interstate who sees a car wreck on the side of the road, I slow down, feeling simultaneously attracted and repelled. I immediately recognize the face, pretty twenty-five years ago and, in the yearbook photo, gorgeous now. Her entry is breezily written, ornamented with exclamation points and ellipses. The style makes me cringe, but the words carry weight. Her highlights since graduation: "Buying a one-way ticket to San Francisco and never looking back; thinking of going to med school, but deciding life is too short . . . winters in Aspen, summers in Hawaii as an ICU nurse . . . living up

and down the coast of California . . . working as a nurse
in the French West Indies, Israel and Mexico . . . traveling to Sardinia, the Italian Alps and Morocco with the
love of my life, a Swiss named Hans . . . marrying Hans
and flying back and forth to our restaurants in Park City
and Mammoth Lakes, CA . . . Hans got his pilot's license . . . later, me too!"

This is the woman whose life I envy. Not the classmate
who wrote three books while practicing neurosurgery, not
the woman with the Wall Street title and the Park Avenue
address, not the beauty queen who married one of the
country's most powerful politicians. I envy the woman
who has lived and worked all over the world, whose life
has been an exotic adventure.

I was an engaged college senior when "make love, not
war" swept the campus, a new bride when Kate Millett
published *Sexual Politics*, a young mother when Ger-
maine Greer expounded on *The Female Eunuch*. Just as
the first woman ran the Boston Marathon, marched at
West Point, and played a TV superheroine, just as Billie
Jean King trounced Bobby Riggs in straight sets, just as
1970s feminism revolutionized every aspect of American
life, I'd chosen a narrower path. In one part of my mind I
saw life stretch out before me; in another, I felt opportunity already squeezed.

The day I am reading my college anniversary yearbook, twenty-five years have elapsed, and not only have I
never lived alone, I'm still living in the city I grew up in.
I close the book with an unsettling realization: I want to
backpack across Europe, study at Oxford, live like
Thoreau in a cabin in the woods. I want to be back in

my twenties but without the responsibilities. I want what I missed.

"Parts of ourselves that are undeveloped reside in a state of unconsciousness," explained Patricia Vesey-McGrew, a Boston Jungian analyst. "At some point we need to go back and get in touch with these unlived lives in order to become whole." So many women I interviewed affirmed Jung's theory of development. Debra, who dropped out of a doctoral program in Far Eastern languages, left to teach English in the Orient. A woman who had to work her way through community college, always juggling classes and jobs, left to be a full-time student at a prestigious university. A woman who had become a professional singer instead of the minister she wanted to be entered seminary. English novelist George Eliot anticipated Jung's theory when she said, "It's never too late to be what you might have been."

That's what Rebecca believed, and in her story more than any other, motivations overlapped and intertwined, revealing the multiple layers woven through a woman's journey.

Rebecca is a painter who lives in New England with her second husband. She described their relationship as "happily domestic," yet when I spoke to her the first time she was preparing to leave her home and husband to spend the winter living and working in Washington, D.C. Rebecca spoke for more than two hours about the reasons underlying her time-out. She talked first about her yearning for another landscape. She appreciated the beauty of her wooded, coastal environment, but not its isolation. She respected her carpenter husband's love for the house he had built himself, its structural design and artistic charm, but she was tired of the rural living that came with it. She longed for the pulse of a city and the energy of human interaction, so she could find new stimulation for her life, new images for her art. "I don't need to be with a lot of people," she said, "but I need to observe them. I'm not a nature artist."

Talking about art led Rebecca to the subject of immersion. As a single parent at twenty-three, she didn't feel she could be a responsible mother and an artist, too. She had to earn a living. After years of a multitude of jobs, she felt it was time to give her creative impulses a dominant place in her life. "Immersion is what art needs and deserves," she said. "It's crazy not to be able to commit to something that is so intrinsic to human historical experience." Immersion was her unlived life, the past she needed to revisit.

Rebecca then talked about spiritual growth and a pressing need to make her inner life a priority. She had long wanted to participate in the life of a metaphysical church, but her small town didn't have one. There were only twelve such churches in the United States, one in Washington, D.C. Her conversation segued to landscape again, a love of Washington, where she had once lived. The city was the setting for an earlier crossroads that she had successfully navigated and, as such, was imprinted in her mind as a place of strength.

Finally, Rebecca talked about time and space to think about her marriage. Every marriage has issues, and Rebecca's was no exception. The question for her, as for every other married person, was how to live with them. She already knew the pain of divorce; she didn't consider that an option. She already knew the frustration of asking, pleading, and fighting for what she wanted but getting no results; that option had expired, too. Her husband was content, saw no reason for change, but Rebecca wanted a different way to coexist, and for this she needed breathing space. She was clear about her motive. "I don't want another man," she said. "What I want is knowledge."

And then she was talking about milestones and midlife. "I just turned fifty and feel I've just awakened."

Rebecca's last words remind me of the quip—lament, actually—about Sleeping Beauty: She slept for a hundred years and when she woke up she was fifty. Carol Gilligan, Jean Miller Baker, Allen Chinen, and others have said that to survive, girls hide their true selves and like Sleeping Beauty hibernate psychologically, like the Little Mermaid silence their voices. At midlife, women wake up, *must* wake up to avoid unhappiness later in life. We have to stop waiting for something external to change our lives and start listening to our own voices, take responsibility for our own fulfillment. As Rebecca said, "A spouse cannot meet all our needs, and why should he?"

For some women, taking responsibility for their own fulfillment means a journey away from home—to learn more about themselves, the world, and their place in it. If a woman feels fragmented, she wants focus. If she feels off-center, she wants balance. If she feels restless, she wants direction. If she feels incomplete, she wants expanded consciousness so her knowing is greater, her loving deeper. She leaves to achieve a dream, conquer a challenge, find the missing piece, become whole. *She leaves to change the rhythms of her life.*

Whether the decision is a natural extension of a woman's interests or a defining moment of her life, it's not a passing whim or an angry act. Some women talked of waking up from a dream or having an epiphany. Others described a moment of crisis: What now? What next? What's left? Accidents or physical symptoms sometimes felt like signs. One woman spoke of a hunger that became an obsession, others said shock waves went through them or a thunderbolt hit. Sue Bender heard a voice telling her to live with an Amish family. "I think of myself as a sensible person, not someone who hears voices, or follows them," she wrote in *Plain and Simple*, "but this voice sounded so loud and clear and came from such a deep place in me, that it seemed like the voice of a stranger. I had to listen."

A voice, a dream, or a sign speaks to the spiritual nature of the journey. So does a sense of urgency. When a woman feels that she "has to listen" to the stirring within, when thinking about the experience fills her equally with joy and with terror, when it's so important she is willing to endure great difficulties, when the decision honors a deep and genuine need, then a powerful spirit is at work.

If the desire lies in our conscious dreams and subconscious yearnings, if it's natural to want to grow, to develop our talents, to find new meaning in our lives; if independence and risk taking and a sense of adventure are qualities we supposedly admire; if bookstores are filled with titles urging us to go after our dreams, then why isn't leaving felt or perceived as natural? What makes it so difficult?

3

FEARS

I told my husband what I planned to do,
shouting like a drill sergeant in heavy army
boots, declaring my certainty, afraid that if I
stopped long enough to take a breath and
discuss it reasonably I'd lose my resolve.

—SUE BENDER,
Plain and Simple:
A Woman's Journey to the Amish

I was forty-one when I landed the job of my dreams: features editor at a new metro newspaper, the first city daily to start up in the United States in fifty years. I loved being part of a journalistic adventure with a sense of mission, a paper designed to revolutionize the industry. The $25-million enterprise generated media coverage from New York to London. Henry Kissinger dropped by for a tour. In a gently curved building of emerald green glass, soaring 188 feet above the St. Louis riverfront, a state-of-the-art newsroom featured floor-to-ceiling windows illuminating the city skyline, impressive by day, breathtaking at dusk.

Only a glass wall separated my office from that of the publishing tycoon who flew in from the East Coast with his $400-million fortune, his private jet and chauffered BMW, his visionary ideas, his cosmopolitan charm. I loved the invitations to the gourmet lunches in the executive dining room. I loved the Dove bars in the executive kitchen. I especially loved my salary—double that of my previous job. I couldn't wait to walk through the marble-walled lobby each morning. I didn't need caffeine to get through the day—I got a rush just being at the daily editorial meeting, the only female section editor at the table. "This is as good as it gets," I thought to myself. "Finally, my work life is in place." Seduced by the atmosphere, consumed by the challenge, I started off working ninety hours a week. By the time I got to a manageable fifty, the paper folded.

Today I cannot think of that time of career headiness without also thinking of the price it exacted. Guilt clings to the memory. My younger son spent too much time alone at home, set off a smoke bomb at school, got suspended, became surly and depressed. My older son was in the midst of college applications, but why research academic scholarships when money was abundant and time scarce? Nine months of being in the top 5 percent of women wage earners in the country led to four years of tuition bills steeper than we could afford. And the part that haunts me still: When I started the job, I had a grandmother I adored, who was just beginning to show signs of dementia. Each month I had intended to visit her; each month I couldn't find the time. The day after the paper closed I went to see her. By then she was in a nursing home, her expression unknowing, her eyes empty.

I left the best part of my life—my family—for an unknown that beckoned. I can't help but wonder as I leave town for three months if I'm doing that again. What if Jim becomes injured or sick while I'm a thousand miles away? What if he dies?

He is my emotional anchor. I rely on him as much as I do on the air I breathe. I know he relies on me equally, but he seems comfortable with his need for me. I wrestle with my need for him. On the surface I look like an independent woman and I know others see me that way. I've earned a living wage all but five years of my adult life; I supported three of us when Jim was in graduate school. I know I can take care of myself financially. But that's only one kind of independence, and I'm afraid I lag in others. I think this feeling comes in part from a learned helplessness that seems inherent in marriage—for both men and women—a helplessness that comes from dividing tasks, which most couples do.

On my first date with Jim, he picked me up in a sleek red sports car, a Firebird 400 so gleaming it looked like he had driven it out of the showroom. To buy it, he had worked two summers trimming trees, and his parents and grandparents matched his earnings. Jim loved that car, the way it was built so low to the ground he could "feel the road." Unknown to the family investors, he raced it during college. For the first seven years of our marriage, it was the only car we had, and for Jim maintaining it was a loving ritual; washing it, a weekly relaxation. When we bought a second car, he automatically took care of it as he did his own. To Jim a car was investment, hobby, and passion. To me it was a tool and a closet.

It was easy to let him take care of my car because it was one less thing to worry about. For years I didn't give the matter much thought. Then one day it hit me that since gas stations had gone to self-serve, I had never put gas in the car. Suddenly one less thing to worry about meant one less thing to master.

"Stop washing my car and filling it with gas every week," I snapped at him one Sunday. "Stop doing all the maintenance. Here I am running a department and I can't run my own car."

I raise my voice about once every two years, so Jim looked up from his desk, startled.

"I had no idea you felt that way. All you had to do was say something."

"Well, I'm saying something."

The next year I got pulled over and handed a ticket because I hadn't renewed the license plates, almost destroyed the engine because I forgot to add oil, called AAA repeatedly for a dead battery, all the while suffering through higher dry-cleaning bills because the grime on the exterior stained my clothes. I didn't feel much mastery that year, actually, but the second year I did. When your spouse has taken charge of the cars or the finances or the laundry for years on end (because, like Jim and our cars, their standards are higher), your knowledge of the subject steadily decreases because someone else was there to know for you. This domestic interplay reinforces the broader illusion that someone else will always be there to do it for us, an illusion that leads first to dependence and then to feelings of incompetence.

I think this is what happens to a lot of men with housework. Their wives have higher standards, therefore do most of the work, so that over time their husbands acquire a learned helplessness in this area. When my mother could no longer drive, my father had to grocery shop for the first time at the age of seventy-five. He was a mathematical and electronics whiz who had gone to MIT and was board-certified in two medical specialties, but he got lost in the grocery store, came home without the things he went for, spent hours searching for the missed items afterward, never got used to going, never liked going. I don't want to have to learn survival skills during a crisis, when emotions are already jumbled.

Psychological dependence is trickier because it's harder to admit, therefore harder to penetrate. I can't think of many decisions that I have to make on which I don't seek Jim's input. I'm continually asking him: What do you think about this job, this story idea, this article, this computer, these contact lenses? "What do you think?" could be my mantra. I don't necessarily follow the advice I've sought, but since his responses are thoughtful and intelligent, I instinctively ask the next time, so the cycle continues. Here's my concern: If he's always there to ask, does that mean I'm less than what I could be? Does his continual presence handicap my decision-making capabilities? Or have I, in fact, assimilated his best qualities—his perspective, his resilience, his calm—but don't know it because they are more pronounced in him than in me? Or do I just think they're more pronounced because they were when we began our lives together?

I'm having trouble gaining perspective on myself. Independence feels like a dress that I bought without trying on because it looked so great on the rack and then came home to discover that it doesn't hang right on my ectomorphic frame. I want the swathe of matte jersey to move with me, not hang loosely like a thing apart. I want a better fit.

I need to know that the self-sufficiency I project is grounded internally, but I'm not sure it's possible with him at my side. I often wonder: How would I be without him? Who would I be without him? When the boys were little and he went out of town, we'd eat out of cartons on the living room rug, using napkins for plates. I'd serve peanut butter for breakfast and cereal and ice cream for dinner. I'd let clothes and papers and sinks pile up, then race around like a charwoman before he returned. The truth is, he civilizes me.

He also helps me stay focused, headed from point A to point B, when my nature is to take a lot of side journeys. Without him would I stay on course? I'm afraid to find out I need him more than I want to need him. And I'm just as afraid to find out I don't need him at all. That's the greater fear, actually, because if I don't need him as I think I do, what happens to our marriage then?

Some contemporary spiritual thinkers believe there are only two basic emotions from which all others flow: love and fear. In a sabbatical, a woman leaves the known for the unknown. Why wouldn't it be fearful? The unknown means risk, and risks are real. In the sacred stories of many cultures, the gods kept complete knowledge from man, so there was always temptation, always risk. Adam and Eve could eat from every tree in the Garden of Eden but the Tree of Knowledge; when they ate the forbidden fruit, they were banished from Paradise and condemned to a life of suffering. In Greek mythology, Psyche was told she must never look at the face of her lover, who came to her each night at dark; after she held a lantern to his face, she had to journey to the underworld and back to reunite with him. In another Greek tale, Pandora, the first mortal woman, was given a golden urn as a dowry for her future husband with the divine injunction that she must never unseal it; when she opened the jar, she unleashed upon the earth every human misery. In European folklore, Bluebeard gave each new bride the keys to his castle with the instruction that she could open every door but one; when she unlocked the forbidden door, behind which were the skeletons of his previous wives, he killed her. The message in bibles and myths is that the desire for knowledge will cost us. Consciousness always extracts a price.

Disapproval

Jessica is an interior designer who has created a water-front home on the West Coast that is sought after for catalogue and magazine photo shoots. She enjoys interior design and has built a profitable business, but her heart lies increasingly in her writing. She went back to school to study fiction, hoping to complete and publish her novel-in-progress. Away from the academic structure, however, she found it hard to justify the time, so progress slowed. The only way, she felt, to make writing a priority was to isolate herself at a writers' retreat. Her desire to go away had little to do with Richard, the man she loved and had lived with for fourteen years, but the fears aroused by her longing had a great deal to do with him.

From the beginning I wanted to apply for the maximum time, which was two months. But when I got the application, I said to Richard, "I'm thinking of doing this for two weeks." I went upstairs and worked on the application for a while. Then I came down and said, "You know, I think a month is a nice length of time. I'll probably go for two weeks, but I think I'll ask for a month." I went back upstairs, worked on the application a little longer, then came down and said, "You know, I think six weeks would be good. I'll just ask for six weeks." I went back upstairs, worked on the application some more, then came down and said, "Well, I finished it and I asked for two months. I won't get it, but that's what I applied for.

Testing out the different times was all about worrying about Richard. When I was accepted for two months, I was scared to tell him. I didn't even know how I was feeling because I was so worried about how he was feeling. Over and over again, I asked him, "Are you going to be okay with this?" I was worried that he'd be so lonely without me that he'd literally die of a broken heart. But that's so narcissistic when you think about it. One of the reasons he's attracted to me is because I'm a strong woman. Why do I act like a wimp? Where is it coming from?

The answer to Jessica's question is a favorite lecture topic of John Gottman. Considered by many to be the foremost marriage researcher in the United States, Dr. Gottman runs a couples clinic, dubbed "The Love Lab," at the University of Washington in Seattle. He believes that women have trouble permitting themselves to have life dreams that are not related to families, to being good wives, good mothers, good daughters—the only dreams society has promoted as legitimate for women. As a result, he said, "Women are all too willing to give up their dreams for the sake of relationships, but the truth is, relationships are helped, not hurt, by honoring women's dreams."

Dr. Gottman thinks that the incidence of depression may be so high in women because they don't pursue their dreams, and that women must pursue them if only for the sake of their mental health. He believes so strongly in this subject that he leads workshops to give women the permission they have trouble giving themselves. "I tell them, 'You're not going to help anyone by giving up on your dream and you're going to lose a part of yourself.' It's a hard message for a lot of women to hear."

It's hard because most women can't think about their dreams without worrying about how those dreams affect everyone else. It's hard because women want to preserve their relationships, and they are afraid the people they love will resist or reject their dreams, and then what? The fear is realistic. Since the subject was first studied, the conclusion has been unchallenged: Support for dreams is less likely to be present in the lives of women than in the lives of men.

What research has documented, Jessica had intuited. She anticipated criticism and a lack of support, with the result that for a long time it wasn't just Richard she was afraid to tell. She was embarrassed to tell her friends. "What I was doing seemed pretentious," she said. "I was afraid they'd think, 'Oh, she must fancy herself a writer.'"

Jessica was also afraid to tell Richard's parents, afraid they would think she was abandoning him. Richard wasn't afraid to tell them and he wasn't worried about their reaction, but the evening they planned to share the news, Jessica worried the whole time. "All night, I kept praying silently, *please Richard, don't tell them the length of time.*"

And finally, Jessica was afraid to tell her own parents. Because she was in the midst of renovating their home, she knew they wouldn't like her absence. Because they had been married fifty-two years and wouldn't sleep apart one night, she knew they wouldn't approve of it. "I was nervous about telling my mother. When I did, she said, 'What about my house?' If it hadn't been the house, she would have said, 'What about Richard?' I knew she wouldn't be happy for me—and she wasn't."

Jessica is one of a number of women I spoke with who were afraid to tell their mothers, and many of these mothers confirmed their daughters' fears. From an older generation, these women did not feel the same sense of freedom and economic security as their daughters, and their marriages adhered to more traditional conventions. Seeing a daughter leave her home and husband to fulfill a dream can unleash a Pandora's box of emotions: regret, if she didn't live out her own dream; envy, if her daughter is doing the very thing she wanted to but didn't; worry, if the experience involves physical danger; fear, if she depends on her daughter for care. Fear, too, if she thinks her daughter will lose her husband in going or—maybe a greater fear—that if she doesn't lose her husband what does that say about her own choices all these years? Any or all of these emotions can surface as disapproval, and disapproval is one of the risks women take.

Sometimes it's just a stiffening of the body or a steely look in the eyes, a beat of silence. *What makes you so special?* is the unspoken question.

"Well, that's a very long time," said one mother-in-law, eyebrows raised, voice clipped.

"Friends said if I did this my marriage was over," said a woman who left for six months with her husband's support.

"All my co-workers thought I was terrible to leave my husband and son for three months," said a nurse whose husband and teenager felt fine about it.

"His family is hard-shell Southern Baptist," said another woman. "Even though no one said anything, I knew what they were thinking: *There she goes, focusing on herself, forgetting about him.*"

Even though no one said anything . . . Just the impression I got . . . She didn't say it aloud, but the underlying message was: "You don't leave your family when you have one." Body language can easily reveal disapproval, and women are good at detecting the meaning behind gestures and vocal tones. When the faces are neutral and the voices silent, however, our reactions become a mirror to our own feelings. We have to ask what's really registering—their disapproval or our guilt?

It can well be our guilt because guilt comes from the internalized "should," the critical voice within. Whether that voice comes from parent or culture, the result is the same: It heightens our sensitivity to others' reactions, leading us to perceive disapproval even where none is intended. In her insightful book on the subject, *Guilt Is the Teacher, Love Is the Lesson*, Joan Borysenko distinguishes between healthy guilt, which teaches us conscience, and unhealthy guilt, which makes us hypersensitive to criticism. Expressions of unhealthy guilt include worrying about what others think, fearing others' anger, wanting to please everyone, caring for everyone but ourselves.

If a woman's history has been to care for everyone but herself, her decision can stir a litany of guilts. She can feel guilty because she's excited about doing something that doesn't include her husband, or because he might like a similar experience but cannot so easily leave his work or give up his income. She can feel guilty because he'll have to live alone, sleep alone. She can feel guilty about walking away from her share of household responsibilities, about leaving a mother who is ill or a grandchild she baby-sits.

A woman can feel guilty about spending money on herself, even when she earns as much as, or more than, her partner does; even when she is paying for the experience and covering home expenses in her absence; even when she is independently wealthy. A women can feel guilty because, if she has been conditioned to put everyone else's needs before her own, a sabbatical feels like selfishness. Guilt comes from pleasing yourself if you have been raised to please others.

Guilt is the hallmark of the first time away because guilt comes from changing the status quo. Guilt comes from moving away from traditional expectations, moving toward a new way of relating to the world. Guilt comes from saying no to others when you have always said yes, from taking care of yourself when you never saw your mother take care of herself. Guilt comes from the emotions, not the intellect, so no matter how legitimate a woman's desire, how supportive her husband, how genuine their devotion, how deep their pockets, if it is the first time that *she* is doing the leaving, then it can feel emotionally upsetting. A rope of guilt wraps around emotions that feel wrong, and with each disparaging remark, each look of disapproval or surprise, the rope tightens. "Guilt's pain is an indication that we are searching for our worthiness in the wrong place," writes Borysenko. "In saying yes to guilt, we begin saying no to life."

Jessica's guilt led her to expect disapproval, but with the exception of her mother, she didn't get it. Her story reveals a woman's fears. Megan's absence of guilt led her to expect approval, but with the exception of her husband, she didn't get it. Her story reveals other people's fears.

A thirty-year-old artist, Megan had been with her husband for six years (living together for five, married for one). She was still noticeably in love with the man in her life, and she had left him twice for two months to paint. Her first time away evoked shrugs; her second, disapproval. Megan was the same woman, exuberant and ambitious, loving and lovable. She was earning the same living teaching art, refinishing furniture, and painting murals for children's rooms. She was devoted to the same man and going to the same place for the same purpose for the same duration. The second time, however, she was wearing a wedding ring. That changed everything.

Her best girlfriend said, "Don't you think that's a long period of time to be away from Jeff?"

A second girlfriend said, "What are you doing going away? Are you hiding something?"

Her sister said, "Can't you go for a shorter time?"

Her mother said, "You are making a big mistake."

Married friends, "every one of them," thought she was running away to have an affair. That thought quickly led to the next: Wasn't she worried Jeff would have one if she weren't home? Her friends let her know she was taking a risk.

Her mother let her know she was taking a big risk. *You're putting your own needs above your marriage*, she warned her daughter. *Every time you leave, you open the window for something to happen.* Megan understood that, like all her married friends, her mother had never gone away by herself for herself. Megan also knew her mother was still hurting from her divorce, still angry at Megan's father for leaving her for another woman, someone he'd met when he was out of town on business. Megan respected her mother's Ph.D. intellect but faulted her logic. Who's to say that the same thing wouldn't have happened if her mother had accompanied him on the trip? Who's to say that the dynamics of one marriage have anything to do with another? Their argument escalated into a fight and then, a few weeks later, into a second one.

What created a problem for Megan weren't her fears but other people's. What caused her both stress and distress was the way others jumped to conclusions, assumed wrongdoing, predicted disaster, communicated a narrow band of thought: *Married women shouldn't leave home.*

"I don't know what everyone's reactions were about," said Megan, "but they had nothing to do with me."

The reactions had nothing to do with the woman receiving them, everything to do with the people expressing them. They reflected not an individual relationship, but a public ritual; not a *concrete* reality, but an *assumed* reality. The collective reaction projected a collective fear relayed through a collective message: *Married women shouldn't leave home.* This is the voice of hundreds of years of cultural conditioning. a husband's entitlement, a wife's duty. A supposed clause of the marital contract filtered down through time and generation: "Good" wives don't leave home. "Good" wives stay home.

In Greek mythology, the message-bearer is Hestia, goddess of the hearth. To ensure the sacred fire never died, Hestia ceded her throne on Olympus, the only deity to do so. Her sacrifice was rewarded: Among men, she was the most venerated of the goddesses (though in text books, her story claims the least space). The myth of Hestia, ever-watchful, ever-present, is the myth of female containment. That others reacted so negatively to Megan's leaving home reveals a society still invested in the myth. The message needs deconstructing not only because it is based on fear rather than reality but also because the presumptions it makes are psychologically unsound, spiritually repressive, and culturally destructive.

Presumption 1: There's only one type of good marriage, and that's joined at the hip. In 1937, a popular book called *New Girls for Old* described marriage as "a perfect consummation of both personalities that will involve every phase of mutual living." This viewpoint is still with us, thirty years after sociologist Jessie Bernard wrote in her landmark book *The Future of Marriage*, "The most important task for women in the marriage of the future is to become autonomous women."

Consider: In the fall of 1998, a caller asked radio host Laura Schlessinger whether she should take a job that would require her to be away from her husband four weeks a year. "Dr. Laura's" response, heard by more than 18 million listeners, more than half of them women, was both rigid and archaic: "You've got to decide whether you want a career or a marriage." She advised the caller against taking the job. In a 1997 article entitled "Rules for Married Couples," *McCall's* magazine also turned back the clock fifty years by telling 5 million female readers: "No commuter marriages. No separate vacations." In a 1987 *Newsweek* cover story entitled "How To Stay Married," the writer explained the success of one couple's twenty-nine-year marriage: "They worked at staying close. They've never been separated for more than a week."

Many marital guides today promote the same ideology. In one such manual, structured as case studies, the author discussed a client who came in distressed because her husband wanted to live in a cabin by himself for ten days. The marriage counselor described how she guided the wife to use her wiles to get him to cut his trip short. In *Learning to Love the One You Marry*, Gary Kinnaman preached that marriage was never meant to be bent to our individual purposes. Among those who agree is psychologist Diane Medved. "You'd better be prepared to spend the rest of your life alone when you depart for that self-defining private space," she wrote in *The Case Against Divorce*. "That you even desire solitary self-fulfillment shows a nonmarriage mentality." Clinical psychologist Willard Harley, author of half a dozen books on marriage, is equally adamant. "Any career that takes you away from your spouse overnight is dangerous to the health of your marriage," he declared in *Love Busters*. Harley recommends—in his writings, on the phone, and to the hundreds of couples he's counseled—that a husband and wife never spend one night apart. When Linda McCartney died, media reports highlighted that in twenty-nine years of marriage, she and Paul spent only eleven days apart, and those were involuntary (when Paul was jailed in Japan for possession of marijuana). In good marriages, in great marriages, we read between the lines, spouses are together all the time.

This joined-at-the-hip mentality is fine for couples for whom it works, but what happens when personal codes become media messages and individual convictions become general prescription? That divorce rates in the United States are among the highest in the industrialized world, that marriage doesn't work long-term for tens of millions of people in this country, that 67 percent of couples marrying today can expect to divorce seem to indicate a need to *loosen* the cultural straitjacketing, move beyond dictates about how married life should be.

When a friend fears "two months is too long" and a therapist counsels "not one night apart," they reduce marriage to one-size-fits-all. A woman in her twenties can be excused on the grounds of naïveté or inexperience, but a therapist is a relationship professional, who more than

anyone else should understand the complexity and variation in individual marriages. Instead, one reductionism is
based on another:

*Presumption 2: Physical closeness means emotional
closeness.* An informal poll of friends who have divorced
will reveal that most, if not all, stopped making love with
their spouses long before they separated physically. In the
film *American Beauty*, the Burnhams portray this marital
truth, one every person who grew up with battling parents
knows: Living in the same house is not a barometer of
emotional intimacy. The Burnhams have been married
sixteen years and, to the outside world, appear to be an attractive twosome, driving to work together or smiling
while they watch their daughter cheerlead, but inside
their elegant home the atmosphere is cold, the conversation brittle. They sleep in the same bed every night, but
the marriage is sexless and joyless, and has been for years.
Carolyn Burnham, played by Annette Bening, has transferred any interest she once had in her husband to her career in real estate. Obsessed with financial success and
image, she rages when he quits a deadening job and
spurns his desire for spontaneous sex because it might
ruin the fabric on her $4,000 sofa.

Although Carolyn's transfer of focus and withdrawal of
affection are extreme, married women take emotional absences all the time. Whether it's a high-pressure job, a political campaign, a start-up business, or a degree, intensive focus can mean partners sleep in the same bed but
not much else.

When I was working twelve- to fourteen-hour days at
high-profile jobs, I received—to my face, anyway—comments that revealed only curiosity, admiration, or envy.

Technically I was living at home, but my energy and focus were on work. I kept in touch through the telephone. Harriett Woods, former president of the National Women's Political Caucus, said of the years she campaigned for public office: "Even when I was home, which wasn't often, I wasn't there. My time and mind were elsewhere. When you become a candidate for office, you're not going to fulfill the vows to your marriage." And yet these types of absences, like commuter marriages, are accepted, respected even, in a way that Megan's absence was not.

Presumption 3: A job is more important than a dream, even if that dream will lead to a new career or new meaning in work. A temporary absence is a temporary absence. To consider it more acceptable when there's a paycheck attached is to say that life's foremost value is a monetary one. To consider living apart as natural behavior for movie stars and heads of state but not for the couple across the street is to say that individuality in relationships is bestowed only upon the cultural elite. To hold those with a stay-at-home profession to a different standard than those whose work requires travel is to engage in parochial thinking, what one woman called "a prejudice against choice over necessity." Duty to self, to talent, to one's dream is not only as important as duty to an employer, it is far more important, because duty to an employer is temporary, whereas duty to self lasts as long as we live.

Presumption 4: A woman can pursue her dreams only when she's single. Through the ages, the world's great thinkers have advocated duty to self. And none that I am aware of qualified this duty as applying only to the unmarried. When Megan's mother chastised her for putting her own needs above her relationship, when therapists write that individual desires and self-defining private spaces are antithetical to marriage, they discount duty to self. They are saying that with the ritual—the institution—of marriage comes an automatic transmission: A man's needs are now more important than a woman's. Journalist Danielle Crittenden says exactly this in her 1999 book, *What Our Mothers Didn't Tell Us.* In order for modern women to have the marriages we want, she writes, we have to stop being so preoccupied about our identities. Crittenden, though in the same generation as Megan, relays the same message as Megan's mother. When Megan's mother approved of her daughter's time away to paint when she was single but not when she was married, she was making this presumption. The subtext here is that once a woman marries she doesn't need to pursue her dreams. All she needs for emotional contentment is the right man.

I believed this when I married at twenty-one, and as a reminder I keep a photo from that time in my office, an image of a young couple on a beach, his eyes focused on the horizon, her eyes focused on him. Years of maternal indoctrination and media messages conjoined to create in one unformed mind one fervent belief: Now that I had found the man of my dreams, all my problems were over. Like Sleeping Beauty, whose long sleep the good fairy charmed with sweet dreams, our culture beguiles women into marriage with this lie—that emotional contentment will come with the right man. (Men are beguiled with an equivalent lie—that contentment will come with financial success.) After twenty-eight years of marriage, I believe that intimate relationship is essential to a satisfying life, but it is not the only essential. We all need to develop

our talents and contribute them to the world. That the realization of those talents requires time away from home
does not affect their legitimacy or discount their importance.

Elsie Roth, a New York native, was a forty-five-year-old
mother of five when her first husband died of a heart at-
tack at their home in Ballwin, Missouri. She entered
nursing school, not because she deeply desired to be a
nurse but because she thought it would be a good profession that would take her anywhere she wanted to go.
When she graduated at fifty-four, she chose public health
and the streets of the world. With her children grown, she
spent months at a time in Ethiopia and Israel tending to
those in need, and she served five times as a volunteer in
the Israeli army. Then in 1986, Roth remarried. During
the Persian Gulf War, she left her husband to volunteer in
the main trauma center in Tel Aviv for six weeks until just
before the war ended. Three years later, she led four separate missions of nurses taking medical supplies to Sara-
jevo during Bosnia's civil war. Her work has attracted
newspaper and magazine articles and earned honorary
awards, including being chosen as one of *Time* magazine's "Local Heroes." "My friends never said a word
when I was single and left on missions," she said. "Once I
remarried, most of them didn't understand that what I do
best, and what I want to do, I'll continue to do in the marriage. They saw only that I was leaving my husband alone.
They never looked at it from the other side, that of making a difference in the world."

Cautionary comments may not seem surprising coming
from Roth's friends, who like her are mostly in their sixties, but they do seem surprising coming from Megan's

friends, thirty years younger. Caution seems surprising coming from women one would assume to be more autonomous: professionals in their thirties, forties, and fifties with advanced degrees (like Megan's mother). The comments seem surprising when they come from college students in the Northeast, not believing a fifty-year-old woman would study so far away from her spouse: "How could you leave your husband like that?" Who disapproves obviously has less to do with age than with mindset, less to do with educational background or professional status than with the assumptions people grew up with, and with whether those assumptions had ever been tested in their personal lives. Since a diverse culture produces diverse viewpoints, what surprises is not the opinion but the sources of the opinion. What they reveal is that *the role of women in marriage has not kept pace with the role of women outside marriage.* Women who have taken sabbaticals of varying lengths and types over long-term marriages said they had seen people's responses become more accepting over the years, but that change has come slowly.

Presumption 5: A man cannot take care of himself. A double standard still exists. When a woman left, people said: You're what? You're leaving? How will he manage? They worried about his eating right and offered sympathy dates; they said they'd "look after" him. When a husband left, noted women who had experienced both situations, no one was concerned about her food intake, no one asked how she would manage. Comments like these are not only demeaning and unfair to men, they are counterproductive for women. As long as women make comments of this nature, and women made them as much as—if not more than—men, as long as women relay the message that men are incapable on the home front, their husbands will live up to their expectations and the women will continue to shoulder the domestic work. What's important to remember about the tale of Hestia is that no one forced her to tend the hearth. No one even suggested it.

Presumption 6: A woman cannot be lonely so long as she has a husband by her side. Another comment rooted in gender stereotypes, voiced not to Megan but to women leaving on long solo journeys: Won't you get lonely? When one woman answered "maybe," her female questioner said, "Well, then, why would you want to go?" We can, in fact, feel lonely when our partners are in the same house, the same room, the same bed, and that may be the worst kind of lonely there is. Solitude does not mean loneliness any more than living with someone means the end of loneliness. Unfamiliarity with solitude underlies others' fear of it, and the fear underlies the view that a temporary absence for creativity or study or reflection is more transgressive than an equivalent absence for a job. Doris Grumbach, who temporarily left her longtime partner (a woman), wrote in her memoir of the experience, *Fifty Days of Solitude*, "I had told people of my intention to be alone for a time. At once I realized they looked upon this declaration as a rejection of them and their company. I felt apologetic, even ashamed, that I would have wanted such a curious thing as solitude, and then sorry that I had made a point of announcing my desire for it."

British novelist Doris Lessing found a married woman's wanting "such a curious thing as solitude" a worthy subject for a short story. "To Room Nineteen" revolves around a married mother of four who for twelve years has not had one moment alone. Even when she locks herself in the bathroom, even when she turns a guest room into a private retreat, she still hears everyone calling her: "She could never forget herself, never really let herself go into forgetfulness." To fill her need, she decides to rent a room in a motel, where she revels in solitude in the afternoons before her children come home from school. Her pleasure doesn't negate her anxiety. "I think there must be something wrong with me," she says to herself. "I need to be alone more than I am." She feels so strongly that her desire is unnatural that when her husband asks where she goes in the afternoons, she tells him she's having an affair rather than reveal her strange need to be alone. When he admits he's having an affair too so why not be civilized about the whole thing and all four have dinner together, the thought of having to reveal solitude as her phantom lover so horrifies her that she kills herself. Lessing's story raises the question: Why does the desire for solitude make women feel there is something wrong with them?

Like the duty to self, the great philosophers and psychologists through the ages have articulated the need for solitude. And, again, none that I am aware of qualified that need as being only for the unmarried. In *Letters to a Young Poet*, Rainer Maria Rilke advised his protégé "deliberately and like a tool spread out your solitude over wide country." Abraham Maslow, founder of humanistic psychology, believed that a need for privacy and detachment was a characteristic of psychologically healthy, self-actualized individuals. Psychologist Barbara Kerr concluded the same thing when she analyzed the lives of thirty-five eminent women by looking for the shared factors that set these women apart not only from women in general but also from the thousands of gifted women who do not achieve eminence. The first characteristic she found, as she reported in *Smart Girls, Gifted Women,* was the ability to be alone, which gave them essential time to develop their intellect and skills.

No matter what researchers find, a culture where some 70 percent of the population is considered extroverts will not value introversion. Most American parents don't reward their children for wanting to spend time alone in their rooms; most parents probably think there's something wrong with their children when they spend too much time alone in their rooms. A 1998 study by Roper Reports discovered that people rarely venture out in public for unaccompanied leisure; just 5 percent of Americans regularly eat at a restaurant alone; and only 3 percent take weekend trips alone. After the age of fifty-five, only 2.5 percent of Americans travel without a companion. No wonder self-sought aloneness is suspect. Within a marriage or family, most suspect of all.

"If it's a job, it's okay to leave because it's perceived as being in service to the family," said clinical psychologist Bill Bumberry. "But to go out to do something alone is taboo in some families because you're taking time away from the others. As if the measure of a relationship is spending every possible moment in each other's presence, rather than going out to do something to make yourself more interesting and enliven the relationship. It's saying that people would rather drown, clinging together, then take a chance on swimming side by side."

When a woman takes a sabbatical, it forces others to look at their own marriages and wonder if they would survive such time alone. We all have unspoken fears about our marriages, and a sabbatical hits at everyone's fundamental fear of being alone or abandoned. The fear is so primal, the reality so frightening, that some people can't even discuss it.

When I call to interview a nationally renowned psychiatrist, the author of numerous books on marriage, the woman who answers the phone, on hearing the topic "marriage sabbatical," says: "He will never support that."

"I'm not looking for him to support it," I respond. "I just want his thoughts on the subject."

"Well, I'm his wife," she answers heatedly. "We've been married thirty-seven years, and he will not talk about that subject, I can assure you." She hangs up on me.

That the subject threatens so speaks to deep and collective illusions: Our partners can fulfill all our needs. Our partners belong to us. Our spouses would rather be with us than anywhere else at all times. Our marriages will stay exactly the same, happily forever after. Relationships are permanent. These illusions deny a universal truth: The only guarantee in life is impermanence. All relationships are temporary; we are just on loan to those we love and they to us. In the end, we are, each of us, all of us, alone.

I think back to seven years ago when my dream was to teach at a university. After two years of writing letters and talking to department chairs, I was assigned my first class. The excitement I felt through the spring and early summer faded as the semester neared and anxiety took over. The night before my academic debut, fear had become full-blown panic. Jim listened as I rehearsed the class; for an hour and a half he was shrink, cheerleader, best friend. His support was important, maybe critical, in helping me reach that first day, but I was alone in the classroom. No one could do it for me.

No matter how wonderful our partners are, no matter how long they have been with us, we fight our biggest battles in life alone. We are alone when we struggle to scale the heights of a mountain or pull ourselves up from the depths of an addiction. We are alone when we interview for jobs, give speeches, take exams. No one can survive tragedy for us. No one else can decide what will give our lives meaning. At its most fundamental level, isn't marriage just a way to buffer ourselves from the reality that we are essentially alone in this world? This last realization can be the most frightening one of all, so frightening that some people will do anything to avoid it, even stay in a bad marriage rather than have no marriage at all.

"I think the reason so many people are unhappy in marriage is because they think marriage is the answer," said Alice Brand-Bartlett, a psychoanalyst at The Menninger Clinic in Topeka, Kansas. "But it's just a vehicle in which we go through life. Some people are in it, and some people are out of it, but it's not the endpoint of anything. It's what you do as an individual that's the challenge."

A sabbatical is something a woman experiences as an individual, which, therefore, can stir whatever marital fears others harbor. Disapproval is the outward expression of those fears. In the end, a woman's own comfort level with what she's doing determines how others' responses affect her. Maybe the reason I hear so many raised voices on the phone, why others' reactions can temporarily knock me over is that I feel unsure of myself, because I feel guilty about my desire. Women like Megan who felt totally comfortable with what they were doing have an easier time letting other people's opinions roll off them. Even Jessica discovered that once she got past the hurdle of telling everyone, she became comfortable with her decision, and once she became comfortable, so did her parents. After they had time to adjust to the idea, they expressed interest in her experience. When Pandora defied the gods and opened the lid of her Grecian urn, she unleashed not only the problems but also the possibilities. After the swarm of mortal afflictions flew out to infect the earth, she looked inside the container and there at the bottom lay Hope.

Affairs

It's a crisp, sun-drenched autumn day. I'm talking to a professor at the university where I teach as an adjunct instructor. I'm walking across the newly landscaped quadrangle, thinking how much I love working on a college campus, connected to a world of ideas, creative problem solving, progressive thinking. I tell him I won't be teaching next semester because I'm going away for a while by myself to write.

"How does your husband feel about this?" he asks.

"He's fine with it. He's making a list of things he's going to do while I'm gone. Projects at home, lectures out of town. He's got friends who always want him to go out for dinner or a drink, but he never goes. So he's planning to go out with all of them."

"Ah, I see the list. One, go out with friends. Two, clean the basement. Three, have an affair."

When a married woman leaves home, it makes no difference whether she's thirty or fifty, married one year or two decades. It makes no difference that statistically at least one-half of married men and women are faithful to their spouses. The first thought many people voice is that her husband's going to have an affair or that she is. A woman can be a devout Catholic, monogamous for twenty-five years, and still hear: What's he going to do—put a chastity belt on you? Her husband can be equally devoted and faithful, and she can still hear: We'll keep a close watch on him.

Presumption 7: Men and women cannot sublimate sexual energy into other pursuits. This presumption leads to a host of media-fed misconceptions: That affairs are what life is about. That we are all sexual machines and if our spouses aren't there to service us, we'll have to substitute someone else (and someone else will be just as good). That the only thing that keeps us from having affairs is the fear we will be caught. That the switch regulating self-control is wired into the landscape rather than the brain. That fidelity is a whim rather than a decision.

In 1971, I was newly married and working as a reporter for a university news bureau. One morning, an older male colleague walked through the front door of our office and headed for my desk rather than his own.

"You know that campus police officer who's always walking around outside?"

"Yeah."

"He wants to go out with you."

"What'd he say?"

"He asked if I knew whether you were available."

"What'd you say?"

"I said I knew you were married. I didn't know if you were available."

The sexual revolution was in high gear, more than 5,000 people worked on campus, and I spent a lot of time out of the office on interviews, wearing skirts so micromini I saved them to show my future grandchildren. So conversations like this were typical of the time. I found them flattering but insignificant. I still idolized—and idealized—Jim.

After a few years, life changed. I had a baby; we moved. Now in postgraduate training, Jim started working long hours. He became self-absorbed, often tired and irritable. I had a job I loved, as a writer and editor at another university, and a terrific group of co-workers. One of my favorites was a photographer, a bohemian type I've always been attracted to, maybe because I was living in married student housing when my contemporaries were in communes, maybe because it represented my undeveloped self. The two of us covered lots of assignments together, sometimes in the evening. He was attractive and interesting, and he was interested in me.

I didn't think about fidelity the day I got married. It was a given or why get married? I may have voiced the commitment to be faithful on that day but I didn't make the commitment—didn't even know what it meant—until I was tested. It happens a few years down the road, if not to everyone then to nearly everyone. It happens when there is vulnerability and temptation. Five years after my pledge at the altar was when I first thought about fidelity and the thought I came to was that an affair was not in my values. Crossing that line would mean bringing deception into my marriage and dishonesty into my life. It would mean losing trust in myself, becoming someone I did not want to be. So I chose fidelity, not because he was a co-worker and others might know, not because Jim might know, but because I would know. Over time propositions diminished because once I chose fidelity in the core of my being, I didn't give off the signals I must once have. (Also, as my knees got older, my skirts got longer.) Over time I also discovered its advantages: Those you're attracted to but don't sleep with can become lifelong friends; fantasy is better than reality in many ways, safer certainly; deep commitment to one person can be counted a personal achievement.

In short: If I were going to have an affair, I would have had one long ago. If I were going to have an affair, I wouldn't need a plane ticket.

The issue isn't proximity. Affairs can occur anytime, any place, at the office behind closed doors or at home on the kitchen table, with a colleague, a classmate, a neighbor, a friend. During a sabbatical an affair is easier, perhaps, because no one's watching, but as most marital therapists will tell you, people have affairs less because of physical opportunity than because of emotional need.

And what most women need on sabbatical is time to themselves, not time shared.

What most women need is one less expectation, not one more.

What most women need is to rediscover who they are, not who they are in relation to someone else.

An interesting paradox: For those to whom a sabbatical is a dissonant idea, their first thought is that a woman is leaving to have an affair, but to those women who were doing the leaving, an affair was not a thought at all. "Not even in my consciousness," said one woman after another. It was so far removed from my own mind that I didn't even ask the question to the first group of women I interviewed. Only after men—and women—responded as the professor I work with had, did I realize I had to go back to pose not only that question but another one: Did you have any fears your husband might have one in your absence?

No, said many women. Not in his nature, not in his moral code, not one of his life challenges, not one of our issues. Or: Been there, resolved that, no longer one of our issues.

Yes, said some women, especially those looking at the longest separations, and from men who were attractive, supportive, good listeners—seductive qualities they knew created the potential to cross the line. Besides planning visits as often as they could afford, they said that talking about the fear openly and honestly with their spouses proved the best shield against the fear's materializing.

And then for others, the specter of temptation for their husbands was not a fear as much as a thought. "Aren't you worried Jim will have an affair?" a female acquaintance asked me. The question was both surprising and irritating, so I gave her the short answer: No. At home that night I found I had to give myself a longer one. I thought about our history and said no. I thought about the day long ago when he said he would never have an affair while we were living together, that he would move out of the house first. (I imagine he arrived at this decision after *he* had been tempted.) I thought about his promise and his integrity and said to myself, *no*. Then I was glad that one of our sons would be at home with him and that I'd be away during the winter when the beautiful single woman in the neighborhood wouldn't be outside in her shorts. And then that was the end of it.

For some women the worry floated around, causing them to give it more thought than I did. They recognized the possibility, hoped it wouldn't happen (didn't want to know it if it did happen) but accepted it as part of the risk, something that was *his* choice, something they ultimately couldn't control. As one woman who went on a six-month adventure said: "I didn't want our marriage to fall apart, but I had to find that place where I could accept the worst fears and know that if it did fall apart, it wouldn't be the end of me. I was willing to take the risk because I knew I had to do this for myself."

Some women were so driven toward their goals that they didn't recognize the risk until after they left. And some women saw no marital risk—not before their experiences, not during, not after. Said Megan:

> Everyone thought I was taking a huge risk. They don't get it. We could sleep in the same bed every night and he could have an affair with someone at Kinko's. I didn't see my leaving as a risk to my marriage in any way. I am not just a body and a lover. Jeff married me for my passions, and the better artist I am the better lover and partner I am. The only risk I saw was living in a prescribed way by society. Rigid thought is what gets you into trouble.

Children

The fear of leaving children is so deep-rooted that most women I interviewed who were mothers waited until their children were teenagers or had left home. Images of the good mother are as dramatically etched in our cultural psyche as those of the good wife. Good mothers are always there sacrificing for their children. Though this hallowed archetype has been refuted by the lives of millions of working mothers, the struggle to puncture it is proving to be a cultural crawl. We're battling half a century of psychoanalytic theory, which gave mothers the responsibility for raising emotionally healthy children, leading to the late twentieth-century creation of child-centered homes.

Two events at the century's end revealed the staying power of the archetype. In 1997, Deborah Eappen, a Boston ophthalmologist working three days a week after her second baby was born, was vilified when that baby died under a nanny's care. Eappen had cut back to part-time work after investing eight years in postgraduate training, had a husband to co-parent, and was still mourning the death of a child, yet people were quick to call her neglectful, selfish, greedy—a bad mother. Many people apparently still believed that mothers should not leave a child, that mothers held sole responsibility for a child's fate. Two years later, Judith Rich Harris created a firestorm when her book *The Nurture Assumption* said that parents—societal subtext, "mothers"—were not the primary influence in a child's environment. The public outcry to the "nanny" trial and Harris's book revealed that our culture still has a strong investment in perpetuating the sainted-mother archetype, always sacrificing, always at home, always contained.

It's not surprising then that married women who left children to pursue an individual passion received negative reactions. *How can you do that? Why do you have to go so far away? Why do you have to go now? Why can't you go locally? How can you leave your children like that?* I doubt that those casting aspersions on a woman's leaving children at home with their father for three months would aim similar barbs at a woman who has divorced her husband and sent her children to live with him for the summer. In essence the situations are the same — the fathers are caring for their children full time — but they evoke very different reactions: approval when the children are the ones to leave, since the mother remains at home; disapproval when the mother is the one to leave, since she's not at home. The result of this thinking, again a prejudice against choice over necessity, is that divorce gets a higher public approval rating than a temporary absence within a committed marriage.

Critical remarks like those above relay the message that the *proper* place — the *only* place — for married mothers is at home. Female containment, however, produces a no-win situation for both mothers and children. When mothers stay home but sacrifice their own desires, they feel resentful and their children bear the guilt that self-sacrifice engenders. When mothers attend to their own desires but leave home to do so, they feel guilty and their children bear the resentment that absence engenders. (Women who stay home with children because they want to be there may avoid these problems, but their dominance on the home front can lead to overinvolvement in their children's lives, creating greater difficulty on both ends when it's time to disengage.)

Two contemporary movies illuminate this no-win situation. In his 1996 film *Mother*, Albert Brooks plays a middle-aged, blocked writer who goes home to live with his mom (Debbie Reynolds) to find out why his relationships with women always fail. After living together for a few weeks, a situation that makes them both prickly, he discovers short stories his mother once wrote, hidden in a hatbox in his bedroom closet.

"When did you do that?" he asks her.

"You weren't even born then."

"You must have stuffed the creative part of yourself way down there."

"That's all in the past," she says, averting her eyes.

"That past is plopped all over our lives," he counters.

He continues questioning her, demanding answers, until he's figured it out: His mother raised children whom she resented for killing her chance of doing the one thing she loved. And she resented him more than his brother because as a writer, he was a continual reminder of the talent she had sacrificed. When she admits he's right, he is exultant because now he understands not only the source of their conflict but also the way that conflict affected both his work and his relationships with other women.

In her 1992 film *This Is My Life*, Nora Ephron portrays the domestic fallout when a mother does take care of her own needs. Dottie Ingels, a divorced mother of two and an aspiring comic, leaves her daughters in New York for three months with an assortment of eccentric but caring sitters while she follows her dream to Hollywood. The climax here occurs when Dottie returns home, her dream fulfilled, her children furious. One at a time, her daughters vent their anger, stomp off to their bedrooms, and slam their doors. In the middle of the night they run away to find the father they barely remember.

The next morning Dottie says to her boyfriend, "I spent sixteen years doing nothing but thinking about them and now I spent three months thinking about myself and I feel like I murdered them." He tries to comfort her with the familiar refrain, "Kids are happy when their mother is happy." She disagrees. "Kids are happy when you're there," she says. "You give kids a choice, your mother in the next room on the verge of suicide versus your mother in Hawaii in ecstasy and they'd choose suicide in the next room, believe me."

Taken together, the films say that a mother is going to suffer either way, now or later, and her children are going to suffer, either way, now or later. And for both story lines, resolution is possible. In *This Is My Life*, Dottie's daughters return home, tears and apologies and hugs all around. In *Mother*, Brooks and Reynolds say goodbye with a new understanding of each other and themselves; he drives back home, she dusts off her typewriter. To create a trilogy of sorts, we need a film that focuses on the relationship between the mother who attended to her own needs and her once-neglected, resentful child as an adult, a movie I hope one of these gifted screenwriters will make.

If suffering is the inevitable by-product for both mother and child (and having tried every possible work/child-care combination, I can affirm that it is), a situation psychologists call "a double negative," the question isn't what's right or wrong or better. The question is why we equate a temporary tantrum with permanent damage. Why does a woman fear that if she leaves a self-sufficient teenager who's an honor student and debate champion, he'll automatically turn to a life of crime or fry his brains with "George of the Jungle" cartoons? When we make this leap, we're "catastrophizing," and, according to Joan Borysenko, imagining the worst is another expression of unhealthy guilt. When we cling to the idea of female containment, we're setting ourselves up for a healthy dose of unhealthy guilt.

I think now about that time twelve years ago when I was asked to work in Connecticut for three months. Why, when my sons asked me to stay, did I just shelve my own desires? What fears lay behind the ease with which I acceded to their requests? And they were requests, nicely asked, not tantrums or demands. Was I worried that I had cut back on my career to stay home with them when they were little and therefore had too much invested in them to leave the scene? If I left, they might not make A's, win school awards, pitch no-hitters, that their lives would dissolve into chaos? Or was I just afraid they would love me less? In light of what happened two years later, when a job did consume all my time, maybe I made the right decision. What disturbs me today isn't that I stayed home. What disturbs me is that as soon as I met the mildest resistance, I submerged my desire, didn't *consider* the possibility of going. What I wish is that I could have weighed the situation. Instead of imagining that they couldn't survive without me, I might have wondered whether they needed to learn to survive without me. Rather than worrying they wouldn't like me as much, I could have figured that in missing me they might discover why they liked me in the first place. I feared they'd find me guilty of "bad" mothering when maybe they would have revaluated their notion of "good" mothering, no longer an expectation but an accomplishment, maybe even a privilege.

One thing I do know: The morning after I made the decision not to go, I was secretly happy I could stay secure. So the waters stayed calm on the surface, but underneath a current was roiling. Over the next ten years, I increasingly felt beleaguered that the boys were always coming to me for help with their homework, their projects and problems. But if I was always there, making myself irreplaceable in their lives, what other scripts were there? When a woman feels she's the one who has to be there to hold everything together, she shoulders the responsibility and, then, the work. I'm convinced we collude in our own caretaking burdens. If we don't give ourselves the permission to unhook from family life, no one else will. And why should the permission come from anyone but ourselves? Why do our children need to like everything we do? If we're waiting for universal approval, we'll be waiting all our lives.

Every time we board a plane and the flight attendant gives instructions for an emergency, we hear that as the cabin begins to decompress, we must put the mask first on ourselves, then on our children. Women have to save themselves before they can be of value to anyone else. As the bumper sticker says, "If momma ain't happy, ain't nobody happy." Women may buy this truth intellectually, experience it emotionally, yet when they take care of themselves, still feel vulnerable to the charges: selfish, neglectful, unnatural. The result is that women can end up doubting their own desires, battling conflicting voices in their heads. *The voice of convention:* Am I just rationalizing when I say that this time I'm spending on myself is going to enrich all my relationships and, in fact, I am being selfish? *The voice of her inner self:* Or is this unfair to me, who wants to grow and learn and achieve and who really does want loving relationships in my life? What do I have to give if I'm not a whole person?

The only thing we have to offer others—ever—is our own state of being. Many psychologists, Erik Erikson and Abraham Maslow among them, established that self-care leads to a stronger identity, and a stronger identity makes it easier to give. When we are confident in who we are, strong in our talents and filled up within, caring for others becomes easier and more authentic. When we nurture ourselves, caretaking feels like generosity rather than obligation, derives from grace rather than guilt. We can wonder ad infinitum whether we're being self-nurturant or self-indulgent, but it's an energy-wasting debate. Since self-nurturance means "caring for ourselves" and self-indulgence means "giving way to our desires," what difference does it make? Let's just call it self-indulgence and ask a different question: What's wrong with self-indulgence? If a woman spends a good part of her life for ten, twenty, or thirty years caring for others, and taking time out for herself helps her to spend another ten, twenty, or thirty years caring for others, maybe self-indulgence is exactly what more women need in their lives. In good relationships, people take care of each other *and* themselves, yet during the long, stressful years of raising children, few married mothers spend on themselves— even once—the energy, the time, the money, the care they lavish so freely and consistently upon those they love. Until I researched this book, I'd never known a married mother who had.

After Libby became a mother, she chose to stay at home, later to work only part-time jobs, so that parenting two daughters could be her priority. Home, she felt, was an important place to be. Libby wasn't struggling to balance child rearing and a full-time job, like two-thirds of married moms today, but she was struggling with the same inner conflict: how to reconcile the desire for time with her children with the demands of a material world, how to balance her creative drives with her maternal responsibilities. The question that dominated her thoughts was that of every married mother: How do I integrate a single soul and a familial heart?

Because Libby didn't marry until she was twenty-eight, her single soul had time to develop. Using an inheritance from her parents' early deaths, she backpacked around the world for four years. When she met her husband, backpacking too, she had traveled alone through fifty countries and felt "as good as I'd ever felt in my life, strong and alive and in control." Libby loved being a wife and mother, just as she had loved being a single woman, but after eleven years of parenting she felt her vitality ebbing. "Ideas were always rushing into my head," she said, "but the reality of daily life gave me no place to go with them, no time for development or execution."

Libby felt as though she were in a bog, not a place she wanted to be. She wanted to move to firmer ground, to recapture the qualities of the woman her husband had married. When a friend suggested she go away for some time to herself, Libby thought the suggestion a good one and borrowed a deserted beach house in winter. "When I left for two months, my friend was shocked. She had meant go away for the weekend." But a weekend, Libby knew, wouldn't give her what she needed, time to get back in touch with the natural world, time to reenergize and think. Just as she once had stepped back from a mountain to gain a better view, she wanted to step back from daily life to gain perspective on how to integrate these two sides of her self.

One of the ideas that grew out of that time, and into a developing passion, was polarity therapy. Certification in this alternative health field would enable her to work on her own terms, at home and part-time, with a skill that resonated with the life she wanted. All the programs nearby offered weekend formats, which meant it would be three years before she could practice. In a full-time program, she'd be certified in seven months, but she'd have to go to school 2,000 miles away.

Her first time away, Libby anguished only about leaving her daughters, then eleven and seven. Five years later, she worried about them again. Even though the second time they were older, sixteen and twelve, the duration was longer. Her fears followed the same lines both times. Her first worry was: Can I do without them? She knew how much children can change in a short time, and she was worried about not being there for those changes (each absence would overlap with a daughter's birthday). Her second worry was: Can they do without me? She was afraid that they would feel she didn't care about them, that in spite of years of proving otherwise they would think she was neglecting them. "I kept asking myself, 'Is it okay for me to be doing this as their mother? To be leaving them alone?' What I had to remember was that I wasn't leaving them alone. They had a father they adored, who was willing to take on the responsibility."

This is the cognitive leap I didn't make at thirty-eight. Not for one moment did I consider that my sons had a father who canceled his appointments on Halloween night when they were little so he could take them trick-or-treat-ing, who for nineteen years never missed a parent-teacher conference, who for ten years coached their Little League teams, who not only made sure they got to every game they played but got other kids on the team there, too.

Thus, *presumption 8: Mothers are the only ones who can care properly for a child*. This premise can lead to only one script with tired themes and stereotypes. It needs a rewrite. Keep the domestic scene and story line but lose the abandoning mother in the leading role. Recast in the lead a nurturing father, a man who can parent, a man who might actually want to parent. This is the way Libby reframed the scene; other women framed it this way from the outset. Each woman who had left children at home said the same thing: They trusted their husbands, were fully confident they'd be loving, responsible caretakers. The women recognized that their husbands would parent in a different way, but they did not view "different" as inferior. Letty Cottin Pogrebin, in fact, said that a secondary motivation in going away to write was to *give* her husband the opportunity to be the primary parent and her children the opportunity to have him as their primary parent. She mitigated her anxiety about leaving them with her intellect and feminist beliefs, which told her the experience would be as valuable a gift for the four of them as it would be for her.

Like Pogrebin, most women who left children were comfortable leaving them. Some knew from having missed an important event in their children's lives because of work that the child's memories centered on what their father did in celebration, not on what their mother didn't do. Most did not agonize as Libby did, but she was leaving for the longest time—two fourteen-week semesters, with a two-week visit home in between. What swayed her decision both times was the awareness that her children were impressionable creatures, learning from her every day.

My mother's dying words to me were, "Don't let your needs be forgotten when you have children, like I did." She had shown us so beautifully how to care for others. We had no idea she was dying and needed to be taken care of herself. I think we teach more by example than by what we say. We can tell our daughters, "You can be anything you want," but if we're not doing what we want, what is the real message they're getting? In the end, I decided that what was most important was becoming the woman I wanted them to have as a mother.

There are no dictates here, no "acceptable" age to leave a child, no "okay" time to be away, no black and white, right and wrong. There is only a woman's soul-searching and this: It is from their parents that children learn their future patterns of behavior. When a mother leaves home out of enlightened self-interest with a willing father on the scene, her children will see a disruption in family life, but they will also see an egalitarian model for parenting. They will see a mother who is not a "perfect" caretaker, but they will also see a mother who is a separate person with an emotional life of her own and interests beyond their care. They will see a woman who may cause them moments of anguish, but they will also see a woman who gives them a lifelong image of independence—a woman who, by claiming her dreams, may help them to claim theirs.

The Unknown

No one can know what lies ahead. There are no guarantees that a woman's experience will be enriching or fun or even comfortable. No assurances that her arrival will be smooth or her return joyous, with expectations met or goals achieved. As poet Adrienne Rich wrote, "The door itself / makes no promises / it is only a door."

Fear of the unknown is the fear no one escapes. It can be more acute in a woman leaving for one month to study at an elite university in a major U.S. city than in a woman leaving for two years to teach in a primitive classroom in a Third World village. The intensity of the fear has little to do with duration or distance, everything to do with the individual woman, her experience with risk taking, her personality, her confidence, her conditioning. The nature of the fear, however, connects to the experience. For some women I interviewed, it focused on what they were going toward. Fear of injury, said those embarking on a physical challenge. Fear of bears, said two women hiking the Appalachian Trail. Fear of failing, said women leaving for intense programs of study. Fear of getting lost, said those traveling to foreign countries. Others feared what they were leaving behind. Fear of financial disaster, said those giving up incomes for graduate degrees. Fear of getting lonely or of his getting lonely, said those who had never been separated more than a week. Fear of leaving their jobs, said those with full-time, management positions. Fear the work wouldn't get done or their staff would flounder or they would jeopardize their standing with the company, *fear of the repercussions.*

"My biggest fear was what would happen to my job," said Darcy, a creative director at an ad agency.

Darcy had found her niche in the world of advertising. For fourteen years she had worked at the same boutique agency where she scripted local radio and television commercials and had won more than twenty industry awards. As dedicated as she was talented, she saw a client one day, gave birth the next, six weeks later returned to the office. Her boss, the agency owner, had been generous in granting her flex time and she did a lot of work at home.

Darcy was thirty-nine when she began teaching a class in advertising one night a week. When the university asked if she wanted to teach a summer class at its campus in Holland, she wanted to go. She didn't fear leaving her husband or eleven-year-old son for two months. She feared leaving her boss.

"We were like Lou Grant and Mary Richards," she said. "I'd been with him longer than I'd been with my husband. Loyalty was important to him, and I knew he'd see it as, 'You don't want to be here as much as you want to be somewhere else.' He would feel that I wasn't committed—almost the same as with a family."

A few months before she planned to leave, she approached him.

"Have you ever heard the word 'sabbatical'?" she asked.

"We're in advertising," he answered. "We don't have that."

Darcy plunged ahead, described her opportunity, asked her boss to think of it as a second maternity leave. Since he had three children to her one, she thought the rationale might work. It didn't.

He hunkered down. He glowered.

"This is outrageous!" he said.

He didn't want to let her go, but given their relationship and her track record, he didn't feel he could stop her.
He admitted he would do the same thing if he were in her
position, but he was furious just the same. "He was both
resentful and jealous, and he started pulling away immediately," said Darcy. "I was determined to go, but I was
afraid of what I'd come back to. I decided the worst that
could happen was that I'd get fired, and I felt I could live
with that. I needed a change in my life and I was willing
to suffer the consequences."

According to Eastern philosophy, the obstacle *is* the
path. The fear a woman faces, the friction she encounters,
is what delineates her desire and fuels her determination. A
woman like Darcy, who was not brought up to take risks,
who except for one semester had not even gone away to
college, can find that as departure looms, misgivings esca-
late and multiply. And then one day she can wake up at 5
A.M., as Darcy did, her body cold with sweat, her mind racing with fear:

> Why am I leaving? I waited so long to have a happy mar-
> riage and a child. I have a comfortable life. Everything's
> okay. What am I doing? All of a sudden I realized I wouldn't
> be there for the end of my son's school year. I would miss
> the whole summer with my yard. Suddenly the experience
> took on dramatic meaning. It felt like a test of courage. I
> said to myself, "If I can go alone to another country and not
> get lost, then I can do anything."

The fear that underlies all others is the fear of freedom
itself. No matter how greatly desired, freedom is frightening because once a woman knows she *can* act upon her

desires, she also knows that she *must*. She must make her own decisions, based on her desires and no one else's, and take responsibility for the outcome of those decisions. Once she knows that she can act freely upon her desires, she also knows she can succeed at whatever she wants. *If I can go alone to another country and not get lost, then I can do anything.* The fear of freedom is really the fear of her own evolution, the fear of her becoming someone new.

We can't have it both ways. We can't change our lives yet stay rooted where we are. We can't leave on an adventure yet control everything at home. We can't meet our own needs yet everyone else's, too. Risk, by definition, means no security, and no security means fear.

Fear travels in both directions, however. The fear with security is that we'll coast or stagnate, dry up or give up, harbor a feeling of life lost or diminished. The fear with risk is that we're hurtling into the unknown, and we're alone on the journey. When it's time to leave, Carol Pearson wrote in *The Hero Within*, wanderers will feel alone whether they are married or not.

Fear is the reason most of us never fulfill our dreams. When fear keeps us from taking the risk, however, the result is only the illusion of security, because real security does not come from our husbands, who may one day die or leave, or from our children, who will assuredly leave, or from our jobs, which grow increasingly obsolete. Real security comes from our evolving talents and strengthened selves.

Only we can decide which is worse: the fear of going or the fear of staying; the fear of risking the unknown or the fear of cheating ourselves. "To do it was painful and not to do it was painful," said a therapist who left her husband in the States to study Jungian analysis in Zurich. "In the end I knew I'd never forgive myself if I didn't go."

"In the end" is something we need to consider, as this therapist knew. When in later years we look back on our lives and examine them—a developmental stage of adulthood called "the life review"—we will confront a psychological balance sheet of all our dreams, yearnings, and goals. In one column will be those we achieved; in another, those we abandoned. Every dream will count. Every yearning will matter. When our unrealized dreams make up the longer column, we face a bleaker and more difficult aging because what beats us down is the unused life, the potential we didn't test. In the struggle to ward off regret and depression, bitterness and despair, nonriskers feel older, look older. Pursuing dreams will cost us, too, but rather than brood on the past, we move forward and more deeply into life. In this path there's passion, and in passion we find vitality and self-esteem.

Every time we break a pattern in life, we feel anxiety because every time we break a pattern, we take a risk. It is the risk, however, that gives the experience meaning, the risk that catalyzes growth. If risk tells us that challenge and learning lie ahead, fear tells us we're human.

4

HUSBANDS

"Guido," said Holly, "we have a better marriage than most people. We like each other more. We are better friends. We have more fun. . . . But I think we are getting very used to it. Life is simply going on and on. I want to do something daring for us. I also need a little space for myself. I think some deprivation will do us a world of good."

"There isn't any stopping you, is there?" said Guido.

"No," said Holly. "Listen, darling, I know you think I'm being willful. You think I make decisions out of the sky and spring them on you. Well, I do, but not very often. I went away before we got married for a good reason. Most of the time we simply dovetail. I think that's dangerous as a steady diet and I know I'm right."

"I'd like to strangle you," said Guido.

"You're being unreasonable."

"Unreasonable!" shouted Guido. "You're the

one who's leaving me."

"I am not leaving you," said Holly. "I am going to France for a little while. We are getting very smug and used to each other and I will not have us taking each other for granted. My instinct tells me this is right. It isn't for me alone. It's for us."

"It's for you," said Guido.

"You don't want to understand this," said Holly. "You want to feel as if you're being badly treated. But you aren't. I feel that our love is very secure—at rock bottom, I mean. I want to miss you and I want you to miss me. If you believe in me, let me go. It's only for a little while. . . . Trust me, this is good for us."

—LAURIE COLWIN,
Happy All the Time

Chris remembers the exact moment her dream took hold. It was the fall of 1960. The first communications satellite was launched, Chubby Checker topped the charts, and Senator John Kennedy was running for president. Sixteen years old, Chris was sprawled on her living-room floor doing homework. Her father, sitting nearby, was watching Kennedy give his campaign speech on television. When Chris heard the senator lay out his proposal for a Peace Corps, she dropped her pencil, closed her book, and said to herself and her dad, "I'm going to do that someday." A conscientious student, Chris was so captivated by what she'd heard that she left her homework unfinished for the first time. When she was a senior in college and the Peace Corps was four years old, that "someday" arrived. She applied in the fall, and, two weeks after she received the acceptance letter with her assignment to teach in Jamaica, her boyfriend proposed. "It sounds like a cliché," she said of the Air Force Academy senior she was in love with, "but he was tall, dark, and handsome, head and shoulders above the others in intelligence and assertiveness. It wasn't just sexual attraction. I saw so much in him that I admired. I knew he was the man I wanted to marry."

When David proposed, Chris was startled, thrilled, and confused all at the same time. She had mapped out her life: the Peace Corps for two years, then marriage to David when she returned. Now she found she had to choose. "I was really torn," she said. David didn't want to wait to get married. A war in Vietnam was escalating and he was in love. "Marry me," he said, "and maybe we can do the Peace Corps together sometime." In David's words Chris found her answer, a way she could have both dreams. They married in a big church wedding, and Chris put the Peace Corps on hold "for a little while."

"A little while" turned into thirty years, thirty years of being married, raising four children, working as a teacher, and living in six states across the country. Family life delayed the dream far longer than Chris had antici- pated at twenty, but a dream deferred did not mean a dream diminished. Four months after her forty-ninth birthday, Chris suffered an agonizing injury. In bed for eight weeks, unable to walk, she had time for some deep thinking. Her youngest son was entering his last year of college, her daughter had just announced her marriage, which meant grandchildren might arrive soon, and after a lifetime of being in good shape, her body was relaying the message that her health was unpredictable. It was time, she decided, to fulfill her second dream.

"I knew this was going to be hard on David," she said, "because in my heart I knew he would not want to go with me."

Though not manipulative by nature, Chris chose her time carefully and broached the subject as gently as she could. She asked David if he remembered their conversa- tion about the Peace Corps before they married. He sur- prised her by answering, "Yes." When she asked if he would consider going with her, it was his turn to be sur- prised. "You can't be serious?" he said. When she assured him she was, he thought about it. He could take a healthy sum from their savings and go with her. Financially it was feasible. But logical? He had retired early from the air force to go into business specifically to earn additional income for college tuitions. Joining the Peace Corps would mean he'd be spending two of his peak earning years making seventy-five cents an hour. Also, joining at forty-nine would mean he'd have to struggle to re-enter the work force when he was over fifty. "I thought about it but I didn't get too far," he said. "The altruistic side of it was the plus, but at the expense of my other goals? No, I just couldn't do it."

David assumed that if he didn't go, neither would Chris. He wasn't prepared for what came next.

"I need to do this," she said. "I gave it up for you the first time. I've waited thirty years. You had to know how I felt. Every time I saw an ad for the Peace Corps on television, I said, 'I'm going to do that someday.' I don't want to wait until you retire or die. I may have arthritis and be unable to go. I may have grandchildren and not want to go."

It was a long evening and the beginning of a long ten months, during which time Chris applied, was accepted, and made preparations to leave for her teaching assignment in Africa. David fell through a kaleidoscope of emotions, the same stages people go through when they suffer loss.

There was denial. "I thought she might not get accepted. When she got accepted, I expected her to change her mind. When our daughter announced she was pregnant, I was sure she would. Even if she left, I figured it'd be too hard and she'd quit after a short time and come home."

There was anger. "You'd leave me for two years? Who leaves their marriage to go off for two years?"

"It's such a small stretch of time in our life together," she answered. "And I'm not leaving you. I wish we were doing it together."

Then came bargaining. "Why can't you join Vista or some other organization here in the States? Why can't you go 100 miles away instead of 8,000 miles away? I understand your desire to make a difference in the world, but I don't understand why you can't do it closer to home."

"It's a good question," she said, "but I can't answer it. I feel called to join the Peace Corps."

The final stages of grief—confusion and reorientation—would come later.

Separations had always been a part of their marriage. As an air force pilot, David had been away on many missions, often for as long as three months. He'd been gone on a yearlong tour of Vietnam. "I never thought about his absences," said Chris. "I just accepted them as part of his work."

"If your husband is disapproving," she continued, "you feel you are making a choice. I was at a point where if he had given me an ultimatum, I still would have taken measures to go. I can't think of anything else I felt that way about. I believe we're on this earth to help one another. My marriage vows meant everything to me, and if I was willing to give them up, it meant my desire came from the soul."

The closer the time got, the worse their relationship became. In the face of David's resistance, Chris plunged into preparations to make his life easier in her absence. David, in turn, grew irritable watching preparations he considered unnecessary for him and a misuse of time for them. When David initiated marriage counseling, Chris was surprised but pleased. "It was out of character for him but really helpful," she said. "The psychologist asked each of us what we thought might happen. I was afraid our philosophies of life would be further apart when I returned. David was afraid I wouldn't come back."

Men's Fears

Fear is the reason men have trouble honoring women's dreams, just as fear is the reason women have trouble honoring their own dreams. What arouses fear isn't the surface message: I'm going to join the Peace Corps, hike the Himalayas, drive cross-country, study abroad. Nor is it necessarily the duration. "Anything longer than a month," said David, "and I would have felt the same way." What arouses fear is the subtext: Change is ahead.

Human nature resists change, and some natures resist it more than others. The more methodical we are, the more fixed in our routines, the more in control we need to feel, the greater will be our resistance to change. For a career military officer like David, who since the age of seventeen had spent most of his waking hours in the highest of structured environments, the battle he now had to wage on the domestic front was as tough as any he'd waged in enemy territory. He didn't like the loss of control, and he was used to being in control. He didn't like the element of surprise, and he hadn't seen this one coming.

What did he think of her desire to join the Peace Corps before they married? "I never took it seriously," he said. "There was a war going on." The problem then was that the stint in the Peace Corps, which had always dominated Chris's life plan, never had been a part of David's. The decision that propelled her life forward threw his in a tailspin because the joint mission she had seen in full view, he hadn't even glimpsed in his peripheral vision.

Chris shared that initial assumption of a journey together with a number of women I interviewed, who assumed their husbands would go with them as they pursued their dreams. Like David, however, these men did not want to go with their wives—not now, not later. The open invitation that led Georgia O'Keeffe to her first summer in the Southwest included her husband, and for years O'Keeffe asked him to accompany her. Stieglitz, however, had no interest in the Southwest, nor did he want to leave his work, his gallery, his friends, his life in Manhattan. The only summer place he wanted to go was upstate New York, to the place he always went, the family compound at Lake George. Stieglitz was a creative genius who transformed photography from curiosity to art form, a visionary whose famed Gallery 291 introduced modern art to America, exhibited the work of Picasso and Rousseau before anyone else in the world, a daring artist who scandalized the public with his sensuous nudes of O'Keeffe, a bohemian who lived an unconventional life with an unconventional woman—in other words, no ordinary man. But in this marital situation—when O'Keeffe wanted to go to New Mexico for two months without him—he reacted the same way David did. He resisted.

For a man like David whose marriage was more traditional, with his work primary, his departures customary, a wife's solo journey diverges more radically from the marital pattern. And the more radical the divergence, the more likely resistance can flare into righteous indignation. Doesn't "to love, honor and cherish" mean she has to be there? Billy Joel must have thought so (before two divorces) when he sang on his *Piano Man* LP, "You're my castle, you're my cabin and my instant pleasure dome / I need you in my house 'cause you're my home." To David, Chris's decision to be away from home felt unfair and arbitrary. Where in their marriage contract was it written that with good behavior she'd get a two-year stint in the

Peace Corps? This wasn't *his* idea of marriage and until now had not been *their* idea of marriage. In his eyes she was not only betraying their wedding vows, spoken aloud before God and friends and family, she was also breaching the psychological contract that accompanied them, the unspoken one with which the marriage began. The old saying comes to mind: Women enter marriage with the expectation that their husbands will change. Men enter marriage with the expectation that their wives will never change.

"A lot of people hold on to the idea that once you marry, no one has the right to change or be different," said marriage counselor Bill Bumberry. "Often when couples are fighting I hear the defense, 'But I haven't changed at all. I'm exactly the same person as when we got married.' Implicit in the comment is the idea that growth and change are not to be tolerated, that the relationship gets laminated when you say 'I do' and then that's the pattern forever."

Married women who embark on solo journeys relay the opposite message: Relationships are fluid. In Eastern philosophy, there's only one law in the universe, and that's change as the only constant. In the West, we don't approach change as serenely, so it always causes anxiety. Resistance, whether plea or grumble, fury or threat, may be the only way a man knows to communicate that he is anxious—more, terrified—of the changes that lie ahead.

First, a man fears the change in his own life for the period of time his wife is away, the extra responsibilities he'll have to take on, the adjustments he'll have to make—the disruption of his routines. And he fears the lonely days ahead without his lover, roommate, companion, maybe best friend—the disruption of their routines. It's generally harder for a man when his wife leaves than the other way around because for many men their wives are their only confidantes. While most women have large social support networks, many men rely solely on their wives for support and intimacy. Studies have found that married men are far more likely than married women to name their spouses as their best friends. As a result, *men generally suffer more from the absence of their wives than women do from the absence of their husbands.* In letters they wrote to friends, Georgia O'Keeffe described her first summer in New Mexico as "bliss"; Stieglitz called it "maybe the most trying" experience of his life.

On a deeper level, a man fears the change that will occur in her. Underlying the words "I am going" is another subtext: I am going to experience something new, tackle something hard, learn something valuable, achieve something wonderful. His fear is that she'll return a different woman, stronger, more creative and capable. An unspoken emotional thread weaves through this fear: What if she changes so much she doesn't want me anymore? What if she becomes so strong she doesn't need me anymore?

Just as John Gottman lectures on the difficulty women have honoring their dreams, he gives equal time to the difficulty men have honoring women's dreams, which he thinks derives from their fear of women's power. To illustrate his point, he describes a Sumerian and Akkadian culture that began before the births of Judaism and Christianity, a culture that for 700 years worshiped both gods and goddesses who reflected the actual roles men and women played in society. In this ancient culture, women invented writing, poetry, medicine, science, and song. Women developed new technologies such as cooking, baking, and sewing. Women started the first schools and universities. The end of this culture gave way to the beginning of the domination of male gods over female goddesses, a shift which came at great cost: devaluation of the status of women and domestic life, and revaluation of warfare. In cultures where women and their dreams are honored, Dr. Gottman explained, men are more likely to take care of infants and less likely to go to war.

"We are living through a renewed dialogue with this ancient struggle," he said. "I think the future of our species depends on honoring women's dreams."

In the ten years of their relationship, a second marriage for both, Joe had routinely honored Ellen's dreams. She was a political media analyst and actress; he, a businessman who shared her love for the stage. After meeting at an audition, then landing the romantic leads, life imitated art, and when the play ended its run, they heightened the drama and married. In the years that followed, if Joe wasn't sharing the spotlight with Ellen, he often helped focus it on her. When she performed in productions that needed help backstage, he joined the tech crew. When she hosted a cable-TV show and needed a last-minute guest or cameraman, he filled in. As often as her talents attracted opportunities, she grabbed them. Joe was used to hearing her say, "Guess what!"

So the day she said "Guess what! I've been asked to teach political media in Europe next summer," he said what he always said: "Great! What a terrific opportunity."

His first thought was what it meant for her and from the blush on her elegant cheekbones it meant something wonderful. For him "it" meant something abstract, distant in time and amorphous in shape. They didn't talk much more about it, but when Ellen mentioned the subject Joe seemed interested and supportive.

Then one day Joe heard Ellen on the phone, her well-modulated voice making an overseas flight reservation. The abstraction had suddenly taken the shape of an airline ticket, and reality set in. She was leaving for two and a half months. Then his reality set in. They'd be separated and he'd be alone. They had been apart very little, never more than ten days, and spent almost all their leisure time together. Yesterday, had anyone asked, he would have described their marriage as a decade of solid devotion; today, all he could think was the worst. *What if she loves it so much she doesn't want to come back? What if she finds someone else?* "I was worried," he said. "I was afraid I'd lose her."

Joe didn't know what to do. He loved his wife and wanted her to be happy. He knew that standing in the way of this opportunity was going to make her unhappy. At the same time, he knew that this particular way of her being happy was going to make him miserable. He couldn't afford to go with her, but he didn't want her to leave him and go alone. He wasn't the type of man to say no, in their relationship never had said no, didn't really want to say no, but he didn't want to say yes, either, which was a problem because he'd already said yes, wished he'd never said yes, didn't know what he was thinking when he said yes. He desperately needed someone to talk to, but since the only someone he knew was the person causing the problem, he now had another problem. Besides not knowing what to do, he didn't know where to turn. His thoughts reeling with ambivalence, his anxiety spiraling out of control, he finally voiced the anguish he felt: "Why are you doing this?" he asked Ellen. "Why are you abandoning me?"

In the river of fear coursing through men's psychic landscape, the currents of loss and loneliness flow from the same source of change, fluctuate with the seasons, gathering momentum as they converge, whirling into rapids of anxiety, crashing into dams of resistance, and if by journey's end they haven't flooded onto the banks of despair, they empty into the sea of abandonment. These are primordial waters, spreading wide, running deep, exerting forces so powerful they can both erode age-old shores and sculpt exquisite new ones.

The fear of abandonment can manifest itself in a one-night lapse of self-pity or months of pervasive agony. Even men in the strongest of marriages, even men who regularly leave town themselves, even men who are confident of their wives' return can feel a momentary twinge. *She's leaving me, and I'll be all alone.* If a man like Stieglitz can feel it—by birth, beloved, privileged, financially secure; by lifestyle, surrounded by family and friends; by ideology, dedicated to freedom of expression; by talent, recognized by the world, with nothing left to prove; by profession, nurturing of the dreams of others—if a man like this can feel it, any man can.

"If you perceive it as abandonment, it hurts you, scares you, makes you realize how dependent you are," explained Dr. Bumberry. "I don't know that men have a greater fear of abandonment than women, but with men it's more subterranean because it's not acceptable. Socially you can't admit it, so you have to go out of your way to prove you don't have it. You can't expose it or puncture it, so the fear just gets bigger and bigger."

That may explain why one husband responded enthusiastically to his wife's four-month overseas opportunity, bought her Tumi luggage and a Seiko multizone clock so she could plan phone calls home, then after she left became noncommunicative. That may explain why another man bought his wife her airline ticket, took her to the airport, and kissed her goodbye, then spent the next three months begging her by e-mail to come home. That may explain why Joe's response deflated from pride to panic.

Denial is the first and most primitive of emotional defense systems. A man like Joe might think the trip will never materialize or, if it does happen, that it won't affect him. A man whose nature is self-absorbed may be so involved in his own life that he doesn't take time to think through the consequences; if his nature is nonreflective, it may not even occur to him to think through the consequences. As personality can play a role in the delayed reaction, so can programming. A man might make the first response simply from habit, in the same way he says, "Let's have lunch sometime," and then two weeks later becomes surprised, irritated even, when the other person calls to make a date, because he has no interest in meeting that person for lunch, never did want to meet for lunch, just said the words because, well, that's what people say.

What the lag time reveals is the difference between rhetoric and action, the long, hard stretch from intellectual feminism to emotional feminism. It's one thing for a man to support his wife's dreams by cooking dinner three nights a week, but it's another thing when it means sleeping alone for two and a half months. It's one thing to support her self-fulfillment; it's another thing when it means less dedication to his self-fulfillment. In the past, walking the talk proved a manageable feat, a two-mile run he could fit in three times a week, work up a good sweat, feel virtuous the rest of the day, consider himself an athlete. Now he discovers he's facing a marathon, the discomfort gauge guaranteed to accelerate from mild to torturous, but no guarantee that he'll reach the finish line or, worse, that his body will ever be the same. He's undergone training but not enough for this, and he has no idea how or where he'll acquire it in such little time. He didn't sign up for this race, never would have signed up for it, in fact, his wife signed him up when he wasn't paying attention, and now that she's told everyone, he can't very well pull out, but that's exactly what he wants to do, because just thinking about running twenty-six miles makes him sick.

If two and a half months is a stretch for a woman, it's an equal—if not greater—stretch for her husband. As Thomas Moore points out in *SoulMates,* a soulful connection sometimes asks for an extraordinary degree of adaptability and flexibility. Since practicing an extraordinary degree of any virtue is tough, how does a man push past such primal feelings of fear and need? How does he keep from devolving into the tearful toddler who won't let mommy go, the unhinged teenager whose girlfriend jilted him, Stanley Kowalski standing at the bottom of the stairs in his undershirt screaming *"STELL-LAHHHHH!"*

O'Keeffe gave her husband the help he needed by asking a mutual friend to accompany her to New Mexico, a friend who promised Stieglitz frequent letters detailing his wife's activities. Ellen gave Joe his lifeline, too, though he didn't need as short a rope as Stieglitz. When Ellen realized that what she considered a brief time Joe viewed as an eternity, when she saw his attitude derail from support to resistance, she knew she had to help him conquer his fears. This is what she said:

> I know this is going to be hard and lonely for you. I'm not asking you to like the idea. I'm asking you to accept it. I need to do this to love and respect myself, and I need to love and respect myself to be a total partner to you. My love for you is so great that there is no question of abandonment, but to assure you of it, I will live very frugally while I'm away and use part of my stipend to buy you a ticket so that you can join me at the end. If you can hang in there for this adventure of mine, we'll have an adventure together.

The words were balm; the ticket, cure. With this gesture Ellen showed Joe that she too would make a sacrifice for their marriage and, more important, she reassured him that he would see her again. With the ticket she also made her opportunity his opportunity. Just as concrete evidence of her trip had escalated his anxiety, concrete evidence of their reunion eased it. The ticket, however, was not a magic potion. It didn't keep Joe from suffering while she was gone or counting the days until she returned. It didn't eradicate his fears, but it enabled him to control them and, in controlling them, to end his resistance. It enabled him to say goodbye, feeling shaky but acting stoic, to write letters and talk on the phone, focusing not on his distress but on their reunion. It enabled him to stay connected as the supportive husband he had wanted to be.

The Matter of Entitlement

Compounding their own fluctuating emotions, men fear what others will think, just as women do. Men have trouble explaining to their friends and families what their wives are up to, just as women do. Some men, in fact, don't tell anyone that their wives are leaving so they can head off the questions that others typically hear. *How can you stand to be alone for that long? What will you do for food? Aren't you worried your wife is going to meet someone? Why would she want to do a thing like that?* If a man is conflicted to begin with, comments like these stir his ambivalence and exacerbate his fear. No man likes hearing the comments, but he understands their origin: Five thousand years of entitlement, men as lords of the manor, women as serfs.

From this legacy of possession comes the comment that rankles men most. *I cannot believe you're letting her go away like that.* Men who hear this remark, or some variation, are often at a loss as to how to respond because it reveals a value system so antithetical to their own that they feel they've been zapped onto the black-and-white set of *Pleasantville.* A man can find the remark amazing or absurd or disturbing or disappointing, depending on what kind of day he's having and who's making the comment. He can bristle, ignore it, or deflect it with humor, but what he feels like saying is rarely what he does say. Men who start out irritated generally end up philosophic. In the words of one man, who spoke for many: "In the beginning, the comment bothered me, but I decided it said more about the person making it than it did about me. I doubt people would make the same remark if the roles were reversed."

Probably not, and yet this sense of possession can surface just as easily and often in comments from women. At first, when I told female friends and acquaintances I was leaving for three months to write, I was surprised at the responses I heard. *I could never do anything like that. My husband doesn't want me go away for the weekend without him* . . . *My husband can tolerate my being gone for one week—that's it* . . . *My husband would never let me leave for that long.* I'm not talking only about conventional women. I'm talking about women who returned to work the week after childbirth, earned advanced degrees, stayed political liberals, married men of different nationalities, races, and religions. I realized I, too, was guilty of making an assumption. I thought that women who were nontraditional in their personal and professional lives would be nontraditional in their married lives—an ironic assumption given that my own experience had already disproved it.

San Francisco, 1989. We were on vacation, walking toward a cable car one colder-than-expected day in August when I saw a *Chronicle* newspaper stand. I immediately went over to buy a copy, flipping through it until I reached the commentary page. And there it was, just as I had hoped and predicted, Jim's byline in the "Open Forum" column. With the surge of adrenalin that comes with recognition, I ran to show it to him. I knew he'd be pleased, and he was. He glanced over the article, asked when he'd get a check, then wanted to move on with the day's plans. I, on the other hand, wanted to savor the moment so I sat there rereading every word, feeling wonderful because my instincts had been on target. At dinner about a month before, Jim had been relating some fascinating stories and statistics about athletes' obsessions with winning. "What a great subject for a commentary," I said. "Write up what you just said, and I'll edit it and send it out. With the Olympics in three weeks, I guarantee you it will get printed all over the country." I had no such guarantee, of course, but knowing he didn't like to spend time on projects that didn't produce results, I figured it was the only way he'd write it. And he did, and now I was reading the first of what would be half a dozen published versions. After the euphoria wore off, I could feel the familiar irritability rising. *I* had always wanted to write commentaries that would appear in wonderful newspapers far and wide. Why was I doing for him what I wasn't doing for myself, making him the carrier of my dreams? About to ruin an otherwise beautiful day, I started to sulk. We'd been through this scene before, so he knew what I was thinking. His voice was patient but weary.

"Have you ever written an essay and sent it to news-
    papers all over the country?"
"No."
"Well then, how can you be upset?"

It was his usual reality therapy I had come to know and not love. I had heard it when he sold his first magazine feature (before me), when he first got published nationally (before me), and I would feel it again when he received his first call from the *New York Times* (before me).

Although I've worked hard to raise my sons free of gender stereotypes, for most of my marriage I have given my husband's career a higher priority than my own. I would have attracted more job opportunities and generated higher incomes had I gone to graduate school myself. Instead, I supported him financially while he earned his degrees, and while working full time, wrote two of his papers, edited the rest, and typed and edited his 200-page dissertation. Twenty years later, while working full time, I was editing his online column and helping him get published in places where I had yet to submit my own ideas. And I was the writer.

The role of women in marriage has not kept pace with the role of women outside marriage because emotional feminism is different from intellectual feminism, and women struggle with the difference just as men do. Some women manifest the struggle by deferring to their husband's career; others by saying "he'd never let me." According to psychoanalyst Alice Brand-Bartlett, "Even feminist women play an enormous organizing role in men's lives. Those who say 'he won't let me' may be taking care of their husbands, protecting them, because they are worried about how their husbands would survive in their absence. Wanting something apart from your spouse is going to be uncomfortable and hard, and some women prefer to keep the relationship where it's comfortable. Saying 'he won't let me' is also easier than struggling with what you really want to do with your life. It's the old existential dodge. We all avoid taking charge of our destinies, but some of us more than others."

The existential dodge—that was the one I identified
with. I never said "he won't let me," I just wouldn't let
myself. It felt safer to transfer my ambitions onto him,
throw myself into his work as a way of forestalling con-
frontation with my own because, the truth is, for the first
ten years of our marriage, I didn't know what I wanted to
do, and for the next ten, I was afraid of what I wanted to
do. Maybe I put energy into publishing his ideas as a way
of building confidence to publish my own. Rather than
admit our fears and inadequacies, it's less threatening to
blame someone else for them, displace disenchantment
with ourselves onto our partners, our marriages.

When Sue Bender traveled around the country talking
to women's groups about her experience living with the
Amish, she said someone in the audience would invariably ask, "How did you get your husband to give you permission to leave?" Although many women apparently
still believe that freedom is given to them by someone
else's permission, neither Sue Bender nor the other
women I spoke with asked for permission. Hypotheti-
cally, what would you have done if your husband had resisted your going? I asked women whose husbands were
supportive throughout. One woman said it was "stretch-
ing her head" to even think about it. The majority said
they would have worked hard to persuade their husbands. Some said they might have compromised on the
length of time or found a program closer to home; a few
said they *would* have compromised if the objection had
been strong and the reason valid. Joint consensus, they
felt, was essential.

Many women, however, said that resistance would not
have swayed them, but it probably would have been detri-

mental to the relationship. "If I had been married to a man who continually crushed those impulses," confided a woman, sixty-four, of her annual sabbaticals, "I don't think I could have stayed in the marriage." Her words echo those of Carl Degler, who wrote *At Odds: Women and the Family in America from the Revolution to the Present*. Historically, women petitioned for divorce, he said, when they found their desire for autonomy within marriage thwarted by men's insistence upon their subordination to the family.

It's a contemporary narrative for divorce too, but given the twenty years of social change since Degler's book was published, a narrative that needs revisiting.

The setting, at home. The time, evening. The protagonists are a happily married couple who have been together three/five/seven years. He's an entrepreneur; she's a real estate agent/copywriter/graphic designer. She's also a good photographer. She'd love to become good enough to exhibit her work in galleries, maybe even change photography from hobby to career.

She begins:

I got this brochure on a photography workshop in Paris/New York/Chicago. I'd really like to go.

When is it?

Early April.

How long?

Two weeks.

That's not a good time for me to get away from the office.

That's okay. I was planning to go by myself.

By yourself? You're going to leave me here all alone
for two weeks while you traipse off to Paris?
It's only two weeks.
What's the point of being married if we're going to go
our separate ways?

One of two things now happens. Either she doesn't go, or
he takes the time off from work and goes with her. If he
goes with her, during class she's aware that he's waiting
for her to be finished; after class she's aware that the other
students are hanging out together, talking shop. Either
way, she doesn't get the immersive experience she
wanted, so resentment wedges its way into the relationship.

Two brochures/jobs/anniversaries later, she tries again.

He grumbles, she bags it. She may appear conciliatory
on the surface, but somewhere within she's angry—at
him, because he didn't make it easier; at herself, because
she didn't persevere. Anger at him becomes resentment;
anger at herself, depression.

The next time she wants to do something on her own,
away from him, she thinks: He won't like it. Now she has
internalized his reaction and doesn't even begin the conversation. Now he doesn't even have to resist for her to retreat and resent.

One day, after five/ten/twenty years together, she sees a
fence around her marriage and the gate is locked. She
looks at him across the dinner table and announces she
wants a divorce. He feels devastated, pleads with her to re-
consider. She refuses, and the once-promising relationship
crumbles like their four-tiered mocha/coconut/chocolate
wedding cake.

In the years afterward, she will tell friends and acquaintances that she got a divorce because she was suffocating and needed to grow; her husband didn't want her to go anywhere without him. Other women will nod their heads sympathetically. "Men are such babies," they'll say.

Are they? His initial response was an emotional one and, as such, it was honest. He was telling her how he *felt* about her leaving, and he couldn't control how he felt. (Who knows how many women might instinctively respond the same way?) What he was saying was that he didn't like the idea. He was not saying that he wouldn't tolerate it. As we know, what people say and what they do are two different things. She, however, suppressed her emotions because she didn't want to start a fight, was afraid to make him mad, afraid to hurt his feelings, afraid to jeopardize the relationship. So she dropped the discussion, relaying the dishonest message that her desire was not so important as his, or important at all. Instead of mustering the courage and expending the energy to fight for what she wanted, she retreated to her familiar, comfortable role of peacemaker/good wife/good girl, deferring to his emotions, acquiescing to what she thought he wanted. What he really wanted was a partner who was in love with him and with life. That's what she wanted, too. In the end, neither got what either wanted because she blamed him for his emotions, which he couldn't control, rather than for his actions, which, out of fear, she never tested. In the end, the accommodation she thought was saving the relationship sabotaged it.

The reason marriage still contains women is that women accommodate containment. As much as we may not want to live a contained life, as long as we are afraid to be difficult and fight for what we want, as long as we are unwilling to do the hard and uncomfortable work necessary to make a change, it is exactly the life we will live. The institution of marriage may order the fence, men may fortify the wood, but if we're securing the lock on the gate while hoping someone discovers the key, we're driving in most of the stakes ourselves.

Beyond Stereotypes

Just as taking center stage is historically radical for women, placing women center stage is historically radical for men. Both remain radical for the culture. Millions of years of male dominance and female submission don't get eradicated in one generation anymore than the words we've scrawled on a blackboard during a three-hour class get erased in one three-second swipe. We have to move the eraser back and forth, sideways, longways, over and over, and even after we've obliterated the words, chalk residue smudges the blackboard and eraser dust coats our clothes. The past thirty years have produced dramatic awareness of gender inequities, resulting in revolutionary changes in laws and policies, but just as action trails insight, emotion trails action. That's why a man can be aware of the double standard, recognize its unfairness, say the politically correct words, make the politically correct gestures, yet not feel the words, not yet have incorporated them as a heartfelt value, still long for the days when a man could expect his wife to be at home, taking care of him and his career and his children.

Many marriage counselors I spoke with said, based on the men they see in their practices (men in their twenties and thirties), the traditional male viewpoint hasn't changed. Some therapists said they didn't think it would ever change, that when it comes to daily living, placing a woman center stage will always be a radical idea for a man. The men in marital therapist's offices, however, are those whose relationships are in trouble. Looking through a different lens, reflecting marriages that were functional rather than dysfunctional, I discovered men who gave their wives two-month dream trips as birthday gifts, helped them research distant schools and programs, studied up on the countries they'd be living in, typed their itineraries, bought their sleeping bags, loaded their cars, and drove them to their destinations.

These men cannot be categorized or stereotyped. They are not distinguishable by socioeconomic background, educational level, profession, or age. They are as easily in their seventies as their thirties, as easily truck driver as physician, artist as engineer. Their rationales may be intellectual or emotional, pragmatic or philosophic, instinctive or learned, one or many. They are as diverse as the men who expressed them, but one man's story expressed them all.

When Peter and Sally met in Alaska, he lured by a teaching position, she by an adventure education, the landscape was just the background against which their romance developed. Landscape doesn't remain background long, however, when it's an environment of extremes promising a constancy of contradictions, astonishing beauty and severe hardship, risk and refuge, a land evoking fear, requiring faith—a frontier that could be a metaphor for their marriage, for any marriage.

In their life together at first, Peter wanted to see if he could make it as an artist on the East Coast, so they moved to New England. That was all it took for him to realize how much creative energy he drew from the Arctic landscape, how much he missed Alaska. After a number of teaching jobs on both coasts, he got his opportunity, and the couple headed north.

Peter had known he wanted to be an artist and art professor long before he met Sally, and he knew where he wanted to live as that artist shortly afterward. Focused and driven, he had no trouble claiming the time and space he needed for his work, just as he had claimed the landscape he needed for his inspiration. Since Sally hadn't found her focus as Peter had, her work accommodated his. She left a city for a job he wanted when she needed just one credit to graduate from college. She earned a master's degree in a field that wasn't her first choice but was available where his next position took them. Although she had many good jobs, she didn't have something she thought of as her life's work. She was always trying to figure out what that could be, and she and Peter talked a lot about the difference between having a gift and becoming good at many things. Sally was good at many things; what she wanted was to feel she had a gift.

When Peter was forty-two, Sally thirty-eight, she started talking about social work as a profession. Knowing she couldn't get a degree where they lived, Peter took her increasing interest as a sign she would need to leave to achieve her goal. Knowing she hated living in Alaska, he took her increasing vocalization of these feelings as a sign she would *want* to leave to achieve her goal. When five years after first talking about it, Sally made up her mind and was ready to act, Peter was ready, too. He helped her research the best programs, finding the one she chose to attend, 3,000 miles and a twelve-hour plane trip away.

Artists by nature tend to enjoy standing out from the crowd, and Peter recognized that his behavior was probably atypical. But his support didn't come from a desire to be different; it came from a desire to be fair. "I don't think I did a great thing," he said. "I did what I should have done. It would have been unfair not to support a dream like that. It was a refreshingly clear-cut, ethical decision."

What may have been inconceivable to a man in his twenties or thirties can look very different at midlife. As Sally revealed and Peter confirmed, he wasn't particularly supportive during the earlier years of their marriage. He liked to work hard without distraction, which meant holing up in his study for long periods of time, leaving for two weeks at a stretch to paint in the Brooks Range, a wilderness as pure and remote as any in North America. Sally resisted his going there because it meant she was left alone to battle the elements in his climate of choice, not hers. In accommodation, Peter didn't go for longer than two weeks, but he claimed his two weeks.

Over five, ten, or twenty years, however, a lot can happen in a man's life and his perspective can change.

He can experience professional success. Men like Peter who voiced a sense of fairness — "her turn now" — have usually achieved their dreams, and with their wives' help. Like the husband in the fairy tale *The Wife Who Would Be King*, they were willing to reverse roles, let the limelight be hers. They recognized the career sacrifices their wives had made for them, a common theme in many long-term marriages of women over forty-five. Claire Fejes, the grande dame of Alaskan art, was enjoying a promising career in her native New York in the 1940s when her husband wanted to follow his dream to mine for gold in Alaska. The only wilderness Fejes had ever known was the Bronx Park, and her idea of adventure was riding the subway into Manhattan, but she packed her stone-carving tools and paint supplies, said goodbye to family, friends, and colleagues, and went with him. Twelve years later, when she wanted to live out her dream among the Eskimos, her husband showed her how to pitch a small mountain tent and work a two-burner gas stove. At a time when most men didn't want their wives even to work, he took over the primary care of their two children. He was more than a generation older than Peter, but they shared perspective: *I've lived my dream, and with her support. Now she needs to live her dream, and with mine.*

Just as achievement can change perspective, so can crisis. Fejes's husband realized his dream, but his gold-mining venture wiped them out financially. Fejes not only stayed with him, she refrained from criticism. Whether the setback is a financial reversal or job loss, a five-year bout of clinical depression or a struggle with alcoholism, a man knows it was a difficult time and he was a difficult person to live with. That his wife not only stood by him but also helped him through it means it's now his turn to show loyalty and gratitude. If a man is in a long-term marriage, the relationship has already weathered crises, not necessarily his. Even the fourteen-month separation Peter faced does not seem a major loss when compared to the death of a parent or sibling or child, a traumatic illness or injury. When couples have survived crises together and stay married, they tend to have gained a broader perspective that enables them to face change and manage conflict with more equanimity.

If a man isn't in a long-term marriage, a divorce can have altered his perspective, making him a different man in his second marriage than in his first. Maybe his first wife was a traditional woman and he discovered the burden of having a woman totally dependent on him. The next time around he decides he wants a career woman who can share the load. While he may not like the absences that accompany her ambition, he figures that if intellectually that's the kind of woman he wants, then emotionally that's the compromise he'll have to make. Or maybe a man's first wife was an independent woman, and after a painful divorce, he reflects that thwarting her independence had been a mistake, a mistake he isn't going to make twice.

A personal crisis does not have to stem from a marriage or occur during a marriage to affect it just the same. Peter was a widower when he met Sally. "When my oldest child was born two weeks before my first wife died," he said, "I felt incapable of caring for her and took her to my parents for six months. I still feel guilty that I did what was best for me and not what was best for my child, and I don't want to feel that kind of regret ever again. That experience helped me to do the right thing this time."

The inner-motivated man sees marriage not only as a contract with another person but also as a contract with himself. He's supportive because that's the kind of person he needs to be in order to feel good about himself. A man like this doesn't see his wife's leaving as a loss of power or control, a threat to his marriage, or a wound to his ego. He sees it as a means to a more emotionally satisfying life. He figures that if his wife does something she really wants to do and goes without hassle or resistance from him, she'll be happier when she returns. He knows that when she's happier, he'll be happier, too. He figures that if he can tolerate discomfort now, he will reap reward later. Even if he isn't particularly interested in what his wife is learning or doing, he can appreciate what it means to her. Even if she's climbing Everest and the only "tent" he'll sleep in offers room service, or she's writing poetry and he reads only engineering manuals, even if her idea of bliss is his idea of prison camp, *he can identify with her desire for the experience.*

Peter had no interest in studying social work, but as a professor, he could identify with Sally's desire for a degree that would lead to meaningful work. As an artist, he could identify with her desire for an immersive experience, which he had in graduate school and continues to have every time he helicopters into the Brooks Range to paint. He understood the need, valued it, believed in its transformative power.

Intellectually empathetic, vocally encouraging, physically helpful do not necessarily mean pure in heart or conflict-free. A man can help his wife research camping equipment, shop for it, pay for it, and pack it, yet still feel uneasy inside. Emotionally, he may not like her leaving any more than Stieglitz or David or Joe. He may feel envy that she has the freedom to go but he doesn't, that her work is more accommodating and her income less critical. He may resent that she's taking off for a five-month walk in the woods while he has to mail the packages she needs to survive or that she's driving across the country while he has to manage without a car. He may resent the cultural burden of financial success that makes him feel this particular door is not open for him, makes him wonder if it ever will.

A man can find his wife a degree program 3,000 miles away, be supportive from the first moment to the last, yet still feel anxious inside because he recognizes the risk. Peter knew that Alaska was his heart place, not Sally's. He knew she was there only because of him. Now she was leaving this town of 20,000, with its miserable climate and isolated culture, for a city of 2 million, where she could take a walk in winter, eat outdoors in spring, see foreign films year-round, experience a richer, more stimulating way of life—a place, in other words, she could love. Empathy works both ways, and just as leaving Alaska had made Peter realize what he missed and had led to his return, he could see that leaving Alaska could make Sally realize what she had been missing for years, and lead her not to return.

Whatever the conflicted emotion, the inner-motivated man downplays his anxiety or keeps it to himself because he doesn't want to interfere with her dream or add to her struggle. He follows the marital advice of the late, great thinker Joseph Campbell: "As a drop of oil on the sea, you must float, using intellect and compassion to ride the waves." Peter told himself that Sally's going away would give him more time to do more of what he loved doing, more solitude to devote to his painting, extended time to spend at the Brooks Range. He told himself that when Sally returned, she'd be more amenable to his desire for longer immersions in the wild, in part because he'd supported her solitude but mostly because once she'd experienced it herself, she would return with greater understanding of its benefits. Peter's support was an act of compassion and love, but it was also an opportunity for him to transcend the past and shape the future, honor a contract he made with himself, nurture the contract he made with another. The way Peter saw it, being supportive of his wife's journey away from him was in his best interests. The way John Gottman sees it, for a man to be supportive, he *has* to see it in his best interests.

Keith didn't doubt for a moment that supporting his wife's solo adventure was in his best interests. He didn't need to evoke empathy or recall sacrifice, hide resentment or quell fear. When Ann landed an opportunity to work for six weeks at the summer camp she'd attended as a child, he encouraged her to go. When the camp director asked her if she could extend her commitment to two months, he said, "Do it!" Ann was a little surprised at his reaction, both the response itself and the quickness. She thought he'd say, "No, that's too long," but the thought never occurred to him. He was looking forward to her going as much as she was.

As a couple, they didn't spend much time apart. Keith ran his own business, never left town for work, and Ann worked with him, never more than a cubicle away. Living in her hometown, they spent weekends with her friends and holidays with her family. Marrying into another family is usually an adjustment, and so it was for Keith. Ann's family was Jewish and close-knit, he said, "with a different concept of family and togetherness than I was raised with."

The forty-five-year-old entrepreneur grew up in a town with a population of 500, offering the safe, secure atmosphere that typically comes with small-town living. His childhood was all space and freedom; from the time he was four, he had no supervision. "The first years of marriage felt a little claustrophobic," he said. "My wife's always worked with me, she likes everything to be 'ours.' But I felt her life was too tied into mine. I thought this was a good opportunity for her to take ownership of something on her own."

He also thought it was a good opportunity to live his life just the way he wanted. "Married men don't control their social lives," he said. "We set ourselves up for that, but we usually end up with our wives' friends. It's not that I don't like them, but I'd just as soon spend weekends with people I haven't met yet. I enjoy the company of strangers."

Before Ann left, neighbors, friends, and family expressed concern for Keith, promised to care for him. Either directly or through Ann, he was quick to relay the message, "I appreciate the thought, but please don't bother me. Don't call. Don't ask me to dinner. And, for god's sake, don't bring me any casseroles."

"All my friends were envious," he said. "They wanted to know how I managed to pull it off."

Keith didn't erect barriers to his wife's freedom because he wanted his own—his adventure (a solo dinner out), his time alone, his breathing space. The freedom lover isn't pushing his wife out the door exactly, but her leaving does not have to be carefully presented, couched, negotiated, or discussed at length. He immediately sees that her opportunity is his opportunity. A time not to have a schedule, to eat what he wants when he wants, to stay for a drink after tennis or golf instead of racing home for dinner. A time to smoke, drink, watch TV, turn up the stereo, play computer games, eat at the kitchen counter, or guzzle out of the juice carton without comment or criticism. He doesn't just enjoy time alone, he revels in it, can't imagine anything worse than spending every night together. He can't relate to that kind of need, readily admits there are times when he doesn't want his wife with him at all, doesn't want to have to worry about whether she's happy or not happy, entertained or not entertained — times when he wants to think only of himself. Why shouldn't there be times when she feels the same way? And why shouldn't he make the most of them?

What leads to a man's being both supportive and conflict-free can be background or lifestyle or ideology. When his behavior stems not so much from the personal as from the political, a man can harbor a philosophy of life that goes beyond the marital bond. His deep and abiding belief in personal freedom means that no matter how much he loves his wife and treasures their relationship, individual freedom is more important than the marriage. English philosopher Bertrand Russell said it in 1929: "If marriage is to achieve its possibilities, husbands and wives must learn to understand that whatever the law may say, in their private lives they must be free."

And finally, some men are both supportive and conflict-free by nature. Of all the supportive types, these are fewest in number, probably because they're fewest in general. Upbeat by temperament, the perennial optimist views life as an ongoing adventure for everyone, and everyone includes his wife. *Go for it*, he says, *what the heck, you only go around once.* It doesn't occur to him to react any other way. He likes that his wife surprises him, that something's always stirring — he'll tell you that's one of the reasons he married her. He loves to watch the way she lives her life, wonders what she'll do next, just assumes he'll benefit from her adventure, whatever it is; in fact, he already has and she hasn't even left yet, he's enjoying just hearing about it, talking about it, having a new subject to study and a new place to visit. He draws energy from his wife's experiences and doesn't see that this one is any different from the others. The natural-born enthusiast exemplifies Joseph Campbell's definition of marriage: "the grace of participating in another life." Margaret Sanger's husband Noah was not an optimist and he complained often about her lengthy absences to promote birth control, but he tolerated them, biographers have concluded, because he considered her the greatest adventure in *his* life.

And what about my own husband's reaction when I decided to leave for three months? I don't know what he thought of my going because I didn't ask. I was afraid if I asked and he expressed any hurt or reservation, I'd feel guiltier than I already did and I couldn't take on any more guilt. But I knew he wouldn't resist. It isn't his nature, and it isn't the nature of our relationship. I think out loud, so there was no defining moment or conversation. It was, rather, evolution over many years, more process than announcement. He knew every time I applied to an out-of-town program, every time I thought about going somewhere by myself. He knew I had missed a developmental stage of being on my own, and as a result of seeing my conflicts with it, he advises his clients not to marry before they have lived by themselves for a while. The man who was so outgoing when I married him is still a strong presence, but today he's a quieter one. He didn't talk about his feelings. He remained focused on me and on what he could do to help me leave. That felt right somehow. After writing this chapter, however, I am ashamed to realize I didn't attend to his feelings. I knew he could take care of himself physically. I knew he could weather it mentally.

But in my heart I also knew it wouldn't be easy for him. So to finish this section, I do what I probably should have done a year ago. I ask him, "How did you feel about my leaving?"

"Even though you'd talked about it for years, I always figured if I didn't say anything, you'd eventually talk yourself out of it. So when it actually happened, I wasn't ready. There was a sense of mild irritation that you were so excited about doing something without me. But I felt if I resisted it would destroy our marriage. After twenty-five years of doing psychotherapy, I have learned that the tighter you hold people to you, the stronger their impulse to leave. I believe that love is an open hand. People have to be free to go if their staying is going to have meaning."

By the numbers, how typical are these men who support their wives' adventures away from them? Based on the 3,000 couples he has studied since 1972, John Gottman has found that one-fourth to one-third of married men support their wives' dreams, his data from newlyweds indicating the numbers are rising. What are the statistics when those dreams mean a physical separation? "I never thought to measure it," he said, "but the numbers would be much lower. The men who do, however, are emotionally intelligent because they can have partners who really love their lives. Being married to a depressed woman is no picnic. Who would want it?"

Dr. Gottman calls the "emotionally intelligent" man the next step in social evolution. Emotional intelligence does not mean that a man is superior in personality, upbringing, or moral fiber. "It just means he's figured out something important about marriage that other men haven't figured out yet, that sometimes he needs to yield in order to win. Time and again, I can separate the happy couples from the unhappy ones based on whether the husband is willing to accept influence from his wife." In his long-term study of 130 newlywed couples, Dr. Gottman found that even in the first few months of marriage, men who allow their wives to influence them have happier marriages than men who resist. And according to two economics professors, men with happier marriages have heftier bank accounts. Calculating the high cost of family disruptions, David Blanchflower and Andrew Oswald concluded in 1999 that a good marriage is worth $100,000 a year. Combining both studies, the man who values his wife and accepts her influence is investing in a partnership that one day could be worth millions.

Gottman's findings lend scientific credibility to an age-old truth, delightfully portrayed in the fourteenth-century tale of Sir Gawain and Lady Ragnell. In this tale, an unarmed King Arthur finds himself at the mercy of Sir Gromer, a powerful chieftain eager to avenge an old score. Just as Gromer is about to wield his sword, he decides to give Arthur a challenge and a chance to escape his doom. He has one year to find the answer to the question: *What do women desire above all else?*

Arthur accepts the challenge but with little hope. He's a wise man who senses the answer is something unexpected, and he feels certain no one in the kingdom has it. Returning to the castle, he shares his plight and pessimism with his nephew Sir Gawain, the finest knight of the Round Table, noble, brave, handsome—and optimistic that his uncle will succeed. Two days before the appointed hour, however, Arthur has no answer, and riding deep into the woods to think of a way out of his predicament, he comes upon a grotesque woman.

"I know your dilemma," she says, "because the man who issued your challenge is my stepbrother. I am Lady Ragnell, and I have your answer."

"Tell it to me!" exclaims Arthur, "and I'll give you a large bag of gold."

"I am not interested in gold," she answers. "What I want in return is that Sir Gawain become my husband."

Arthur is incredulous. The woman was not only repulsive, she was crazy.

"He's his own person," he says, "not mine to give."

"I don't want you to give him to me," she answers. "If he agrees to marry me of his own free will then I'll give you the answer."

Now Arthur is really depressed. When he tells his nephew what happened, Gawain is thrilled to be able to save his uncle's life and agrees to the marriage. When Arthur describes the would-be bride, Gawain stands by his agreement. At the fateful hour, Arthur gives Gromer the answer Lady Ragnell gave him:

What a woman desires above all else is the right to exercise her own free will.

Arthur's life is spared, Gawain's wedding sealed. That night in their bedchamber the revolting hag turns into a radiant beauty. To a shocked but delighted Gawain, Lady Ragnell explains:

"My stepbrother thought me unwomanly because I refused his commands, so as punishment he used sorcery to change my shape. Only when the finest knight in England chose me as his bride would the spell be broken.

You have broken the spell, Sir Gawain, but only partially. Now you must choose: You can have me beautiful by night or by day, but not both. Which do you want?"

"The decision has to do with you and your person," answers Gawain. "Only you can choose."

With these words the spell is broken completely. The last condition set by Lady Ragnell's stepbrother was that after marriage to the most splendid knight in the land, her husband must give her the power to exercise her own free will. The emotionally intelligent man may not have reached critical mass in the culture, but as the legendary Sir Gawain demonstrated, he's been around a long time.

The Issue of Fidelity

Skeptics might say at this point that emotional intelligence is a façade, that men who support their wives' solo journeys are really thinking of affairs. Some might say that men who find themselves in this position *should* be thinking of affairs. *You should just let go of fidelity while she's gone*, said one colleague. *No way would I go without sex for that long*, said another. Here's the question I asked: Did you feel your wife's leaving gave you the permission to have an affair? Here's the response I heard more than any other, in one variation or another, from men in their thirties as well as men in their fifties: Her leaving may have given me the physical freedom, but it did not give me the mental freedom. Geography, they said, didn't change their expectations of each other. "I probably could have rationalized it," said David, "because I didn't support her going to Africa. But that's not me." Some men, in fact, said one of the reasons they didn't tell any-

one about their wives' absence was to safeguard themselves against sexual advances. Some men found my question offensive.

A celibate season isn't something any husband looks
forward to, but most men I spoke with didn't see the loss
as one that could be remedied by a substitute or pre-
vented by resistance. They didn't consider possessiveness
a solution. Possessiveness often characterizes the early
stages of a relationship, and because screen romances typically focus on beginnings, our media images of romantic
love often appear possessive, based on need rather than
want. As country western singer LeAnn Rimes croons,
"How do I live without you? How do I breathe without
you? If you ever go, how do I ever, ever survive?" Over
time and as relationships mature, however, possessiveness
diminishes the potential a marriage can achieve. Possessiveness says that what we want is more important than
what our partner wants, which means it's a selfish desire.
Possessiveness clings to that which must change, which
means it's an unattainable goal. Possessiveness grasps to
avoid the pain it's guaranteed to inflict, which means it's
self-defeating behavior. In Buddhist belief, all earthly suffering comes from grasping, and only by letting go can we
find inner freedom and peace. In relationships, that
means loving lightly, without making our need our partner's burden. "Most of us love as cannibals, as food for
ourselves," wrote Simone Weil, the French philosopher
and social reformer. "To love purely is to consent to distance, to love the hunger in another."

Those who love purely, lightly, who consent to distance, those who intend to be faithful themselves can still
worry about their wives' fidelity in their absence. When it

comes to thoughts of affairs, committed husbands react like committed wives. They are clear about their own moral codes but have to trust their partners feel the same way. Men looking at long separations were the ones most likely to worry. Voicing the fear out loud and talking about it with their spouses were the ways they worked through it, if they did. David never stopped worrying that Chris might meet someone during her time in the Peace Corps. He worried the ten months before she left, and he worried the two years she was away.

Many men I spoke with, however, didn't voice this fear, said if it hadn't happened when they had reason to fear it might happen, then they didn't expect it would happen now. Some said the thought never crossed their minds; others said it always crossed their minds, but awareness didn't translate into fear. In the words of one man, "I'm aware of the risk every time my wife leaves, but if my marriage was based on narrowing my life to the point where there'd be no risk, then it wouldn't be much of a marriage."

Men's Sabbaticals

Men take marriage sabbaticals, too. At the age of sixty, novelist John Steinbeck temporarily said goodbye to his third wife and left with a French poodle and a truck to rediscover America. His three months on the road became the now classic *Travels with Charley*. More recently, journalist Gregory Jaynes boarded a freighter and traveled the world for six months. In his rollicking account of the trip, *Come Hell on High Water*, the author said that when he turned forty-seven, he "became disenchanted with the view" and wanted change. He also wrote, "I can say that I did not sail away owing to a problem of the heart. I can say I know no one more special than the woman who told me to go ahead if I must."

Hollywood producer and manager Jon Brown thought his wife of seven years was pretty special, too, when she stood up at his thirtieth birthday party and announced in front of fifty friends: *Here is my gift to you—if we're still married in ten years, I will give you one year out of the marriage, no questions asked.* Brown knew he'd heard something rare and wonderful, possibly something no married man had heard before. He savored the words, memorized them, stored them, didn't mention them for 3,285 days. And then on his thirty-ninth birthday, he spoke them, slowly, verbatim, as he watched a look of horror cross his wife's face. *You remember?* she gasped. *Remember?* he answered. *I've been waiting nine years.* Renee Brown fulfilled her promise but attached three conditions: He had to use condoms, he had to shower before he came home, and he couldn't brag about his exploits to his friends. The caveats proved unnecessary since he stayed in hotels in town and went home to visit every couple of weeks. "She thought it would be about sex," he said, "but it wasn't about that at all. I didn't even have a one-night stand. I'd been a very responsible person for twenty years, a husband for seventeen, a business owner for fifteen, a father for five, and I wanted time off from that responsibility. I just didn't want to have to answer to anyone." *No Questions Asked,* the comic screenplay based on Brown's experience, is in development.

Writer Jon Katz, a husband and father on the East Coast, expressed a number of reasons he left home for six months to live alone in a cabin. "I had settled down," he wrote in his lyrical memoir *Running to the Mountain*. "Any more settling and I would vanish into the mud like some fat old catfish." Katz went to the mountains the year he turned fifty, for change, for solitude, for reflection, but mostly, he said, "to try to be a better human." Byron Scott, a professor at the University of Missouri, left his wife for a year and a half to start a journalism program in Eastern Europe because "we promised ourselves after our last child was through college that now was the time for our adventures." Only one in a thousand Peace Corps enlistees is married, said director Mark Schneider, but it's far more common for men to leave for the two-year commitment without their spouses than it is for women. Humanitarian work, soul work, adventure, challenge, change — men's motivations echo women's. And when men are the ones who leave, they face their own difficulties.

When the great nineteenth-century adventurer Sir Richard Burton ventured forth on his global expeditions, he knew the love of his life, Isabel Arundell, would be there when he returned. Arundell was twenty-four when Burton proposed, and shortly afterward, he set sail for Africa to discover the source of the Nile. When he returned three years later, skeletal from twenty-one bouts of fever, Arundell wrote that she "loved him more than ever." As soon as he regained his health, he left again. Isabel Arundell Burton was strong-willed and aristocratic, an independent woman in many ways, but she was also a product of her Victorian times. During the Burtons' eleven-year engagement and thirty-year marriage, she packed his suitcases before he left and nursed his ailments when he returned. Although she did accompany him on many trips after they married, she often did not. While he journeyed down the Amazon River by raft, up the Chilean coast by horseback, across Iceland by pony and canoe, she edited his memoirs, negotiated with his publishers, handled his court cases, and prayed for his safe returns. Today, men married to women with equal opportunities and incomes have no such assurances their wives will be around when they return, or even that they'll be supportive when they go. When men are the ones to leave, women can have a hard time, too.

When I was growing up in the fifties and sixties, my father left every year on a scuba-diving trip with the same group of men. He started getting ready for those trips sometimes six months in advance. First, there was a meeting to decide when and where they'd charter a boat, based on seasonal water temperatures and everyone's schedules. Then he'd start making camera housings for his underwater photography, practice shooting fish in the pool, and, as the time drew near, work on laying down a protective tan. To my scientifically minded father, every trip was not only an adventure but an experiment. One year, he lugged through customs a disassembled shark cage that he had built, only to come home with the news that none of the men, himself included, was daring enough to get in it. Another time, he wanted to experiment with bait and loaded his duffel bag with tins of anchovies and sardines. Scuba diving was, and still is, one of my father's great passions, and his enthusiasm was infectious. But I felt guilty sharing his excitement because the closer his departure date, the more distressed my mother became. She would say to me, her eyes teary, her voice trembling, "Why does he want to go on a trip without me? I don't want to go anywhere without him." In time, her distress turned to anger, and she would literally stop speaking to my father two weeks before he left. If she caught me talking to him about the trip, she stopped speaking to me, too. The house turned into a morgue, dinnertime a wake. (While writing this book, I asked my dad how long those trips were, imagining they must have been at least a month. "A week," he answered. "They were never more than a week.") Bereft while he was gone, begrudging when he returned, she greeted his stories and slides and sharks' teeth with disinterest, his gifts with reserve.

We went through this scene every trip, every year, but it wasn't until long after I'd left home that I came to understand her reaction. When she was five years old, her father had left her and her mother in their native France to attend a conference in the States. He never returned. Every time my father left, her soul closed in on itself, like mimosa leaves at dusk. Every time he left, she felt abandoned again.

All life is a leave-taking. No one says the parting isn't painful, and more painful always for those who are left than for those who do the leaving.

Of those left behind, parting will be easier for the man who was raised in a secure family, who was not abandoned in his youth or threatened with abandonment. It will be easier for the man who has lived alone or is relatively self-sufficient, who shares the cooking and other household responsibilities. It will be easier for the man who enjoys his work and has some freedom with it, easier still for the man who enjoys a social life independent of his wife and values his own company. The man who handles it best and suffers the least is the one who views his wife's desire not as diminishment of him but as development for her. The man who handles it best doesn't take it personally.

Supportive men may not be the dominant culture — certainly they are not portrayed as the dominant culture — but until more women see men as having the potential to be supportive, we'll never know the possibilities. "Why do you think more married women haven't done this sort of thing?" I asked female therapists. And a number responded, "Because most men would never tolerate it." But if most women would not think of bringing up such a desire or risk pursuing it in the face of resistance, if even independent wives prefer to keep the relationship where it's comfortable, how then can we really know what a man would do?

How can we know, for example, how many men might not react like Sabina Shalom's husband? When friends invited the Florida couple to visit them in Australia, as Shalom related in her 1984 memoir, she saw an adventure; her husband saw a drag. When she said she wanted to go without him, he sputtered: *Are you crazy? Why it's off the map. What on earth would you do there?* When she said if she were going that far she might as well visit her relatives in England, might as well take six months off to see the world, he blustered: *You can't do this. I'm not going to let you go. It's out of the question. We don't have the money. And what about me? I don't know how I'll manage without you.* As she went ahead with her plans, he acted by turns disgruntled, bewildered, and remote. Finally,

Shalom decided she'd had enough. Giving an impassioned speech, she listed all the reasons she needed to make the trip, including that the future of their marriage *depended* on her making the trip—why it was as important for him as it was for her. She followed the speech with a phone call to their younger son to request that he come home to keep his dad company for the duration. The Miami businessman went out and bought her the airline ticket and a new 35-millimeter camera.

How can we know, for example, how many men might not react like Chris's husband David, resistant the entire ten months before she left but then willing to spend more than $12,000 for three trips to Africa to see her and still married three years after her return?

5

PREPARATIONS

To get ready for Portugal, my mother
prepares herself the other 10 months out of
the year. She is always on the lookout for that
perfect beige blouse, the perfect Portugal-
skirt, a new bathroom kit. . . . As she finds
these perfect travel items for the trip, she
assembles them on a shelf in her pie-safe,
stealing, tucking them away until the spring
weather unfolds. All year she anticipates. She
plans. She plots. In her room, she has 43
books on Portugal. And she reads. And she
makes itineraries.

— CHARLOTTE OVERBY,
"SWEEPING UP," FROM
Exposures: Essays by Missouri Women

*I*n Anne Tyler's best-selling novel *Ladder of Years*, the forty-year-old protagonist, in the midst of a quarrel with her husband on a family vacation, grabs her tote bag and stomps off down the beach. She crosses the highway, hitches a ride to a neighboring town, and stays for a year. She goes without leaving a clue as to why or where. In Elizabeth Berg's *The Pull of the Moon*, the heroine also leaves her husband abruptly, without warning. Although she writes a note saying she'll be back in a couple of days, she knows she'll be gone much longer.

Running away from home is both compelling fiction and heartbreaking fact. When Angelina Alioto disappeared in 1974, her husband, Joseph, then mayor of San Francisco, was campaigning for the Democratic nomination for governor. The charismatic, progressive politician had to tell the press he did not know where she was or why she had left, and her disappearance made headlines nationwide. While the distraught mayor issued a five-state, missing-person bulletin for her recovery and hired private detectives to find her, Angelina Alioto rested quietly in retreat, seeking spiritual solace in California missions. When she returned after three weeks, the once-anonymous political wife called a press conference. The *New York Times* reported that the mayor stood beside her with a strained smile as she explained that she loved her husband very much but she felt frustrated and taken for granted. Joseph Alioto lost in the primaries.

Most married women have escape fantasies: to find a room in a hotel somewhere, lock the door, indulge in vapid magazines and a large bag of M&Ms, to forget for a night or a weekend that they are wife, mother, daughter, responsible woman, good girl. Women who take a sabbatical, however, don't act out these fantasies in harmful ways. They don't wake up one morning and walk out the door like fictional characters or Angelina Alioto. Women who take a sabbatical show care in their leave-taking, spending months, even years, talking about it and planning for it.

The sun is bright and the air crisp as I take my daily walk to the mailbox, a midafternoon ritual since I began working at home four years ago. The significance of the mail is inversely proportionate to the degree of excitement in my life, but hope always prevails that somewhere amid the advertising mailers and overdue library notices and bank statements will be good news: an invitation, a fan letter, a check for an article I recently wrote, or better still, a check for a reprint of an article written long ago. Today I see the return address of a writers' colony I applied to. I've been turned down by two, which makes me feel like a high school senior again, waiting for college-admission notifications. I read the letter as I slowly walk back to the house, elation tempered by amazement that I made it happen. How did desire finally become a departure date?

I guess it began with my lists, which I've been composing for as long as I can remember. I find the activity irresistible because it creates order out of chaos and—for a few moments anyway—quells my free-floating anxiety. In high school and college, I scribbled my lists on scraps of old homework paper, in the margins of course notebooks: homework to do, books to read, clothes to buy, hair products to try. After I married, I tucked the lists into cookbooks and novels, crammed them into pockets of jackets and coats: books to read, recipes to try, house projects to begin, Christmas gifts to make, clothes to sew. More lists covered my desk at work: people to call, stories to write, groceries to buy. In my thirties, the lists grew exponentially, written on legal pads and Post-its, the backs of envelopes and library notices: to-do lists at work, to-do lists at home, phone calls to make, appointments to schedule, gifts to buy, people to entertain, books to request from the library, movies to rent.

The one list I never made: Dreams To Pursue.

Then I came across an exercise in a career book that gave me the direction I needed: Make a list of all the things you want to do before you die. Creating a list made me realize I had spent more time planning a dinner party than I had planning my life. I found the exercise so effective that I did it every year, and I replaced the scraps of paper with a silk-covered journal. I like Jung's idea that by taking dreams and fantasies seriously, we can come to know our most secret desires. In my thirties the dreams focused on professional achievement. A decade later, career dreams are still there, but others have become equally important: travel around the world, live in another country, live in New York. City of the arts, publishing capital of the world, New York is my favorite city to visit, the city where I might have gone after college if I had had the confidence, if I hadn't gotten married. I visit there each spring for five days, because that's what I can afford. How can I go for three months, I ask myself, when I can't afford one week? Even if I had a job while I was there, I doubt I could swing it financially. With one son in college, none of these dreams are options yet, but I gather information anyway.

My eyes move down the list: to live in the Northwest, to live in New England, to work at a writers' colony. This last one may be every writer's dream. To work undistracted, to lose oneself in large blocks of creative time without having to stop to prepare dinner, pick up the phone, answer the door, feed the cat, retrieve the car at the shop. Going to a writers' colony has been a fantasy of mine for ten years, since I first opened a book and noticed in the acknowledgments the author thanking the place that gave her free room and board so that she could write. I know only of the most prestigious ones, where Truman Capote wrote *In Cold Blood* and Thornton Wilder wrote *Our Town*. I am plagued by doubt. How am I going to receive a grant to such a place when my name isn't recognizable, when I've never taken a grant-writing workshop?

I head to the library. There are not just a few colonies, as I had imagined, but more than thirty in the United States alone. I discover that many accept writers based on work in progress rather than on work that's already proven. I compile a list, then narrow it to those where I think I have the best chance of being accepted, the newer ones, the all-women ones. I apply for the coldest months of the year, the time I imagine to be the least competitive. I want to go to three, so I apply to six. I spend weeks filling out applications, writing essays, asking people for recommendations. Now I'm looking at the first of three acceptance letters—to writing retreats in Washington,

Wyoming, and Vermont—and I feel both exhilarated and grateful. My unexpectedly giddiest moment comes as I'm pushing my cart down the aisle at the grocery store and realize I won't have to grocery shop for three months. I remember a *New York Times* interview with astronaut Shannon Lucid, who orbited the earth for 188 days. She loved floating around in space, she said, because she didn't have to worry about going to the grocery store.

Later, my emotions take a different shape as I realize the fantasy will come to an end, the "if only" fantasy: If only I had some *real* time, I could change my career, change my habits, change my life. The dream, the adventure, is now a paradox, both what I want and what I fear. Around the edges of the emotional cauldron, irritation simmers. If these opportunities were there all along, just for the asking, why did it take me so long?

The Wait

The time a woman's desire takes hold until the day she acts on it can range from months to years. Sometimes the reasons are practical: She is waiting for a child to grow up or finances to accrue. More often, the reasons are psychological. For many women it is difficult to let go of the fantasy. As long as the dream takes shape only in our heads, we can write the script to glorify the ending. Untested, the fantasy remains safe, protected from disapproval, immune to failure. In fantasy, we can imagine the thrill without risking the danger, stir the passion without suffering the guilt. In our heads we earn a doctorate, write a bestseller, exhibit at the Metropolitan, trek the Himalayas. When imagined glory exudes such pleasure, why wouldn't we cling to it? Not ready, we say to ourselves, not yet. Revisiting the fantasy is familiar and easy; acting on it, unfamiliar and hard. Human nature gravitates to what's familiar, settles for what's easy.

A woman can need time to sort through her emotions, to conquer her fears or exhaust her guilt. A woman can need time to push past the cultural messages that negate the need, dull the desire. When there is so much reinforcement in the culture for women to create a home, breaking free from that conditioning takes emotional and mental strength, attributes that require time to develop, and more time in some women than in others depending on how great the obstacles or how deep the conditioning. Jessamyn West, an accomplished screenwriter and author, took nearly thirty years to realize her dream of spending a summer alone on the banks of the Colorado River, in a trailer she called "Walden on Wheels." Sue Bender was thirty-three when she became mesmerized by the haunting quality of Amish quilts; she was forty-eight when she first went to live with an Amish family to discover the source of that fascination. It takes time because with age women feel freer to follow their own passions and freer not to follow others' expectations. This sense of personal freedom and social power peaks in women during early midlife.

A woman might have a fantasy and not bring it to reality for many years because the ability to enact the fantasy requires an inner shift, and developmental change happens slowly. That's why a woman can spend years living somewhere between the shifts, why some women need trial runs, consciously or subconsciously easing the stretch. Some women see incremental journeys as natural progressions; others, as psychic rehearsals.

Either way, slow change can be the best kind of change. In *The Uses of Enchantment*, psychologist Bruno Bettelheim said that Sleeping Beauty's hundred years' sleep symbolized not deathlike passivity but the importance of growth and preparation, the long, quiet concentration on oneself that is needed to become oneself. Thinking about the experience begins the process. Thinking about the experience enriches its meaning.

The Logistics

Even when she has conquered psychological fears, a woman can feel overwhelmed by logistical ones. How can I leave for six weeks when it's an ordeal to get away for one? How can I find an Amish family to take me in when the Amish don't reach out to strangers? Like a roller coaster going from zero to seventy miles per hour in six seconds, a woman's thoughts can rocket from "Wow, I'm really going to do this" to "How can I possibly do this now?"

Ironically, the woman who appeared to have the greatest logistical problems never saw them as barriers making for an impassable road or even as challenges requiring a superhuman effort. She just saw them as tasks requiring time and attention.

Shelley began teaching yoga in her twenties, and as her fascination with the Eastern discipline grew, so did her desire to go to India. Every year for fifteen years she thought about going. Every year for fifteen years she decided she wasn't ready. Yoga had helped her become strong in mind and body, but her dream of a trip to India aroused fears—that she would become infected with parasites or stricken with dysentery, that she wouldn't be able to handle the poverty she would find there. Then one year she discovered her fears were gone. She was forty-five, and she was ready.

Mentally ready did not, however, mean physically ready, and Shelley discovered that moving from fantasy to reality was like rising from a yoga stretch to run the hurdles. In addition to teaching yoga, Shelley was directing the marketing for a small theater company and working as a waitress. She was also raising a ten-year-old son with her husband, who was a full-time graduate student. At the time Shelley decided to go on her six-week adventure, she was the sole support of her family, had no savings for the trip, no money for child care, no money for expenses at home in her absence, and no scheduled time off from any of her three jobs.

To leave in September, Shelley began making phone calls in June. She asked and scheduled co-workers to cover the eighteen waitressing shifts she would miss. She asked another teacher to cover her twelve yoga classes. She negotiated with her boss at the theater company to let her leave on the condition that she'd work full time when she returned. Then she worked longer hours over the summer to ensure all the marketing was in place for the fall season when she would be away.

The child-care arrangements were the hardest, not only because she had little money for sitters but also because the only time to go to India is after monsoon season, which is during the school year. So Shelley had to ask and then schedule mothers of her son's classmates for thirty rides home from school. She had to ask and then schedule friends and family for thirty baby-sittings afterward. She mapped out a chart, with each day's arrangements, names, and phone numbers. "I couldn't have done it without extended family in town," she said. Extended family for Shelley meant her ex-husband and his second wife, who agreed to cover many hours of her son's care.

Finally, what would have been many women's first thought was Shelley's last: the matter of money. She needed $3,000 — two-thirds for the trip, the rest for expenses at home while she was away. In the midst of her planning, her sister-in-law sent a check for $1,200 with a note saying, "This is to help with your trip. You can pay me back later."

"I was shocked and grateful and worried about how I was going to repay it," said Shelley. "But the worry didn't keep me from taking it." Shelley's husband, meanwhile, was filling out applications for student loans. Since he considered her trip to India the educational equivalent of his teaching degree, he applied for an additional student loan and gave it to her. It took Shelley a year to repay her sister-in-law and five years to pay off the student loan. Still, she said, "It was much easier than I thought it would be."

It was easier than she thought it would be because, once women make the decision and say "I am going," help comes from both expected and unexpected places. Perception is the critical factor. When women reveal the efforts they are willing to expend for the experience, when they make visible the value they attach to it, others come to perceive its value, too. And when others come forward with offers of help, women realize that what may have looked like boulders blocking the road were only stones needing to be moved aside.

Physical preparations are obviously easier for those who are affluent, who have housekeepers, nannies, au pairs, bank accounts, or trust funds that enable them to rent a house, mail a tuition check, or book a flight without a moment's hesitancy. But if taking a sabbatical were only a matter of economics, only wealthy women would take them. The majority of women I interviewed applied for grants or loans, withdrew savings, tapped into pensions, used an inheritance, or worked to buy the time they wanted. Not even these options were available to Harriet Beecher Stowe in the 1840s when she longed to go to a newly-opened water cure in the East. She and her husband were so poor that they had to take in boarders to pay the bills, but Stowe reportedly expressed her desire so often (and the wealthier the gathering, the more loudly she expressed it) that eventually enough donations poured in to pay her way to the exclusive retreat. Limited finances make preparations more time-consuming and angst-ridden, but as women's stories reveal, the issue is one of inner drives more than outer resources.

Jobs can be a bigger obstacle than finances, and some women find their greatest challenge is lobbying for the time off from work. The more one is committed to a job and the more responsible the position, the more difficult it is to leave. "The only real worry I had was telling my boss at the theater company," said Shelley, "because I didn't want her to replace me. I could always find a new place to teach yoga or work as a waitress, but that job I didn't want to lose."

Some professions accommodate sabbaticals more easily than others, which is the reason the women who responded to my requests for an interview came overwhelmingly from the fields of teaching, medicine,
writing, and the arts. A number were small-business own-
ers, who had family in town to take over their shops. A
number were women in transition, many of them students. The few I talked to from the business world were
at a crossroads in their careers, psychologically ready to
move in new directions and, therefore, willing to risk an
unpleasant aftermath. Studies have found that less than
one-fourth of companies offer sabbaticals, which means
most of the corporate world does not embrace the concept. Getting the time off from work is another book and
beyond the scope of this one. But opportunities for sabbaticals are widening as increasing numbers of women
work for themselves, as telecommunications enable us to
work from anywhere, as more companies offer short-term
contract work. What I discovered from fifty-five interviews, albeit with middle- and upper-class women: If a
woman wants the experience badly enough, she finds a
way

The Load Lessening

She will also lessen the load for those left behind.

Mystic Margery Kempe, who owned the largest brew-
ery in the English town of Lynn in the fourteenth century, paid all her husband's debts before she left on her
pilgrimage to the Holy Land. Recalling Kaye Gibbons's
heroine in *A Virtuous Woman*, who made three months'
worth of casseroles for her husband before she died, some

women cook as much as a month's worth of meals and stockpile the freezer. Although packing for a significant time away, some spend their last days doing loads of laundry, cleaning the house, filling the pantry, leaving notes taped on the refrigerator, inside kitchen cabinets, on bathroom mirrors. They make lists: special foods a child likes; gear to pack for a teenager going to camp; instructions for the dog and yard and garden; phone numbers of maintenance people, baby-sitters, doctors, vets. They make sure the calendar is covered, that friends or family or sitters are scheduled to drive car pools, to get their children to music lessons, soccer practices, baseball games, dentist appointments. They detail the bills to be paid and the dates they're to be mailed, address, stamp, and stack the envelopes in chronological order. One woman who handled the finances in her family arranged to continue handling them even though she was leaving for a rigorous graduate program 3,000 miles away. For a woman with children, going away for one month can take six months of preparation.

Women leaving on sabbatical tend to take care of whatever they've been taking care of. I stopped cooking years ago, so I didn't stock the kitchen (what was the point of filling the freezer with carry-out?). But if I had left years earlier, with children at home, I know I would have. Why women do this reveals the essential conflict of the journey. To go toward herself means separation from her family, and separation from her family is hard for a woman invested in relationship. So to ease the pain of separation, she stores, cooks, freezes, labels, prepares. She may do it out of habit or out of guilt, but the meaning behind her actions remains the same: It's a way of saying "I love you," and it's a way of saying "Love me, too." She may do it out of anxiety that her family won't be able to get along without her, or she may do it out of fear that her family will be able to get along without her. She may do it as a way of exerting control over an area in which she will be losing control, and as a way of dealing with her uneasiness over that loss. She may do it for one of these reasons or all of these reasons, but whatever the motivation, the gesture symbolizes a woman's connection to her home and those within it. The gesture reaffirms that her leaving is physical, not emotional.

The Goal Setting

While a woman is arranging for a smoothly running home life in her absence, she is also planning a carefully thought-out agenda for her experience. Just as every dream has a goal, every sabbatical has a purpose: earn a degree, become fluent in French, participate in a mission, complete a course, write a first or final draft. Goal setting reveals intention, and intention is what gives the sabbatical not only its shape but its soul. Joan Mister first thought of a cross-country road trip when she drove home alone after taking a son to college. Eight years later, she began the first stage of preparations. She created a card business to earn the money, visualized the trip every time she got into a car, and test-ran the dream by taking several warm-up trips ranging from three to five weeks. In the second stage of her preparations, she designed an itinerary for each of the 180 days of her trip. She created file folders, with daily logs, for each day's destination. She packed her car with maps and tourist guides and brochures and newspaper clippings of interesting sites, and tapes and journals to record her observations. Her goal was not only to drive 25,000 miles but also to travel the country as a social scientist, to research the land and its people by visiting lunch counters and diners and bookstores—the places where conversations happen.

Women determined to "thru-hike" the Appalachian Trail discovered that planning, shopping, and packing for the five-and-a-half-month trek could take almost as long as walking it. They had to decide what was essential to survive but minimal to carry, buy each item in the lightest possible weight, prepackage some fourteen boxes of provisions, and preaddress them to mail drops along the way so that they only had to carry ten days' worth of food at a time. Even women who just wanted time alone created a plan and a structure for that time. Libby, the mother of two who needed to re-energize and gain perspective, planned to live for two months in a deserted beach house in winter, without a car, television, or radio; to begin each day with a meditation and long walk; to eat only natural foods; to cook them over an open fire. It is this agenda setting, this planning what one wants to accomplish, that is a defining characteristic of a sabbatical, that differentiates it from a vacation.

When people heard that Susan was going to the south of France for six months to read, it sounded like a vacation to them, and an overly long and indulgent one at that, available to Susan because of her wealth and surely one that signified marital disaster. To Susan, the time-out was a sabbatical, a critical time for her work, her relationships, and her inner self, but it was not a vacation.

Susan had gone her own way since she was a teenager and chose to spend a summer working full time as a maid at a nearby hospital rather than fulfill her affluent family's expectations and socialize at their country club. In the years afterward, wherever her interests led, she exhibited the same determination. When she wanted to learn to play golf, she drove to the driving range after putting her children to bed and hit golf balls until midnight. When she wanted to have a say in her children's education, she sat on their school boards. And when she wanted to change the world, she became a community activist, chairing a preschool board in the inner city while working full time as the director of a radio help line for the needy.

Here, Susan discovered her limits, her inability to always mold the world to her will. Obsessed with resolving what were unresolvable problems, she found the momentum that had always driven her interests spiraling around her, the gears of her life stuck in neutral. Surrounded by congestion on all sides and unable to see the road ahead, she felt her balance and perception weakening. She knew she had to get off the highway, catch her breath, spread out a map, and look for an alternate route. She knew the exit ramp marked "time alone" was the one to take.

When mythologist Joseph Campbell dropped out of a Ph.D. program with no idea what to do next, he spent a year and a half in a cabin in Woodstock, New York, reading scholarly works on mythology, legends, and folklore. In a similar manner but with no knowledge of Campbell's background, Susan decided that the way to clarify her thinking and redirect her life was through the words of others. And not just any words, from any others.

She wrote to twenty-five friends who were readers, asking them to send her a list of the ten books that had made the biggest impact on their lives or that they felt were important books to have read. She culled the eighteen responses and 180 titles she received to a hundred "great books," which she bought, packed up in a crate, and shipped to the house where she would be staying. Then she designed her days in the focused and thorough way that was her custom. Each morning and afternoon she would read classic fiction such as Tolstoy's *War and Peace* and George Eliot's *Middlemarch*; epics like *The Iliad* and *The Odyssey*; memoirs ranging from Margaret Mead's *Blackberry Winter* to B. F. Skinner's *Beyond Freedom and Dignity*; the novels of Faulkner, Steinbeck, and Hemingway; the plays of Sophocles and Shakespeare, Chekhov and Ibsen; the humor of P. G. Wodehouse and James Thurber. Then, after dinner and a drive, she would read each evening: ten pages of philosophy—Plato and Kierkegaard, Nietzsche and Tillich—ten pages of poetry from the collections of Dickinson, Milton, Whitman, Frost; and finally, ten pages of the Bible. To accompany her reading list, she packed forty classical music tapes, the symphonies of Tchaikovsky, Mahler, Beethoven, Bach.

While Susan was culling and crating, her female friends took her to lunch to tell her that if she went through with this craziness she would not have a marriage when she returned. "I don't know what kept me going," she said. "I had no idea how long it would take me to read the books or how many I'd get through. But I became excited the moment I started planning. I felt like I was going to a new frontier."

The Leave-taking

As excitement about the experience rises, so can apprehension about leaving. A smooth withdrawal from the scene is easier for those with supportive husbands and self-sufficient children, easier still for those with supportive husbands and no children. But in the end, there is no good time for a woman to leave. Wondering about a good time to leave is like wondering about a good time to be hospitalized. Looking back, a woman can say that it was a good time or a perfect time or the only possible time, but before she leaves, there is no good time when someone won't be depending on her for something. It is time when an opportunity beckons, when the need presses, when the desire will no longer be denied. But there is no good time, and because there is no good time, a woman will experience—at some moment, somewhere—discomfort.

The night before she left for India, Shelley, who had no fears about leaving her husband, no fears about leaving her son, awoke at 3 A.M. "afraid that if I heard their voices while I was away, I'd dissolve into a puddle." That morning at breakfast, she told them she would be too far away to get homesick so she would not be calling. She would only write.

Like Shelley, women take care as they leave, clarifying the steps they'll take to nurture their relationships to preserve connections. They discuss times for telephone calls and visits, give prepaid calling cards, distribute itineraries. For women walking the Appalachian Trail, this was no minor undertaking. They had to study forty-one maps and the terrains of fourteen states to estimate the number of miles they would walk each day, then calculate what towns they hoped to reach each weekend so they could leave names and phone numbers of the nearest lodgings.

If it takes emotional energy for women like Shelley and Susan with supportive families, it takes even more for women with family members who are resistant or worried. Children can be disconcerted at any age, express their uneasiness in myriad ways. They can ask questions: What if I break my arm? What if I get sick? What if I need help with my homework? They can be sarcastic or surly. A teenage daughter whose mother is the disciplinarian can look forward to the reprieve but still need reassurance that her parents' marriage is okay. A daughter can be immersed in college life and supportive of her mother yet still ask, "Who's gonna take care of Dad?" A daughter can be attending college at the opposite end of the country but upon hearing that her mother is going to graduate school in another state respond, "Children leave home, not parents."

Even supportive children can feel uneasy because a new pattern for a mother means a new pattern for a child. When a woman is negotiating a new phase of her development, she is also pushing her children to negotiate a new phase of theirs. Incessant questions, cries of protest, subtle or not-so-subtle digs are their ways of actively expressing this negotiation, of dealing with their own fears—and they have to deal with them. Separation is a part of life, necessary, inevitable, universal. Without it children cannot grow into mature adults. Mastering fears is their path to growth too, and growth is hard for everyone.

The discovery that a mother has a life of her own can be a narcissistic blow at any age. It's hard for children, even adult children, to see their parents as individuals with needs and desires beyond caring for them. Even self-sufficient teenagers or young adult children are not thinking of their mothers' self-development. They're thinking of themselves: How is this going to affect *my* life? Who will take care of *my* needs? Children see it as their right to leave their parents, to move in and out of their lives however they can and whenever they wish, but rarely do they see their parents as having the same right.

The parable of *The Giving Tree* says it all. "Once there was a tree and she loved a little boy," begins Shel Silverstein's classic children's tale. The little boy grows up expecting the tree will always be there for him, available to serve his needs, whatever they are, whenever he asks. And the tree is always there for him, a continually reassuring presence, rooted in the same ground, giving happily of itself whatever the boy asks—its apples when he needs money, its branches when he needs a house, its trunk when he wants a boat. As the story ends, the boy has wizened into a lonely, old man and the tree has been hacked to a stump. And the tree is delighted to be a stump so that her "boy" can have a place to sit. In real life, no mother, no person, can be this happily sacrificial, but if it's an illusion a child harbors, a mother's leaving home will shatter it.

Psychoanalytic theory gave us the term "separation anxiety" to describe the anxiety generated by the absence of someone we feel is necessary for our survival. How much anxiety a child feels when a mother temporarily leaves home depends on many factors. It depends on the child's temperament, personality, and level of self-sufficiency, how much the child has going on in his or her own life. It depends on the father, his relationship to the child and his comfort with the situation, and it depends on the mother, her relationship to the child and her comfort with the situation. Children tend to take their cues from their parents.

Separation anxiety peaks in early childhood, but it is not limited to a certain period of development. It can occur at any age. The difference is that the older we become, the more it feels like a weakness, making it difficult to admit to ourselves, much less voice to others. Separation can be hard even for young adult children if they are feeling vulnerable, struggling with divorce or job loss or financial problems—if they are facing their own unknowns, and their mother, like the giving tree, has *always* been there for them.

Four days before Chris left on her two-year Peace Corps assignment to Africa, her twenty-four-year-old daughter announced her pregnancy. Chris hugged and congratulated her daughter, but tears filled her eyes because she was thinking ahead. The Peace Corps allows only one emergency trip home, and she had already promised her son she'd be there for his college graduation. "I didn't know what to say," said Chris. "I knew I'd be okay with it, and the baby certainly wouldn't know, but I could see and hear her disappointment." Chris tried to reassure her daughter, told her she had her husband and her father and the best medical care in the world. Chris tried to reassure herself, too, that she could make it up to her daughter later, that time would heal the hurt. "She is as independent as I am and she knew what this meant to me," said Chris, "but she did not want me to go. I remember thinking, 'When is the right time for a woman to get the chance to do what she feels driven to do?'"

Psychologist Monica McGoldrick explains the dynamics of Chris's frustration in terms of the family life cycle. In this framework, society has always given men and children a life cycle apart from their roles in the family constellation, but giving women a life cycle apart from their roles as wife and mother is a relatively recent idea and, as such, still not widely recognized. As McGoldrick wrote in an academic paper, "Traditionally, the cultural expectation for women was that they would take care of the needs of others—first men, then children, then the elderly. . . . Rarely has it been accepted that women had a right to a life for themselves."

The conflict for many women like Chris lies not in deciding what they want but in having to say no to others in order to attain it. And saying no to others is one of women's most difficult tasks in life. According to the myth of Psyche, it is our most difficult task. In Greek mythology, Psyche is a mortal maiden who personifies the female soul. To be reunited with her lost lover, the god Eros, she must carry out four seemingly impossible tasks assigned by Eros's jealous mother, Aphrodite. The final and most difficult task is to bring the goddess a cask of supernatural beauty ointment from the underworld. Psyche is given two coins for the ferryman Charon to take her across the river Styx and two pieces of barley bread to appease Cerberus, the vicious, three-headed dog guarding the entrance to Hades. On Psyche's journey to hell and back, hands keep reaching for her. A drowning man pleads for her help; beggars ask for her food, her money. Psyche realizes that reaching her goal will require *all* her energies and resources; therefore, she cannot help everyone she meets, nor can she rescue others from their destinies. When she succeeds in saying no to the out-stretched hands and brings the cask to Aphrodite, not only is she reunited with Eros, she is also given a place among the gods, equal to her husband's.

Using this myth to illustrate female psychological growth, psychoanalyst Robert Johnson wrote in *She* that few women achieve Psyche's level of development, not because they are incapable of it but because "it is out of the realm of their experiences." If it's a faint flicker on our psychic screens, it's because for women trained to take care of others, saying "I can't take care of you right now" feels like a violation of all we were raised to believe, a des-ecration of the feminine ideal. It also feels like aberrant behavior, like not being who we are or who we have been. If few women achieve this level of development, it's also because it is not one for which most married women have models. Many single women have exemplified this de-gree of determined focus, but the model for married women, in contrast, has been the maternal Wonder Woman who reaches the height of personal glory while still taking care of everyone and everything, the woman who rises at dawn, jogs five miles, runs a company by day, then plays the piano for a family sing-along at night. These are the women we're fed a steady media diet of, but most women can't relate to these brilliant dynamos. Most of us can't do it all at the same time.

The ability to say no, because it is such a difficult psy-chological task, is critical to female development. If mar-ried women are going to fulfill their dreams, they will sometimes have to say "I can't take care of you right now," because saying no to others is saying yes to something deeper within ourselves.

Chris could go forward in spite of resistance at home because her faith was strong and her dream powerful, and the stronger a woman's commitment to herself, the less emotional support she needs. But every woman needs some support. Most found it in husbands or friends or family. Some found it in an older woman who had taken time away for herself and still had a strong marriage. Some found it in women they knew only by reputation, women like Indira Gandhi and Georgia O'Keeffe, who had navigated similar marital terrain. "Of all the responses I heard when I told people I was going into the Peace Corps," said Chris, "one of the best came from an older woman who said, 'If you didn't go, after all, what would you be two years from now but two years older?' I wrote it down and carried it with me to Africa."

As soon as I receive the residency grants to the writers' colonies, Jim starts telling everyone about them and how proud he is of me. Suddenly I have forgotten why I am leaving this man who has always been surer of my abilities than I am. The closer the day of departure, the better my life at home seems. My house looks warm and comfortable and familiar, my husband attractive, sweet, and helpful. Two weeks before I leave, I sit on his lap one night after dinner—when was the last time I did this?—and ask him if he wants to come visit. "Sure," he says, "but why don't you wait until you get there and see how you feel."

An insomniac for years, I now find my sleep fitful with nightmares, with rotating themes. One night I dream that the other writers are already gathered at the dining table when I arrive for dinner. They look me up and down, no

one inviting me to join them. One of the writers is taunt-
ing and cruel. I look at him closely, realize he's a guy I
went to high school with. I slink away to eat by myself. I
wake up feeling the pain of high school rejection all over
again as I realize the past is never over. Every time we
face a new unknown, old vulnerabilities surface. A week
before I leave, I read the information packet from the first
retreat. The words "communal bathroom," even for an
all-women's colony, sound ominous, threaten my modest
nature. That night I dream of a harrowing trek through
muddied trails in search of a bathroom, only to find an
outhouse, filthy and insect ridden. I wake up, sick to my
stomach and scared, with no idea what I'm in for. Why do
I need to go away to write when I have a wonderful office
at home? What if I'm trapped with people I don't like,
people who are obnoxious or mean-spirited? And why am
I going to Wyoming in February?

The Friday night before I leave, Jim and I are in his
study. He is setting up his old laptop so I'll have Internet access wherever I go. I'm reading the information on the second retreat. The words "isolated" and "rural" jump off the
page. Suddenly I realize I'll be in the middle of cattle
country, where "snow is frequent in winter" and the nearest
town is seventeen miles away and I won't have a car. Why
didn't I notice these words before? Why don't I ever read
instructions until it's too late? Worriedly, I look up at Jim.

"Do you think I'll feel too isolated, go crazy, lose my
mind?"

"I didn't think there was much left to lose."

"Seriously, how would you feel if you were in the middle of nowhere without a car?"

"Well, I wouldn't like it. But then the whole idea of a writer's colony doesn't appeal to me. I wouldn't want to be stuck in a room all day without a phone or easy Internet access or my stereo. But you're not as dependent on these things as I am. If you feel isolated, just rent a car. Don't worry about the money."

I do worry about the money.

The Sunday before I leave, Jim shops with me for long underwear and winter hiking boots. I think of Thoreau's admonition to beware of any enterprise requiring new clothes, and I feel unsure of the purchases, queasy about my decision. I am still the woman I was raised to be, and fear envelops me like the blizzard I'm sure awaits in Wyoming. "You'll be fine," Jim says. "This is what you wanted. Remember?" I find his words equally soothing and irritating.

At ten the night before I leave, I start packing. I have no idea how to pack for three months; the longest I've been away in years is one week. I throw in all the underwear I own, every T-shirt and sweatshirt, every pair of sweatpants, socks, and tights. When I'm nearly finished, my older son comes in the room and, seeing the size of the bag, tries to lift it.

"What have you got in here?" he asks.

I show him the piles of books, the clothes, the boots, the free weights. My world-traveled son raises his voice in exasperation.

"You can't take these weights. Your bag should never be heavier than what you can comfortably carry."

"But I need them for my muscle tone," I moan.

"Do push-ups," he says.

I look at this strong, confident, funny, twenty-four-year-old and suddenly my stomach constricts and my eyes tear as I think, "How can I leave my son, my little boy?" And then I ask him the question I never thought to ask my husband.

"Are you going to be okay while I'm gone?"

"I'll be fine," he reassures me.

I stay up all night, calculating my portion of our income taxes, then leave the next morning bleary-eyed, carrying a computer I've never used and a duffel bag I can barely lift. Jim drives me to the airport and races with me to the gate, where we hurriedly say "I love you," as we hug and kiss goodbye. I make it onto the plane just as the flight attendant is moving to close the cabin door. "Fifteen more seconds and you wouldn't have made it," he says. Good thing I took out the weights. As I squeeze into my seat, feeling strange but oddly free, I take out a letter my son gave me before I left, with the promise I wouldn't read it until I was airborne.

"Mom—I want you to know that you do not need to worry about me. You only need to worry about yourself now. You are the architect of your future, and you are living out a dream starting right now. You've earned this time, and you deserve it, which is why I'm going to offer you a piece of advice that a good friend once offered me when I began to live out decisions that would forever affect my life. Go all the way, Mom. Do everything you have to do, need to do, want to do, hope to do. Leave no desire unfilled inside of your heart because this is your time. I love you."

I cry halfway to Washington.

6

EXPERIENCES

Stepping from the boat, I realized that I was
on my own, with no husband to help and no
one to speak for me but myself. Perhaps here
among the Eskimos I would find out what I
was really like as an individual and as an
artist.

I felt I had shed the other world and had
been initiated into Eskimo life. Every
defense, every preconception was stripped
away, as though I had undergone a sort of
baptism of the sea.

—CLAIRE FEJES,
People of the Noatuk

I have stepped into a retreat of quiet beauty on Whidbey Island off the coast of Washington. I have my very own cottage, a cedar-shake A-frame with a Scandinavian wood-burning stove, an overstuffed leather chair, a wide, L-shaped desk, and a carpeted sleeping loft with a window of stained-glass peonies. As I walk out the front door, I find myself in thirty-three acres of woods, lush with ferns and ponds, pine trees and cedars. Hiking trails curve in all directions. Deciding which path to take feels like a metaphor.

My thoughts swing wildly from one extreme to another, from exhilaration that I have found this creative paradise to dismay that it took me so long. Thinking of the years I spent looking to my husband to change my life is depressing; realizing that I have accomplished it on my own is empowering. My emotions are tangled and at odds. One minute I'm feeling grateful to Jim for his support of this experience. Thirty minutes later, I'm sitting at the floral window seat, sipping apricot tea in a cup of handcrafted pottery, wondering why I need a husband and home at all.

It's an environmental community where I've landed, part organic farm, part nature preserve. It's also a female community—the first time since college that I've lived exclusively among women. For six writers there is a staff of ten, each one gentle and caring, respectful of the land, the work, and us. We spend the days working alone in our cottages, the evenings communally gathered around a candlelit dining table in a farmhouse modeled after those in the French countryside. The meals are surprisingly exotic feasts—lunches of curried soups and fruit breads still warm from the oven delivered to our cottages in cloth-lined wicker baskets, dinners of cioppino and sushi, salads fresh from the garden. We are not allowed to set the table or dry a dish. This time is ours, they tell us, because women do all the nurturing but seldom are nurtured themselves. There are no page police checking our daily output, no evaluations or grades. Do whatever you need to do to become a better writer, they tell us.

In late afternoon, I walk to the bathhouse, a sumptuous oasis where hand-painted herons grace porcelain sinks and heated quarry tiles warm the floor. As I lie back in a Victorian claw-footed tub, steeped in Epsom salts and sur-rounded by scented candles, I realize I haven't indulged in a bath in twenty years. A ten-minute shower was all I ever had time for.

I thought I was drawn to a writer's retreat as a way to work in another landscape, mentally undistracted, sceni-cally serene. I realize now I was also gravitating to what my soul needed. How can creativity flourish if we feel de-pleted? I'd been working six, seven days a week for years. I was running on empty and didn't even know it.

The Sounds of Silence

A woman may have been fearful and tearful before she left, yet at the moment of arrival sigh contentedly, feeling she is exactly where she is supposed to be. A woman may have left home clear-eyed and confident, yet at the mo-ment of arrival feel disheartened and wonder how her fan-tasies got so out of hand.

She may have imagined a lovely European flat out of a Merchant-Ivory film and, after climbing a flight of stairs so narrow and steep she thinks she's on her way to an attic, discover that her home for the summer may as well be an attic, with the tiniest room she's ever seen, a daybed full of lumps, and a balcony covered with tar paper.

She may have boarded a plane still reeling from excitement over winning a Fulbright award and twenty hours later land on the other side of the world, dizzy and exhausted, to discover her mattress is a slab of wood, her roommate a needy stranger, her host school a third-tier university with no structured program and no understanding of what she's doing there. Aching to call home but unable to find a working phone, she can't help asking the same question her host asked her earlier: What *is* she doing here?

She may have spent months rearranging her schedule to leave her therapy practice to write a first draft of a book and take one look at her computer and panic: Everyone knows why I'm here, even my clients. What if I can't do it?

She may have given up her practice altogether to study Jungian analysis in Switzerland and, after getting lost three times the first day, wander around in the rain feeling cold and scared and alone, able to communicate only with her doubting self: Is this really a step toward growth or the mistake of a madwoman?

Whether she experiences one such moment or many, many or none, a sense of disorientation is inevitable because, like Lewis Carroll's fictional Alice, she has fallen down the rabbit hole and found herself in a Wonderland of reversals. More than the tumultuous whirl of the trip, more than the strangeness of the new and the absence of the familiar, disorientation comes from finding herself in an alternate reality where the usual dimensions of space and time no longer measure. Disorientation comes from the stillness and the silence.

The place itself isn't silent, but it is silent of a woman's individual sounds: the knock on her door, the ring of her phone, the cry of her name, the voices on her answering machine, the scratches of her pencil making to-do lists. The space is silent of those questions needing her answers, activities needing her plans, home maintenance needing her decisions, what to clean, repair, replace, renovate, donate, what to sign, mail, buy, borrow, return — the sounds of caretaking.

When women move away from routines and responsibilities, it doesn't matter whether they cross city lines or continental divides, they are traveling the same psychic route: from a space overflowing with others' needs to a space emptied of others' needs. They can land at a cottage at the beach, a cabin in the woods, a classroom or ashram, but they arrive at the same psychic destination: from time-starved to time-steeped. They can spend six weeks cocooned on a campus or six months backpacking around the world, but they travel the same psychic distance: from an awareness the time is theirs to an awareness the time is limited. As Jessamyn West wrote in *Hide and Seek*, time alone might not be so exciting if we "were condemned to a prison cell or cast away on a desert island, but when the opportunity for solitude must be stolen, as for the most part it must in large families or even in small families of one husband and one wife, it is, like stolen fruits, very sweet."

With the awareness that the days are hers but the weeks are numbered (and those at home are counting), she finds distortion in time merging with disorientation in space, and the reversals continue. When a seven-foot square room expands with the fullness of time and the sign on the door reads "distraction-free," an attic becomes a haven, a sanctuary, a nest, silks of solitude draping the window, stillness carpeting the floor.

Like being alone in the desert, women have to adjust to the silence. While driving more than 30,000 miles, Joan Mister rarely listened to audio tapes or the radio. "I just wanted to be in the silence," she said. Some women decline invitations to socialize and discourage visits from friends because they don't want any intrusions on their time. One woman didn't talk to anyone for four days. Without others to care for and listen to, women first listen to the rain beating against the roof. Then they begin to listen to themselves.

Week 2: I had always imagined that a writer's retreat would be a rustic place, isolated cabins in a camp-like setting. Never had I envisioned a sanctum of elegance. When I edited a shelter magazine, I toured scores of exceptional dwellings, where physical surfaces reflected consuming passions. I now find myself living in a space as exquisitely designed and cared for as any that appeared in the pages of that magazine. As I observe the gleaming fir wood floors and crystalline, arched windows, I cannot help but think of the house I left behind—the house that for so many years looked like a gym, smelled like a boys' locker room. I think of my sons' long adolescent years when it was simpler to close their bedroom doors than groan at the sight of the size thirteen tennis shoes and soccer cleats strewn across their floors, the guitars and amps and music stands, the sweat-stained jerseys, the ripped and swollen backpacks. I think of my husband's study, how I love having his soul in my life but not his things. Not his hundreds of tapes and CDs and albums, not his stereo equipment everywhere, with its tangled wires and thick-knotted cords splayed across walls and floorboards. Not his piles and piles of magazines. And now his room bulges with computer paraphernalia: disks, books, more wires, more mountains of magazines. When I married, I never considered that my house would always be filled with his stuff. Over the years, in bleak or tired moments, I fantasized about a house just for me, one that was spare and uncluttered and pristine. Now I'm living in just such a house, the house of my guilty dreams, and I'm looking at my crumbs on the floor, my dishes stacked in the sink, my papers and books scattered all over the place. I'm smelling something rancid—days-old food in an unemptied compost jar?—and I'm wondering: How did this happen?

A time to forget who we were, and a time to remember who we are.

With the release from caretaking—the sounds a woman creates—comes the first level of stillness. With the release from her environment—the sounds she absorbs—comes the second. She doesn't hear others' voices telling her what she should do or feel or think, the voices of commentary and criticism, opinions asked, advice unasked, the voices of familial skepticism, professional pessimism, cultural admonitions and advisements. In this silence she experiences what Judaic scholar David Ariel calls "feminine divine-time," one of his definitions of the Sabbath because it is free of the critical and competitive elements that dominate the rest of the week. In this silence, a woman doesn't hear the voices that mask jealousy, engen-

der guilt, express disinterest or disdain, the voices that relay her patterns and mistakes, voices that may be motivated by concern but advise caution, arouse fear. Without
these sounds of judgment, a woman is released from others' notions of who she is and their expectations of who
she should be. With this release comes a freedom to experience life *without filters*, to engage in the world more directly and spontaneously than she might with another
voice at her side. Without having to consider someone
else's feelings or opinions, she can leave plans open and
papers strewn, experiment, wander, immerse.

The Textures of Time

Whether the immersion is into a landscape or a language,
a culture or a canvas, a printed page or a blank page,
women discover what immersion feels like, what it
means, what it requires, what it releases. As psychic drains
empty and time collects, energy gathers to sharpen awareness, notice the textures of life.

A concert pianist studying in Vienna played the same
keyboards as Mozart and Bach, felt the surfaces of the
room where Beethoven composed his symphonies, the
concert hall where Chopin performed his études. A folk
artist walking a medieval pilgrimage focused on the dramatic path under her feet as it changed from cobblestone
road to muddy farmland, from vineyard to cow path. A
teacher hiking through piney forests listened to the wild
turkeys, loons, and deer along the trail. A stay-at-home
mother, thinking only of what she wanted to eat, slow-
cooked foil-wrapped vegetables over an open fire, creating a meal so delicious that three years later she still re-

membered its taste. A career mom dining alone at a restaurant for the first time discovered in solitude a comfort food. When a woman prolongs a fifteen-minute walk to class into an hourlong meandering, time expands. When she spends an hour luxuriating in a bathtub in the late afternoon, time disappears. Immersion means surrendering to the experience, connecting to whatever a woman needed to connect.

When Katherine had a sabbatical coming to her from the university where she was a professor, she was all business as she designed, organized, and negotiated a three-month sabbatical in Europe: first, language school in Paris, then jobs with an ad agency in Brussels and the United Nations in Geneva.

Once she landed on French soil, however, her days changed from time-structured to time-textured. Although she spent her first weeks feeling lost and exhausted from having to figure out the money exchange and transportation in a language in which she was not yet fluent, she considered these difficulties minor when spoken in French. A long-time Francophile, Katherine fell in love with the lyricism of the language, and she hoped to become fluent enough to read and understand the French poets. After a morning of language-school immersion, she felt "overwhelmed with pleasure" just sitting by herself at a café. "When you're with other people, you're always worried that they're bored," she said. "When you're with yourself, you know exactly whether you're bored or not. I spent an hour in one room at the Louvre looking at paintings of Catherine de Medici. I never could have done that with my children, and my husband would have become restless. When you're alone, you can really play."

Sensory pleasure for Katherine reached its peak the day she went to the beach. She'd wanted to go from the beginning of her stay, but she didn't have a car. Then a young woman she'd befriended in class invited her to join a group for a trip to the shore. Katherine described the afternoon:

We were racing through the French countryside at a breakneck speed which I'd never drive myself. Turkish, Algerian, and flamenco music were playing at top volume, my hair was flying out the window. We were laughing, passing chocolates all around, and these women, who were much younger, accepted me completely. When we went to the beach, I was the only one without a bathing suit. I took off my clothes and went swimming in the ocean in my underpants. Never would I have done that at home. I felt like a kid.

A time to feel comfortable with who we are, and a time to feel exhilarated by who we are.

Mythologist Joseph Campbell believed that what people are really seeking is not a meaning for life but an experience of being alive. "We're so engaged in doing things to achieve outer value," he wrote, "that we forget that the inner value, the rapture that is associated with being alive, is what it's all about."

When women leave roles and expectations behind, time changes from care-free to carefree, and immersion can feel sensual and uninhibited. Harriet Beecher Stowe could have been the nineteenth-century "poster woman" for a life jolted from other-care to self-care. When the struggling writer, minister's wife, and mother of five arrived at the new Brattleboro Water Cure in Vermont, the Victorian version of today's health spa, she discovered immersion on three levels. Literally immersed in hydrotherapy treatments, she soaked and whirled in the healing waters from the freshwater mountain springs. Immersed in nature, she walked five miles daily along trout streams and wooded trails in the New England landscape of her childhood. She devoured brown bread and milk on the veranda and slept soundly in the cool, clear air.

She was also immersed in a woman's world. After a decade of married life in Cincinnati, where her home was filled with children and boarders, her mind with "anxious thought," where her body was depleted by illness and pregnancy, she left one child with her husband and the other four with friends and family to live with a group of women in a building called Paradise Row. Like a college dorm, it was a setting for reading circles and parlor games, long talks and laughter in each other's rooms. One of Stowe's biographers likened the atmosphere to that of a female seminary because the women supported each other in their spiritual lives. "Not for years have I enjoyed life as I have here," said Stowe. "Everything agrees with me."

Georgia O'Keeffe voiced the same sentiment her first summer in New Mexico. Exhilarated by the silence and the beauty of the desert, she indulged in activities her husband would have disdained. She rode horseback across sacred Indian ground, sunbathed in the nude, slept under the stars, sampled bootleg whiskey, smoked her first cigarette, and learned to drive. In a letter to a friend, she wrote, "I never felt better in my life."

Into these harmonious surroundings comes the ring of a telephone (or in earlier times, a knock on the door with the arrival of a letter), jangling a note of discord.

I hear his voice, immediately sense unease.

"What's wrong?" I ask him.

"I can't believe what people say to me when I tell them what you're doing."

"What people?"

"Men. Friends."

"What do they say?"

"That there's no way they could live alone for three months. They can't believe I let you go."

"What'd you say?"

"What is there to say?"

"A psychologist said he couldn't live alone for three months?"

"Yeah."

"A sixties hippie said he couldn't believe you let me go?"

"Yeah."

"Did anyone say anything supportive?"

"One."

"What'd he say?"

"He said he wished his wife would go somewhere for three months."

The purpose of travel, wrote the French essayist Montaigne, is "rubbing up against others" and learning from them. Married women on solo journeys rub up against two sets of others: those they meet along the way and those they leave behind. Woman after woman said that her experience was not about him. But once away, they discover that while it may not have been about him, it affects him, and what affects him affects her. She cannot foresee a setback at work that leaves him depressed or an inability to reach her that leaves him frustrated. An insensitive comment from a colleague can irritate, a brisk e-mail from her disappoint. She can't know how he'll react after a bad day when he comes home to an empty house feeling lonely for her and sorry for himself, angry because he needs her and she's not there or disgruntled because he needs her and he doesn't like the need. He might want to talk about his feelings, or he might not, only the sound of his voice betraying the truth of his emotions.

Many thoughts go through women's minds before they leave, but problematic phone conversations aren't typically among them. After a time, though, when the reality hits that she's on an exciting adventure while he's overwhelmed by household detail, the conversation can turn prickly, and Paradise Row loses a touch of serenity. Physical caretaking may be on hiatus, but emotional caretaking is not. Concern for him can mean anxiety for her: Will he become irritated if I ask him to send me something? Will it hurt him to hear how happy I am without him? Some women downplay their difficulties so their spouses don't worry; others play up their difficulties so their spouses don't think they're having too much fun.

Harriet Beecher Stowe fell into this last category. To her husband, Calvin, she complained at length about the water treatments, and while some aspects of them were harsh, others were soothing. Invigorated by the physical exercise and female companionship, Stowe was having the time of her life. At the end of the summer, while her husband was readying the house in Cincinnati for her return, Stowe was composing a letter. The message: I'm not ready to come home yet. I need to stay through the fall so that I can return physically stronger. Not yet, she said again before Christmas, convincing him of her poor health while sledding and skating and throwing snowballs in the moonlight.

One hundred and fifty years later, Sue Bender was dealing with weeks rather than months and a very different atmosphere in a simple Amish community, but she shared Stowe's desire to prolong the experience and the calm she felt. "I was worried I may not ever want to leave," she wrote. Bender had told her husband she'd return in three weeks: Not ready yet, she said, after the fourth, fifth, six, and seventh.

A time to feel peaceful, and a time to feel pulled.

Whenever women rub up against others, they rub up against themselves. Experiencing life without filters means that after our surroundings emerge in sharper focus, *we* become in sharper focus. In the third layer of silence, women hear the sounds of contemplation and self-examination, what Georgia O'Keeffe called "the loud ring of a hammer striking something hard."

Like O'Keeffe, Sarah was spending her first summer away from a strong and charismatic husband. Away from his high-speed orbit, she explored her own rhythms. When she wasn't immersed in her studies for a new computer certification, she spent time at a spiritual community which she discovered soon after her arrival. There she was drawn to yoga classes, so she could find that center of calm where her life could be at peace no matter what turbulence others stirred around her. As she was acquiring a new computer expertise, she was also learning a new mental discipline, the focused awareness Buddhism calls *dhyana*. The basis of a spiritual life and the fundamental method of achieving happiness, says the Dalai Lama, is inner discipline. Practices that quiet the mind connect us more deeply to our spiritual nature, lead to inner transformation.

A dream Sarah had soon after she arrived revealed her desire for inner change. In the dream, she was walking through her house when she suddenly saw a secret door. She walked through the door to discover an extra room that she had no idea was there. When she walked through the room, she was amazed to find another one, a massive hall with ten-foot ceilings. "When I woke up, I realized I had been living in just two little rooms," she said. "All I could see were the lack of possibilities. I discovered that all I had to do was take a few steps and the whole world was out there."

The unconscious speaks in dreams and symbols, and houses are symbols for the structure of the self. Discovering empty rooms is about discovering the life within. With immersion come flashes of insight.

A time to open our minds to other ways we can be.

Week 5: I'm in rural Wyoming, in the foothills of the Bighorn Mountains. Rustic red barns, with contemporary and colorful, art-filled spaces within, make up this second creative retreat. It has much the same philosophy and structure as the first one: days devoted to working in solitude, evenings spent with other artists from across the country. Here, there are painters and photographers, too.

A plaque on the wall in my writing studio reads: "No one may interrupt you when you are in your work space unless the building is burning down." No one can call me during the day, no one can come to my studio, which has no phones, no modem, no answering or fax machine. I remember a former boss, a newspaper editor, telling me after the paper folded that I had done a good job in every way but one. "You never figured out how to manage your time," he said. He was right. I never figured out how to block the continual interruptions. Here, I experience time uninterrupted, all day, all mine. Here, the silence and the space feel sacred. For the first time in twenty-eight years, I know what it feels like not to have that space invaded. And I know that I would never have experienced it without leaving home.

Another sensation has been building, the feeling of being cherished as a writer. In twenty years of writing for a living, especially in the last six as a freelancer, I have never known this feeling. It's hard to feel valued when you have to call publications repeatedly for money owed, when you spend months on an article that an editor kills because she waited so long to run it that the subject became obsolete, when friends and family assume that writing at home is not really working. Staying in a profession where fortune is a rarity, isolation a given, and rejection a constant often feels like masochism. But to come night after night to a dinner table, set with floral cloth napkins and flickering candles and tulips in February, and feel like a guest of honor just because "your words matter" is moving and powerful. Then it comes to me why it has been so hard to protect my time and space. If I didn't value my work, it must not have felt worth protecting. And if I didn't feel it was worth protecting, why would anyone else?

A time to lose oneself in the quiet, and a time to find oneself in the quiet.

Focus and Flow

With immersion in creative or intellectual activity, the reversals and dichotomies continue: Time slows and quickens, thought expands and narrows. After energy bubbles, it flows into ideas and words and images. What immersion feels like: waking up before dawn without an alarm because a woman's so eager to get started; or falling asleep every night at eight because she's so exhausted from the excitement of learning; or not wanting to go to bed at all because she doesn't want the day to end. Some women eat ravenously; others lose their appetites. What immersion looks like: dropping one's watch on the floor, seeing it splinter into tiny pieces and thinking, "I didn't need it anyway."

Immersion means work can feel like play, joyful for its own sake. A nurse attending an intensive three-month educational program spent eight hours a day in classes, evenings and weekends in seminars, and most of the rest of the time studying. But with a room to herself and no distractions, she said, "It felt like a vacation—a real rest."

Immersion means Megan created thirty paintings in eight weeks, "three times what I would have done at home." Melissa studied for her law boards sixteen hours a day. Sally completed a two-year graduate program in social work in fourteen months, acing every class. A psychotherapist knocked out the first draft of a book in one month, "what had previously taken me two years." Immersion means such concentration on a discipline that external surroundings disappear. Immersion means the same thing today that it meant fifty years ago when Claire Fejes lived in isolated Eskimo villages, not caring that she had to sleep on the ice or eat seal liver. "With uninterrupted time to write and sketch, I did the best drawings of my life sitting on a rock, the north wind blowing and the dogs howling. . . . It was a revelation to find that I did more creative work in one month than I had accomplished in a year at home."

Psychologist Mihaly Csikszentmihalyi calls this phenomenon "flow." In several books he has written on the subject, he explains that the baseline state of the normal mind is vague, unfocused, and constantly distracted. Flow comes from the opposite state of consciousness, highly focused. It requires clear goals, no distractions, no worries of judgment or failure. In everyday life flow is impossible to achieve, he says, because we're always monitoring our actions to protect our ego, so our thoughts are chaotic and negative, our minds disconnected to our actions. Any intrusion from the world of everyday reality can make flow disappear, and the more ambitious the task, the easier it is to be distracted. Only when we can block out all distraction and silence all disapproval can we attain this optimal mind-body state. In flow, we lose a sense of time and gain a sense of oneness with something greater than ourselves. Self-consciousness disappears as action and awareness merge, insights crystallize and connect.

When women experience flow day after day, week after week, sometimes month after month, they feel at the peak of their powers. And with this sense of mastery come moments of exhilaration, a rush of well-being. The more flow we experience in daily life, writes Csikszentmihalyi in *Creativity*, the more likely we are to feel happy overall. And as long as the flow-producing activity is complex and challenging, it will lead to personal growth. Women who receive a lot of validation from other people discover what it feels like to earn validation from themselves.

When Darcy left a supportive husband, anxious son, and angry boss to spend two months teaching in Holland, she left a frantic culture for a gentle one, and since she didn't understand Dutch, a noisy culture for a silent one.

The whole experience was a way of slowing down my life, of becoming an observer. I'm a real social person and at home I'm continually overstimulated and overbooked. Every second is planned. Add to that the stress of getting ahead. I was always thinking, "I've got to finish this project, win this award." I was never in the moment. When I was away, I let life happen instead of trying to control it. I never felt so great in my life. When you're cut off from overstimulation, everything tastes better, sounds better. A Gloria Estefan concert was on the BBC one night and it sounded wonderful; back at home I heard it on the radio and was switching the dial after five seconds. I had so much contemplative time, I kept a diary the whole way through. It was a time to be the person I always wanted to be.

I missed my family, but I never got bored or lonely. It amazed me that I was never lonely.

A time for serenity, and a time for surprise.

Solitude and Intimacy

For most women, the sense of aloneness does not carry over into a feeling of loneliness—or more than an occasional twinge. Part of the reason is that women have chosen to be alone. And the more we are ourselves, the less alone we feel. Writer May Sarton provides the rest of the answer. "Loneliness is the poverty of self," she wrote. "Solitude is the richness of self." What most women feel on sabbatical is, unquestionably, a richness of self.

Knowing that the people they love are waiting for them to return gives women on sabbatical the ultimate feeling of richness: being alone, yet knowing they have love in their life, and only a phone call away.

In his classic essay "Of Solitude," the French essayist Montaigne wrote, "The greatest thing in the world is to know how to belong to oneself." Most of us have known the fear of being alone and the longing to be alone, but fewer of us have mastered the ability to enjoy being alone. It's an important life skill because the older we get, the more loss we encounter, and the more people we lose, the more alone we become.

Women on sabbatical during their second marriages said the experience provided a different type of aloneness than the one they experienced after their divorces. With divorce, they said, anxieties about aloneness surface, and often creativity and focus are lost in the existential struggle of being alone. On a sabbatical, if a woman becomes afraid or lonely, she can just call her husband, receive an immediate shot of intimacy and connection, then go back recharged to her particular challenge.

Even if not existentially alone, women on sabbatical glimpse being alone. And that glimpse is enough for many to discover two paradoxical truths: They want and value intimacy in their life, and they want more time alone.

"Solitude is very addictive," concludes New York psychoanalyst Ester Saler Buchholz in *The Call to Solitude*. "For couples who are separating from each other, then suddenly have privacy and alonetime, sometimes it comes as a shock how much they enjoy it, how good it feels. And then they seek it more." Buchholz believes that "alonetime" is necessary for all human development: "It's a biological and psychological essential, as important as our need for attachment. Alonetime is fuel for life."

Women may want time alone, but they still want to share their experiences. Keeping the conversation going is a far different undertaking for those with easy access to phones and e-mail than for those in Third World countries, where one telephone serves a village and the mail takes three weeks to arrive. "The only person with a phone was the principal of the school where I taught," said Chris about the African village where she was assigned by the Peace Corps. "I had to beg him to let me call my husband once a week. I went into his office late at night and sat on the floor with a flashlight, the mosquitoes eating me in the dark."

Week 7: My husband has many talents, but talking on the phone is not one of them. His mother and sister complain. Our sons and their girlfriends over the years have complained. On this night, he's just returned from visiting our youngest in California, a trip I'd suggested before I left. He is expansive about the wonderful time they had together, the long conversations deep into the night. He takes me through each day's highlights. He talks about our older son's picking him up at the airport and the long evening they spent together. He feels closer to them than he ever has, he says, is grateful for what terrific boys they turned out to be. I listen, waiting for him to add, "I guess this all happened because you left. What a good thing you did that." Of course he says nothing of the kind. I don't say anything, either, but I feel the last residue of guilt drain out of me.

I share with him what I've learned about myself, why I needed to go away, how it wasn't about him. I didn't fully understand all my motivations before I left, and what I didn't understand I couldn't communicate. Now the words rush out of me, and I know he is listening to every one of them, and I sense an undercurrent of relief.

I ask if he wants to visit. I have waited to ask until only one weekend—just five days away—would work for us both and a ticket would cost a fortune, so I ask not out of my needs but his. "I would love to," he answers, "but I know how much this time means to you, how long you have wanted it. And I know my coming would disrupt that for you. I can wait."

In another of life's paradoxes, what is hardest about being married a long time is also what is best. He knows me as well as I know myself. Sometimes that means he knows me better than I would like. Tonight, that works to my advantage. I have never felt closer to him, never appreciated him more, than I do this night. I don't join the others for dinner. Gratitude and love fill me up in a way no gourmet meal ever could.

A time to feel the strain in a marriage, and a time to feel the strength in a marriage.

Conversations take on a different quality when they become a couple's primary or only means of communication. Instead of talking about the bits and pieces of daily life—*Have you seen my glasses? Did you put the sprinkler on? We'd better call a plumber*—the kinds of conversations we so often have at home, couples engage in meaningful dialogues about the excitement of new activities, the depths of new studies. Within women's experiences, conversations become high points and lows, relay comfort and conflict, reveal surprise. "I had planned to call my husband just once a week," said one woman, "but I ended up calling him every night. It was my way of refueling." Some women said they talked more to their husbands when they were away at graduate school than they did when they lived in the same house. Others reported two- and three-hour conversations, discussing their philosophies of marriage and commitment, what they needed from one another, what they were learning they needed from themselves. When feelings and thoughts have to be articulated, conversations can feel like the ultimate intimacy, passion flowing through the words and the wires.

The Dutch theologian Henri Nouwen, one of the great spiritual thinkers of the twentieth century, wrote that it is a fallacy to think that we grow closer to each other only when we talk, play, or work together. It is in solitude, he believed, that our intimacy with each other is deepened because in solitude we come to realize that we are not *driven* together—by fear or habit or circumstance—but that we are *brought* together by a bond deeper than our own efforts can create. If we base our life together on our physical proximity, he wrote in *Clowning in Rome*, then life fluctuates according to individual moods and desires and attractiveness, so we can easily become clingy and irritated, scrutinizing each other with tiring hypersensitivity. Without solitude, shallow conflicts easily cause deep wounds, and daily life can become so self-conscious that long-term living together is virtually impossible.

"I am deeply convinced that gentleness, tenderness, peacefulness, and the inner freedom to move closer to one another or to withdraw from one another, are nurtured in solitude," he wrote. Nouwen saw solitude as the source of intimacy that transcends the emergencies of daily life—intimacy that endures.

Week 9: Writing retreats are two-thirds solitude, one-third communing with other writers and artists. After two months of this life, I find myself craving total solitude. My older son advised me not to plan every step of the journey. "Leave it open," he said. "That's part of the adventure." I cancel my plans to go to a third colony in Vermont when an artist I meet in Wyoming offers me a guest house on a ranch she owns in Montana. I head to the bus depot in Sheridan. Is it my media-saturated imagination or do half of the men in their tight, faded jeans and scraggly beards look like serial killers? After I arrive in Billings, I pick up a rental car and head to Molt, Montana, population sixteen. I am following a detailed map, but I don't see the street sign I'm looking for. I turn up a road, which I hope is the right one, only to find barbed wire and a dilapidated shack. Another serial killer, I'm sure, lurks inside. As I turn the car around, the wheels lock in the muddy dirt road.

I look around at the vast, open spaces, dominated by a sky so huge I feel I have been dropped into the middle of the earth—or a movie set. I have never before seen so much sky. I don't know if it's because I don't usually study the sky or because here there is nothing to clutter it. No skyscrapers, no strip malls, no billboards, no traffic lights, no cars, no people, no help. Where *is* everyone? All I see are acres of prairie grass and a seemingly endless two-lane dirt road. In a moment of panic, I think of all the ways Jim has saved me. Every time I wanted to quit a job before I had another one, he supported me in my decision, never mentioning the loss of income. Every time I was on deadline and my computer crashed, he got it working again. Who's going to save me now?

Somehow, I manage to maneuver the car out of the ruts, just as a woman in a pickup comes down the road and stops to give me directions. My fears now seem foolish. In strange surroundings, my mind immediately races to serial killers. My fears of dependency on Jim also seem absurd. To navigate our way through life, we all need an outstretched hand, and we can find it in many people, most places.

A time to feel fear, and a time to dispel it.

Exhilaration and Edge

Immersion means experiences will always be stimulating but not always comfortable. An undisturbed encounter with ourselves means we'll come up against our edges. Sabbaticals test strengths and reveal weaknesses, imprint them in boldface. At the end of a ten-hour day of painting, a woman can hate what she's drawn, furiously throw away the canvas, doubt her talent all over again. She can fail her first test, suffer ridicule from a teacher, panic at the sight of a bear or a mouse. Alone in the dark, she can imagine a rapist in the closet or a voyeur at the window. Without distractions and filters, she has no choice but to face her fear and, in doing so, she discovers that no matter how much comfort she derives from her husband, she must develop strength within and learn to comfort herself. A journey with soul means a journey with difficulty.

In the midst of feeling so serene in Holland, Darcy looked out her bedroom window one day and saw a little boy playing with plastic dinosaurs. "I felt sick that I had left my son, that he was more than 4,000 miles away," she said. "That moment, it dawned on me that I couldn't have him, that I couldn't get to him when I needed him. I knew he was okay, but it was the first time I felt disconnected as a mother. That was part of the trade."

Edges emerge from connection and disconnection, from the experiences themselves and from experiences at home. Life's realities follow women wherever they go. If in moments of serenity come feelings of disconnection, in moments of connection come feelings of turmoil. Husbands lose patience, aging parents need help, children call in crisis. Women discover they can mother long-distance when they leave home just as they mother long-distance when their children leave home. They can still check in daily at 3:15 P.M., mediate sibling fights, listen and advise, celebrate and commiserate. They can caretake parents from afar, supervise nursing home moves and hospital stays. What a woman discovers is that total freedom is an illusion, that as long as she is connected to others and they are in need, she will be giving emotional care.

Each conversation relaying need reaffirms the depths of her support system and the entanglements of love, and each conversation reminds her why she left. As her days alone dwindle in number, she feels a greater urgency to shape the space, transform the time.

Week 10: I'm living on a ranch in Montana with 300 Black Angus cows, 225 Columbia sheep, ten quarter horses, one donkey, one Border collie, one Australian shepherd, seven cats, and a family forty yards away that oversees it all. There's no pizza delivery here, no video stores, no television. The myriad ways I anesthetize myself from the stresses of daily life—crossword puzzles, magazines, movie videos, *Seinfeld* reruns—are absent. No radio, television, or magazine ads, no thirty-second seductions exhorting me to be younger, prettier, fitter. I feel so much peace in the quiet. Here, people are plugged in only to the land.

I've been in the West before, but always on a vacation, and spending a week at a dude ranch is being a tourist looking at the experience. Here, I feel I'm living it. As I accompany the three boys next door on their chores, watch the shearing of the sheep and the birthing of a calf, then another day sit in on a cattle auction, I am reminded of the value of immersing oneself in a radically different way of life. It forces you to examine your own more deeply and to ask: Am I doing what I really want to do, or have I been doing the same thing for so long I can't imagine anything else?

Living alone, where no one is watching, I discover who I really am. For a week, I don't take a bath or wash my hair. It feels strange and decadent and wonderful, not to have to bother about looking good, mostly not to have to spend the time. I write all day, take a long walk each afternoon with one of the dogs, then read at night, surprised that my natural rhythms are the same as they are at home.

Then the long-feared blizzard descends, four feet of snow encircling the house, more whipping around it. This is also a day the words don't come, and I can't take a walk to purge my frustrations. Intensity dominates the day. Where are distractions when I need them? By early evening I'm feeling distraught, trapped, and alone. Now I wish Jim were here, but it's too late. In tears, I reach for the phone and call him. For an hour and a half, he listens and soothes. As I go to bed, wishing I could feel his arms wrap around me, I realize a motivation in leaving—unconscious at the time—was that I wanted to miss him, needed to miss him. At home, I never have the opportunity. I think of the many conversations I've had with single friends over the years, who moaned about the lack of sexual intimacy in their lives, maybe for one year, maybe for three. These confidences always intrigued me because they were so removed from my own experience, where the opportunity to make love was almost always an arm's-length away. I realize now I wanted to miss that, too.

A time when perceptions clarify, and a time when emotions intensify.

Connections: Near and Far

No matter how little a woman thought about sex before she left, she will think about it when she's away. And one woman's thoughts will be very different from another's.

Some women miss a regular sex life, some don't. Some said they were so busy and tired that they could not have mustered the energy. Those who were on strenuous physical adventures said they were too grimy, sore, and exhausted even to contemplate it. Said one woman who hiked the Appalachian Trail, "Some nights I slept in a shelter with four or five men. No one was thinking about it. Even couples who were hiking together didn't have much of a sex life."

Whatever their ages, in the absence of sex, women rediscover how they feel about it in general and how they feel about it with their partners in particular. Some discover that they miss the physical affection more than the sex; others, that they miss the physical affection, but not the sex. Some learn to take care of themselves, others how long they can last before they need to reconnect with their husbands, reset their sexual thermostats.

Women discover that fidelity, like faith, is an ongoing test. The thought of an affair may have been nonexistent before a woman left, but if she's feeling free-spirited and meets an attractive man, the thought may surface when she's away. "Never for one moment before I left for the Peace Corps in Africa did I think about an affair," said Chris. "But was I tempted when I was gone? Yes. It was a perfect setup to stray. But I made a vow when I married my husband, and I meant it. We may have our differences, but we have trust."

Even Megan, the thirty-year-old artist who was outraged that her friends thought she was sneaking off to have an affair, met an appealing man whom, in other circumstances, she might have pursued. "I thought about sleeping with him, but I didn't," she said, "because I'm in love with my husband. It's a sacred bond, and once you've broken it, you never get it back."

If some women said they were tempted and did consider it, others said they were tempted but didn't consider it; others that they would never be tempted. What most women experience on sabbatical is an affair with themselves. It's a time to take in their own life energy, exult in the sensual quality of time lavished on themselves, not squandered on a stranger.

When a married woman goes off alone, explained analyst Patricia Vesey-McGrew, she begins to integrate different parts of herself. "If she has an outer relationship, this integration doesn't occur. It's not a matter of morals, it's a psychological reality. But when you're away, you can love yourself enough to indulge in the feelings of being appreciated and desired and appreciating and desiring someone else. There's a way you can just allow the feelings to surface without acting on them or making a judgment on them. Sexual feelings for other people are very natural, and, when women deal with them in healthy ways rather than pretending they're not there, they can add a richness to life."

Disinterest in an affair, then, does not mean disinterest in men, and women enjoy meeting and spending time with men other than their husbands, indulging in schoolgirl crushes on male professors, sharing meals and classes and shelters with men of different backgrounds—a freedom, some said, they didn't have in their workplaces or small towns. The erotic enlivens the journey.

Many women take these heightened feelings of sensuality and infuse them into "conjugal" visits. The old saying applies: It's never a question that lust goes, only a question of when. Sometimes visits become an elixir for what had become a routine sex life: *the most fun we'd had*

*together in years . . . the sex was great . . . felt like we were
having an affair.* "I never thought about traveling or visits
when I left for the Peace Corps," said Chris, "but my husband's visits to see me were very much like a honeymoon.
And they really sustained me while I was away."

Some women want visits but prefer them on neutral
ground, not at the site of their experiences. Others discourage visits, even at the end of their stays; they feel a
need for closure in their own space. Women enduring
long separations like Chris's (though closer than Africa)
have to experiment to figure out how often to meet to sus-
tain the relationship yet not disrupt their experiences or
jeopardize their finances. Some were willing to jeopardize their finances, taking out loans to see their partners
more often. Some described hello fights or goodbye
fights, reflecting the ongoing struggle to find the right balance between intimacy and distance.

When Ellen, the political analyst and actress, went
overseas for the summer to teach, she would have been
content to reunite with her husband at home when she
was finished, but to ease his anxiety and preserve their relationship, she bought him a ticket to visit her in Europe.
His letters and phone conversations focused heavily on
his trip, but it was not a blissful reunion. Into her tiny
room he brought a big presence. He spread his belongings all over the place. "I had been exhilarated from day
one," she said. "It felt so good to have my own space, and
suddenly he was there invading my routine and my independence. We did not connect at all. I felt I had grown,
and he felt he had been left behind."

For several days they snapped at each other, didn't get
along at all. Then their camaraderie returned, and they

enjoyed the rest of their time together. "He needed to picture my life there and feel a part of it," she said, "and having him there eased the burden of communicating the experience to him. In the end, I felt good about the visit. It was important for us both."

A *time to forget our need for him, and a time to remember his need for us.*

Expectations: Met and Unmet

Every woman knows one moment of dissonance or doubt. Some women know many. Sabbaticals are different for those harbored in safe retreats than they are for those battling the forces of nature. They are different for those who spend them in the States than for those in countries where the language is foreign, the climate hard, the food suspect, the technology primitive. The months will take on a different quality for those who aren't under pressure to perform than for those who must pass tough exams. The internship can be disappointing, the teacher critical, the program grueling or boring. When Chris left for the Peace Corps, she wasn't looking for bliss, only to make a difference in the world. She never imagined how difficult that goal would be. In Namibia's drought-ridden desert climate, she struggled to connect with students hardened by years of poverty and abuse. She thought often about quitting. "Ninety-five percent of the time, I was frustrated and in tears," she said, "but the other 5 percent made up for it." The "other 5 percent" came the second year, when her students learned to trust her. One unexpected struggle, however, led to another. Her daughter wrote an angry letter after the birth of her child, ending it with a bitter warning: "Don't think that we can pick up where we left off." Chris cried for three days. "I told her that I hoped she would leave the door open, and I told myself that she would understand when she was my age. I had faith, but I was afraid."

A time to realize that what we thought it was going to be isn't necessarily what it becomes.

When Maria set out for the Appalachian Trail, she had definite expectations.

During the months after her son's death, when she was preparing for the world's longest footpath, walking eight miles to and from her job to build strength in her legs, what kept her going was her vision of lovely, solitary walks in scenic woods.

The first night—in Georgia in March—the temperature plummeted to nine degrees, and seven inches of snow fell on the three-sided wooden lean-to where she slept. After the cold and the snow came the rains, sometimes unrelenting, six days in a row. By the time Maria reached Virginia, so did a heat wave, with temperatures in the 100s and humidity at 98 percent. Hiking with thirty-five pounds on her back, a sun blazing overhead, and gnats swarming all around, she became so uncomfortable that she changed directions, riding a bus to Maine and walking back down to Virginia. "I lost my focus then," she said.

Maria suffered other losses, too. She hadn't expected the terrain to be so rocky, didn't anticipate the strain on her knees from walking eight to twelve hours a day. She didn't think about how tired she'd become of eating the same dried, packaged foods, how grimy she'd feel without her daily shower. She grew so hungry for a decent meal and a soft bed and a hot bath that she stayed in motels more often than she had planned, spending more money than she had allocated. She hadn't expected to become so lonely, the cost of her phone calls home soaring to $400 a month. Her husband had planned to visit her twice, but her escalating expenses eliminated one trip. She never imagined how much she would miss him.

Finally, after five months and 1,000 miles, she boarded a train, homesick, weary, and in pain. "My biggest disappointment," she said, "was that I didn't finish."

As the unexpected brought her worst moments, it also brought her best. Maria had expected to be alone, but she found the trail filled with people. She anticipated a lot of questions, but they respected her privacy. She had arrived feeling alone in crisis but discovered most people on the trail were at a crossroads, too. Sharing shelter with people she ordinarily would never have talked to forced her to look beneath the surface, where she discovered the ties that bind.

Spiritual solace she found. "I felt closer to God out there on the trail," she said. And closer to those she loved. As she walked beside strangers, her individual sorrow became a family sojourn, where the past met the present, and the present, the future. In Georgia, she felt the spirit of her grandfather, who had lived in the state. Moving north, she felt the presence of her late father, who had loved the outdoors, and her mother, who would have liked to walk the trail but didn't feel she could leave her husband, who after he died was too old to attempt it herself but still young enough to accompany her daughter in spirit. In the New

England of her childhood, Maria thought about the girl she had been and the woman she became, and everywhere she thought about the boy she had lost.

"I learned to grieve the same way that I walked—one step at a time, one day at a time. When I rode the train home, I felt physically stronger and mentally better able to handle my life. And I decided I would do it again, and the next time I would finish."

A time of release, and a time of revelation.

Some women, like Maria, feel ready to go home. Some do not. They can be away six weeks or six months yet say with equal feeling, "I did not want to go back."

That must have been the thought in Harriet Beecher Stowe's mind when she prolonged her stay from four months to twelve, then prolonged her journey home. To travel the 900 miles to Vermont by steamboat, stage, and rail took her six days; to travel back to Cincinnati took her two months, as she stopped along the way to visit everyone she knew.

After six weeks in India, Shelley didn't want to leave either.

Before I left, I worried about all the wrong things. What I should have worried about was staying longer. The six weeks went by very quickly. The day I was scheduled to go home, I cried all day. I was still crying on the plane. The woman sitting next to me asked what was wrong, and when I told her, she looked at my ticket and said it was good for another three months. It was a good thing I didn't know that until I was ten thousand feet up in the air and climbing, or I wouldn't have gone back that soon. If I hadn't had a husband and son waiting for me, I wouldn't have gone back at all.

The reason I delayed going to India for so many years was that I was afraid I'd be overwhelmed by the poverty and sickness. They were worse than I could have ever imagined, but it wasn't a problem. I never saw people smile as much as they did in India. I used twenty-seven rolls of film, their faces were so beautiful. In the midst of such poverty and filth, they were joyful. I felt sorry for us feeling sorry for them. I fell in love with the country. I felt like I had found my roots.

A time to learn about ourselves, and a time to learn about others.

Landscape: Oneness and Otherness

Falling in love with another landscape means a woman can feel as though she's lived there before and, thus, gone home. Thoughts of going to her real-life home can then be as fearful as were thoughts of leaving it. It's not that she doesn't want to see those she left behind but that she loves the way she feels when she's away—calm and centered and strong. Women who become one with a landscape decide to return before they even leave. The first experience evolves into another, and then another.

Barbara Overby had not thought about a solo journey until, on a vacation with her husband in Portugal, she met an American archaeologist looking for a drafter for his excavation in Alentejo. "I could do that!" she exclaimed (surprising both herself and her husband), and the following year she arrived in Portugal.

In exchange for airfare, a per diem, and the opportunity to stay as long as she wanted after the six-week dig was over, Overby sat for long hours in the hot sun on the grounds of an ancient villa, drawing meticulous sketches of the site and the artifacts. It had been years, actually, since she'd done architectural drafting; children had inspired a more flexible career as a folk artist and crafts-shop owner. But as she had intuited, she could do the work, and she loved it. For two months she became Doña Barbara, working alongside Portuguese women her age but a culture apart, learning their language, listening to their stories, always asking questions. As she studied their world, they studied hers. *Where is your husband?* they asked. *Doesn't he mind your coming here? Why did you leave your home? Don't you miss your family?*

From the vantage point of another culture, Overby rethought her own. She revalued her independence, devalued the consumer culture that skewed priorities, created need where none existed. As she rinsed out her clothes each night and slept on an army cot, she discovered in a simpler culture the essentials for a good life.

For Overby, insight came less as flash than unfolding. She stopped biting her nails and wondered why she hadn't been able to stop at home. She watched them grow and knew she'd return. Each year, her anticipation of the summer grew stronger; each year, she extended her stay.

The Portuguese landscape wove through her summers like the yarn through her floor rugs, and after the ten-year dig was finished, Overby went back to complete the tapestry, to celebrate the land and the learning. Her first summer on the dig, she had heard about the Camino de Santiago, a footpath across the Pyrenees once traveled by St. Francis of Assisi; her eleventh summer, she walked it. Across mud-baked plains and meadows of wildflowers dotted with medieval hamlets and shrines, she talked to people from all over the world one day, enjoyed being alone in the solitude the next. Although the 500-mile trek is considered a contemporary quest for ancient wisdom, Overby said, "For me it wasn't a search as much as a thanksgiving."

In the tradition of sacred travel, she wanted to acknowledge her thanks. After completing the forty-four-day pilgrimage, she volunteered for a month at a *refugio*, one of the many hostels along the way where she had so often collapsed for the night for a few dollars. She rose at dawn to wash sheets, clean bathrooms, and get everything ready for the day's travelers, coming from twenty-seven countries, speaking as many as thirty-five languages. In the evenings, she kneaded aching shoulders and tended blistered feet, while offering a sympathetic ear. When asked to stay on another month, she accepted. "It was the best summer of my life," she said. "I dreaded coming home."

A time to awaken something new, and a time to reawaken something dormant.

Whether or not a woman is ready to leave, feelings of gratitude can be powerful. Anne Morrow Lindbergh was often berated by her mercurial husband for investing her energy in journal writing rather than publication, but in 1947 he encouraged her to write a series of articles on postwar Europe, and she traveled overseas alone for nine weeks. Days before boarding the boat home, she wrote to him: "I have been lonely, and it has been difficult. I have made mistakes & yet it has been one of the big things in my life. Of all the things you have given me . . . — & you have given me so much — perhaps this is one of the biggest. Your sending me out on this mission alone. (For I should not have done it if you had not pushed me a little & told me I could do it!) I am grateful to you for it. You are always giving me life, life itself. May I make something of it!"

Gratitude suffused Georgia O'Keeffe's correspondence, too. In one letter to a friend, she wrote, "The summer had brought me to a state of mind where I felt as grateful for my largest hurts as I did for my largest happiness — in spite of all my tearing about many things that had been accumulating inside of me for years were arranging themselves — and rearranging themselves."

From alternate realities comes what Hinduism considers the ultimate reality: knowledge of the self. Insight is the reason every woman gave for finding value in her experience, no matter how trying it was. *I learned so much about myself I couldn't have learned any other way . . . I learned I was stronger than I thought I was . . . I learned to be appreciative for all that I have . . . I learned I missed my family and they missed me. That alone made it worthwhile.* Experiences that bring us to awareness bring us to grace. As Jung reminded us, there's gold in those dark places.

Of their travels home, many women reported feeling fed, satiated, full of generosity toward their husbands, their children, the women who had inspired them along the way, a gratitude to have discovered a connection to their deeper selves, to have recovered the woman they had left behind or to envision the woman they could now become.

Week 12: That my own journey is ending in Molt, Montana, feels symbolic. I've done a lot of shedding here—mostly illusions. I thought that where I lived was keeping me from being the writer I wanted to be, or could be—if only I lived in a brownstone in Manhattan or a farmhouse in New England or a ranch out West. I've now been living on a ranch out West, and the writing is no easier here than at home. A blank computer screen is still a blank computer screen. Magical settings can stimulate creativity, but our mental landscape sustains it. I've decided to stop questioning my choice of profession, having concluded here that it chose me.

I thought that in these three months I would regain the body I had in my thirties when I taught aerobics five times a week. ("That's *you*?" my younger son exclaimed when he came upon a photo of me from that era, in class in my leotard. He was the one now going to the gym five days a week, and he shook his head in disgust. "I can't believe you let yourself go like that.") With no demands on my time, I thought I would work out every afternoon. The reality is that I've stretched and walked but haven't done a push-up since the second day. With no responsibilities to anyone but myself, with no boys for whom to keep the pantry and freezer well stocked, I thought I'd lose fifteen pounds. From the way my sweatpants fit, I figure I've gained five. So it's not the demands on my time, obviously, that keep me from looking the way I want; it's my lack of motivation. The realization is painful yet liberating—a sign, perhaps, not to look back, trying to recapture what's impossible to recapture, but to move ahead, a sign, perhaps, that for the second half of my life I need to redirect my time to mental disciplines.

Before I left, I thought that the relationships in my life were draining my energies. Some days, they were. Here, I've been reminded that the same relationships that interfere with my achieving are also my deepest joy and, perhaps, my greatest strength—what has enabled me to live without my husband more easily than he has been able to live without me. I don't know if there is an answer to this one, except maybe to take time alone each year to remind myself of the paradox and become comfortable with it.

This last month has felt as if I've entered an allergy clinic where all foods were taken away from my diet, then slowly, one at a time, reintroduced. Each day alone in the Montana quiet shows in starker relief what I value, what I want back in my life: my husband, my sons' conversations and smiles, my friends, my shower, the *New York Times* crossword puzzle, the movies. Mostly, I want Jim. Three months ago, I couldn't wait to leave. Now I cannot wait to go home.

7

HOMECOMINGS

Max still remembered me. He waved back.
Lucky for me.

—JESSAMYN WEST,
Hide and Seek: A Continuing Journey

I am nervous about seeing Jim. I feel as tingly as I did the weekend of our wedding, when he arrived at the St. Louis airport wearing a khaki suit and carrying a box of long-stemmed roses. I feel that same kind of adolescent excitement. To be married twenty-eight years and have gone through almost everything two people can go through together, seen each other at our worst—moments of agony in childbirth, my features contorted beyond recognition; hours of fear in the emergency room, his face pale, his hand clutching mine—times of grief and humiliation, rages of anger, tears of remorse—to feel this kind of excitement is one I didn't think I'd ever feel again.

I know when I walk off the plane he'll be standing right in my line of vision. Unlike me, who's always racing to meet someone at the airport and rarely makes it to the gate on time, he is compulsively organized and punctual, someone you can rely on to follow through on his promises, to be there when you walk off the plane. Sometimes it used to bother me that he was so together because it made me feel inferior; today I find comfort in these qualities of his.

As soon as I walk into the terminal, I see him. He's thinner, definitely thinner, probably from too many sandwich dinners at the kitchen counter. After all these years, I'm surprised by how attractive I still find him, his basketball-player's body, his natural year-round tan, the classic way he's always dressed. And in his eyes, a look that says the attraction is mutual. At home, on the dining room wall, a colorful banner he made on his computer welcomes me.

As I walk slowly through the house, amazed at its cleanliness, he says he called a service that morning. He shows me the work he had done while I was away: plaster walls repaired, basement floor painted, closets and shed cleaned and reorganized. Walking into his study, I see a new chair he bought for his desk, a large black swivel atrocity, totally incongruous and disproportionate for the cozy, earth-toned room I once designed with care. I cringe, but only inwardly. After all, what can I say? When you leave, you give up control. I marvel over everything he's done. An hour later, as we rise from our rumpled sheets, in the middle of the afternoon, sunlight streaming through the windows, I have only one thought: I should have done this years ago.

Two weeks later:

"You were so radiant the first week you were home," he says. "Every day you look more depressed."

I don't know why this is, but it feels true. And who would know better than a psychologist what depression looks like? Is it because I have to go to the grocery store again? He goes every week, too, but it doesn't bother him as it bothers me. Why not? I ask. "I don't think much about it," he says. Is it because when I sit down to dinner every night, I wonder where all the interesting people are, where's the dinner party? The problem: I feel different, but everything around me feels the same.

Re-entry

Just as a woman's experience is as individual as she is, so is her homecoming.

She can return to gifts of silk lingerie and fresh flowers, to lust in the afternoon and lust again that night. She can return to an excited child and exhausted husband, whose dazed expression says, "Thank God, she's home." She can return to her testosterone-heavy tribe, hear the words, "What's for dinner?" and wonder if she ever left. She can come home on a late-night flight after a difficult experience to find her chronically late husband late once again while her three teenagers lie asleep in their rooms. The tumultuous emotions she experienced when she was away are as tumultuous as these: from irritation that her family planned no welcoming celebration to amazement that the house is still standing, everyone well; from gratitude that the house is still standing, everyone well to delight that obviously she can go away again.

While some women slip back easily into their old lives, particularly those coming home to strong marriages, good jobs, lively children, others find that their greatest challenge awaits. The longer women are away, the harder the re-entry. The more time they had to establish a new pattern of living, the more likely they are to wonder, at least for a moment, *Can I ever go back? Do I want to?* Some women need a period of time to get reacquainted with their husbands, to discover how to remesh two independent lives or to rediscover why they fell in love in the first place. Three years after Chris's return from the Peace Corps, she and David both said, "We're still adjusting."

Women who take grand adventures can find coming home anticlimactic, sometimes downright depressing. On her backpacking trip around the world, Sabina Shalom chatted with Indira Gandhi in New Delhi, lunched with the prime minister of Australia, and met the king of Tonga. She visited shrines and temples in Bangkok, spent a night in a mud hut in Papua, New Guinea, traded her clothes for lodging on Easter Island, and in Fiji barricaded her bedroom door when she realized her hotel was a brothel. Back home in Miami, six months later and thirty pounds lighter, she was delighted to see her husband but sorry to see her time away end. "I felt in limbo, utterly disoriented," she wrote in her memoir. "When the euphoria began to fade, I felt guilty for asking myself, 'Now what?'"

Coming home can mean feeling dislocated all over again. The disorientation comes from returning to an old life with a new sensibility yet feeling unsure how to integrate the two, "like being dropped into a new play," said one woman, "and wondering, 'Now what were my lines?'" The disorientation comes from wanting to hold on to the strengthened woman she has become when those around her want her to be the woman she was before. As habits from their old lives take over, women can feel fragmented in their thinking, cranky in their conversation, as they struggle not to lose what they've gained because women come home having gained a lot. The changes can be dramatic or subtle, immediate or gradual, many or few, but no woman comes home unaffected.

Impact on Women

For some women, it's enough that they lived the experience. Completion is its own reward. In doing what they set out to do, many women reported feeling a deep inner peace. A study published in 1995 in the *International Journal of Aging & Human Development* confirms the correlation. Based on interviews with ninety women between the ages of thirty-eight and fifty-two, it concluded that those who were in the process of fulfilling dreams or had already fulfilled them suffered less anxiety than those who were not pursuing their dreams or had given up on them. Studies also reveal that people who challenge themselves score higher in "life satisfaction" than those who don't.

Concentrating on the self can—and often does—lead to high achievement, and impact for many women lies in the accomplishments they bring home: degrees, certifications, paintings, manuscripts; miles walked, climbed, or driven. Melissa passed her law boards. Jessica completed a novella. Shelley exhibited her photographs of India and won awards for them. With her stack of thirty new canvases, Megan landed four major shows.

Throughout history, married women in the arts have left a luminous trail of achievements after solo journeys. Fourteenth-century mystic Margery Kempe could neither read nor write, but after her pilgrimages she dictated her memoirs, which became the first autobiography in the English-speaking world. When Harriet Beecher Stowe returned home from the Brattleboro Water Cure, she started a school, nursed her family through a cholera epidemic, buried the baby she became pregnant with on her return, then began writing *Uncle Tom's Cabin*. She had hoped the book would strike a blow against slavery and enable her to buy a new dress. It did both, and changed the world besides.

In 1946, Anne Morrow Lindbergh wrote in her journal, "Will I ever write again?" After her nine-week trip abroad the following year, she wrote a series of articles on postwar Europe that appeared in *Harper's*, *Life*, and *Reader's Di-*

gest. Eight years later, her *Gift from the Sea* became one of the most phenomenal triumphs in publishing history, topping the bestseller list for a year. *Plain and Simple*, Sue Bender's 1989 memoir on her experiences with the Amish, became a bestseller, too. Letty Cottin Pogrebin's acclaimed books have influenced millions of women in the way we think about work, mothering, family, and friendship.

Georgia O'Keeffe was already a renowned artist when she spent her first summer in New Mexico, but that summer inspired a new direction in her artistic development. For years she had developed as her husband's protégé, adopting not only his friends, family, and lifestyle but also his subjects for her art. In New Mexico she chose her own landscapes. Her first exhibit to include her work from the desert was widely praised, one critic remarking that it showed "the real Taos and the real O'Keeffe."

After five visits to live among the Eskimos, Claire Fejes wrote and illustrated her first book on her experiences, *People of the Noatak*. It won praise in the *New York Times* and, twenty-eight years later, was reprinted as a classic. When it was selected as a textbook in an Eskimo high school, she called it "the biggest honor of my life." In a later book, Fejes described what fuel that first time away released in her:

> Back in Fairbanks, I painted feverishly for three months and lost ten pounds. Painting became a sacred act. . . . I began to live a life of purpose, not just letting circumstances control my days but choosing to have a voice in the direction of my journey. . . . I emerged with a new persona, a creative rebirth, to find my own voice. All the banked fires within me had burst into flame, and I painted surely, without retracting a single stroke.

At thirty, Megan has not yet earned a reputation like Fejes's, but achievements don't need to claim space in the record books to enhance women's working lives. For women easily diverted at home, the time away produces an enthusiasm to get back on task. "I'm not different when I return," said Megan of her two-month stays at artists' retreats, "but going away turns up the volume. I come home feeling so alive and focused." As valuable as the paintings she created—maybe more so—is her enhanced perspective of herself as a professional. "At home, paying jobs always take precedence over my painting," she said, "and sometimes I wonder who I am and what my work is about. My times away reaffirm that I'm an artist."

Whenever we set a challenge for ourselves and meet it, we emerge from the experience with more respect for our abilities. Whenever we do something hard and survive, we grow in self-esteem. Chris began her Peace Corps assignment in Africa as one of eleven teachers, many of them, like her, women at midlife. When she finished, she was one of four. Fewer than 20 percent of those who intend to walk the length of the Appalachian Trail succeed. On her second attempt, Maria came closer than she did on her first, but more important, she returned home feeling stronger, more peaceful still. A woman who did hike the entire length of the trail said she had been shy and timid her whole life, but after the five-and-a-half month solo trek, "I wasn't shy or timid anymore."

From a one-month intensive, immersive program at Harvard, a woman learned the varying shapes of confidence:

My husband had always taken charge of our getting around when we traveled. It was the first time I had explored a city by myself, and I wondered if I could ride the "T." Here I was running a division with more than 400 employees and a $186-million budget, and I was worried I couldn't manage the subway without my husband. You'd think my confidence at work would have carried over, but with every career success I felt like a fraud. The confidence I gained from going away alone transferred to every area of my life.

It didn't matter if women were executives or full-time moms, with a history of thirteen different jobs or one long career. Many said that going away gave them a self-confidence that nothing else had.

What women gain is as individual as they are, but all come home feeling stronger. All come home more self-aware. Some gain a clearer vision of how they want to live their lives. "More relaxed," said Shelley after each of her two stays in India. "More gently," said Sue Bender after living with the Amish. "More focused," said artists and writers. Women struggling with career decisions return with answers; others, with new ideas and the energy to pursue them. They enroll in schools, leave jobs, change professions, start companies. Some create new careers based on their experiences. They write memoirs and articles, give speeches and slide shows, raise money for humanitarian causes around the world. They design new working lives, more creative and flexible. Jessica went away to write, then surprised herself by coming home with a whole new approach to her interior design business. "I thought I wanted to close it down," she said, "but I figured out a way to have both the design work and the writing in my life. While I was away, I remembered the parts of the business that I loved."

When Susan came home from six months of reading in the south of France, her husband said, "I can't believe you read all those books and you never read a novel." "I read *War and Peace!*" she exclaimed. "I meant bestseller-type novels," he answered. No, she hadn't. She had fed herself only the classics, brain food that had stood the test of time. And when she returned home, she had a direction. She entered a graduate program in urban affairs, after which she ran for and won a seat on her city council. The eight years she spent in local government were the best of her working life. There she achieved two concrete changes in social welfare, the kind that had felt so elusive in her inner-city work. "I came back with more balance in my life," she said. "I realized I didn't have to do everything in such an extreme way."

Susan also returned feeling more comfortable with her own thoughts. It had been the first time in her life that she had been alone, and when her husband died many years later, she said, "I definitely drew strength from that time. It helped me to be alone, and it helped me to cope." Eighty percent of American wives will be widows one day, most of them outliving their husbands by ten years. On a sabbatical, a woman learns to embrace aloneness on her own terms rather than having it thrust upon her. She learns to survive with a safety net rather than without.

When women return with a stronger sense of the woman within, they also return with a desire to hold onto that strength. They realize that it's not just taking the time away that's important but keeping the experience alive, making a psychic container so that they can "go away" in their own homes. Mythologist Joseph Campbell wrote at length about the hero's journey. One of its major characteristics is that the individual brings forth something that wasn't there before. For many women, that something is a shift in psychological makeup. Maybe they vacate roles they played before or maybe they choose to move in or out of them in a different way, but something has shifted in their consciousness. It can be saying "no" to those who drain their energies or distract them from their goals. It can be saying "yes" to more time for themselves. It can be a stronger commitment to take their dreams more seriously, put their own lives first. They recognize that the energy they have given over to others in the past is their own; they can still choose to give it away, but now they know it will be their choice. If they're going to fulfill their dreams, they will have to conserve energy for themselves, sometimes be in retreat in their home lives.

Psychic containers often assume concrete forms. Some women create a room of their own, where they can meditate, work creatively, where the silence feels fuller and deeper. Others move to a new home or redesign the one they have as a metaphor for a new life. Sue Bender felt like a misfit after her return home until she remodeled her kitchen—white, uncluttered, and serene—to reflect the simplicity of the Amish and the state of her mind when she lived among them. "Finally I was home, in my kitchen," she wrote. "No matter how scattered or fractured my day was, when I walked into that room I felt calm." Today, Bender says she still works on creating more "white space" in her house. Some women take annual personal retreats. A woman who spent her sabbatical studying for a theology degree periodically stays at a monastery, what she called "my spiritual home."

As with all the best journeys, sabbaticals continue long after physical movement has ended. Anne Morrow Lindbergh placed a moon shell from one of her solo trips to Florida on her desk in Connecticut as a reminder to be alone for part of each year because "unless I keep the island quality intact somewhere within me, I will have little to give my husband, my children, my friends or the world at large." Above my computer, I keep a glossy color photo of my writer's cottage on Whidbey Island. Looking at it as I start the day helps me to block out interruptions and concentrate on my work. When life feels overwhelming, I retrieve the memory of the time when my mind was focused and relaxed. When I feel weighed down by the problems of others, I can recall the time when I centered on my own needs.

The psychic journey is not a steady ascent, however. Taking one sabbatical, or many, doesn't guarantee overcoming a lifetime of behavior. Some days, a woman can feel the old conflicts stirring, her boundaries slipping, but now she understands more clearly the importance of the struggle and feels better armed for it. She knows which mental muscles she needs to exercise, and exercising them feels more familiar than it did before. Life doesn't cease being difficult. What changes is the strength women draw on during those difficult times.

As growth is inevitable, so is loss. Euphoria doesn't last as long as we think it will. Neither does weight loss. Neither does lust. Children of any age can make a mother suffer for her absence, and a mother's guilt can outlast her experience. Chris came home from the Peace Corps to find her daughter still angry because she had her first pregnancy and childbirth without her mother nearby.

"Today we're closer than ever," said Chris, "but it took eight months for the relationship to heal." Women living in small towns or conservative cities can find on their return a coolness from those who found their time away strange or uncomfortable, raising barriers that weren't there before. One woman called her experience "a lovely thing to have done and a lonely thing to have done." The price of a solo journey is that for all the photos and stories and dinner table conversations, no one at home really shared the experience. Most people can't understand it. Most people aren't interested.

Her first day back at the ad agency, Darcy couldn't wait to tell everyone about her summer in Holland. A few co-workers expressed superficial interest; one said, "You spent all that money and now it's over." Her boss listened for twenty minutes, then made it clear he was through with the subject. "No one really cared," she said.

When Darcy returned to work, she also returned to a redesigned agency. Gone was her private office with a window; her desk now stood in a little cubicle in a big room, all her belongings crammed into a couple of boxes. "That was the beginning of the end," she said. "When I lost my office, I lost my ability to think."

Darcy repeated her sabbatical experience the following summer; upon that return, she found her boss had hired a new protégé. Although Darcy worked at the ad agency for two more years, her boss never got over his resentment, never let her back in the inner circle. "I kept losing power," she said, "and some of it was very painful. By leaving, I fatally cracked the relationship. But I don't regret it. My boss and I needed a divorce. I didn't know how to grow anymore, and leaving to work overseas was like opening the floodgates. I came home feeling I could do anything."

What she did was complete her master's degree, which she had let languish, and move into teaching full time. When she was nominated for her university's outstanding teacher award, she was disappointed she lost but felt validated in her career move.

Darcy was distressed by what happened at work but not surprised. What surprised her was what happened at home.

> When my husband and I met, I was the pursuer. While he'd show up an hour late for our dates, he was an ecstatic experience for me, like when you're twelve years old and the Beatles come to town. When I got home from Europe, I felt like some of that excitement was returned. I used to feel that I cared more about him than he did about me. When I came home, I realized I didn't. I don't think I would have known that if I hadn't left.
>
> The more time goes by, the more I appreciate his support. He gave me no grief about it, never made me feel guilty. It was the ultimate gift.

Impact on Husbands

Liberation, wrote Erik Erikson, is always reciprocal.

When women come home feeling grateful and invigorated—in Georgia O'Keeffe's words, "so alive that I am apt to crack at any moment"—that feeling cannot help but spill over into the lives of those they love. When Shelley returned from India, "broader in my thinking, more laid back, easier to get along with," her husband not only observed the difference, he benefited from it. "From the moment she walked off the plane, there was a noticeable change in her," he said. "She was so calm and peaceful. Before she left she was nervous as hell. An experience like she had changes you forever, and everything she experienced rubbed off on me."

Men who coped by immersing themselves in their work racked up their own achievements. Shelley's husband threw himself into his studies and into sports with their son. While Sally earned a degree in social work, back in Alaska Peter participated in fifteen juried art shows and three solo shows, all while chairing his department. Taking advantage that Sally wasn't around to criticize the amount of time he spent on the computer, he also developed a new curriculum in computer art. It was, he said, "the most productive year I've had since graduate school." Peter rearranged his teaching schedule to accommodate five long-weekend visits to see Sally, a schedule he ended up liking so much he continues it today.

Darcy's husband, whose hobby is home-construction projects, greeted her with a remodeled bathroom, which he installed with his son as an apprentice. Like Peter, he used her absence to do something she would have complained about had she been there, because with their only bathroom gutted, she would have had to use the makeshift one he created in the basement. During the five months Maria hiked the Appalachian Trail, her husband survived her absence by working longer hours at his new job, creating a 55 percent increase in the company's profits that year. While Chris was in the Peace Corps, David worked on new business projects and overhauled the family finances, previously Chris's domain.

When men take over responsibilities usually handled by their wives, a shift in gender roles occurs naturally. All the magazine articles in the world ("Sneaky Ways to Get Him to Do What You Want") won't effect change the way necessity will. An engineer, who used to just dig the garden, planted and tended it, learned to cook, and did all the housework. Others harvested apples and tomatoes, canned applesauce and tomato paste. They braided their daughters' hair, took aerobics classes with their teenagers. Men whose wives had always managed their social lives found that if they wanted to see their young adult children, they had to pick up the phone to call them, and they found pleasure in doing so.

Men discovered their own wellsprings of gratitude for the opportunity to spend extended one-on-one time with their children—a responsibility their wives had been assuming for years. The Families and Work Institute in New York found that 80 percent of men they interviewed wanted a stronger role in child rearing than their own dads had had. Men whose wives take solo journeys gain that opportunity. Every man I spoke with who was a father said he became closer to his children while his wife was away. Some said they grew close for the first time; others, that the time cemented the bond they already had. All with growing children said they developed a deeper compassion for single parents. When men today become primary caretakers, it's usually under duress, when custody battles and loyalty struggles intensify parenting pressures.

Men whose wives take solo journeys assume the role in a healthier environment.

Whirling emotions lead men to their own shifts in consciousness. They, too, rethink identities and relationships. If they had doubts, they learn they can live by themselves. They may have become lethargic and lonely, but they were not debilitated. While his wife was away at seminary, one forty-nine-year-old man lost his job, moved his father to a nursing home, buried his brother-in-law, all while living with a needy young adult child. "It was harder than I ever imagined, and I wouldn't want to do it again," he said. "But I discovered an inner strength I didn't know I had. I used to wonder how I'd manage if anything happened to my wife. I know now that I can survive on my own, and reasonably well. It was a significant realization."

Alfred Stieglitz suffered and strengthened, too. During O'Keeffe's first summer in the desert, he became so distraught he inundated her with letters filled with agony and need. (She once received fifteen in a single day.) But with the help of his friends, he rallied to experience a rebirth of his own. On her return, he greeted her with renewed health and two new passions—flying a seaplane over the Hudson River and playing classical music on his elegant new Victrola. That fall, he opened a new gallery and took more photos of his wife than he had in years. Of their first summer apart, he wrote his niece, "I have learned a lot— & I shall apply what I have learned." The next year, when O'Keeffe wanted to return to the Southwest for the summer, he gave the trip his blessing. "It is almost as though Stieglitz makes me a present of myself in the way he feels about it," she wrote.

Stieglitz never again resisted her desire, but until the day he died he never visited her in the place she called "my faraway." While Harriet Beecher Stowe was at the Brattleboro Water Cure, her husband responded much as Stieglitz did, his correspondence to her full of complaints and woe. After she returned, however, Calvin Stowe responded quite differently to the source of his wife's restoration. For the next two summers, with her encouragement, he was the one to leave home to soak in the healing waters.

Just as knowing that he can be alone reaffirms a man's self-worth, so does his wife's gratitude. When a woman comes home with a new appreciation for life, that includes the man who supported her experience. Is anyone more esteemed than the person who encourages our growth?

It's been six years now since Sally returned to Peter in Alaska. She still writes him notes, thanking him for his support.

"I believe that immersion into some kind of study or intense work changes people, rewires the brain," said Peter. "Men do this all the time, but women tend to do it more part time so they can still take care of everyone and everything. Doing it part-time though, you don't change. My wife came back transformed. She took on a new identity. She felt reborn and rebuilt, and the support that I gave her to do this generated trust in a way that nothing else could."

In the fourteen-month journey from his support to her trust and gratitude, Peter experienced his share of disquieting moments. "I learned I was more insecure than I thought I was," he said. "Sally was so happy with what she was doing that I was very afraid she wouldn't want to come back. Part of the insecurity was realizing how much I relied on her. I felt I was at a scary disadvantage, that she didn't need me as much as I needed her."

Marital research pioneer Jessie Bernard said it twenty-five years ago: Seventy-three percent of husbands overestimate their power in the relationship, while 70 percent of wives underestimate theirs.

It's Sunday morning breakfast, two months after my return:

"I've decided next summer I'm going to walk the battlefields of the Civil War," he says.

"By yourself?" I ask.

"Yes."

I smile. Now this is change.

I am married to a man who has been fascinated by the Civil War for as long as I've known him. He says the fascination started as a child, when his grandfather took him scouting for minié balls in the dirt roads of West Virginia. Jim has read Shelby Foote's three-volume history, as well as his novel *Shiloh*. He's read Bruce Catton. I won't embarrass him by revealing how many times he's seen the movie *Gettysburg*. I think he must have been a Civil War soldier in a previous life. When I'm working crossword puzzles and he knows the five-letter name of a Civil War general beginning with M, my eyes light up, but when he talks of taking a vacation together to walk the battlefields, they glaze over. He stopped mentioning it years ago, but I knew his desire hadn't diminished. I imagine the reason he never went was that he would have felt selfish using limited vacation time just for his own desires. My going away alone seems to have given him the permission he couldn't give himself.

Some days I think my leaving had more of an impact on Jim than it did on me. It forced him to leave the cozy familiarity of his study with his stereo and his computer. He started several new activities, laid the groundwork for a new business.

For a number of years before I left, I often went alone to social gatherings. As a writer working at home, I tend to accept every invitation I receive, if only for my sanity. Jim, on the other hand, sees clients on Saturdays, rarely wants to go out on those evenings with anyone but me. So he stayed home many a Saturday night, relaxing with Bach and the Internet, while I ventured out alone wherever we were invited. After I came home, we received an invitation to a gathering, and I said what I always say, "I'm going. Do you want to come?" And he surprised me by saying yes—and to every invitation since, *yes*.

Impact on Marriages

The Greek philosopher Heraclitus said that we can't step into the same river twice. The second time we approach it, the river is different and we're different. So too when a woman steps back into her marriage.

Strong marriages grow stronger. The separation becomes another bond, leads couples to treasure each other anew, promise not to take each other for granted. They feel confident they can be apart in the future and, most said, probably for longer durations. Some rediscover a comfort and security in the relationship that they had been too stressed or distracted to appreciate. "I discovered how much I missed his daily attentions, his nurturing," said one woman, "just having him say, 'Would you like a cup of tea?' I brought back a whole new appreciation for him. If you don't go away, I don't know how you ever see that."

As a woman continues to reap rewards from her experience, she continues to appreciate the man who helped her attain them. In the words of marital researcher John Gottman, "If you have a partner who follows her dream and sees you as an ally, my God, there's real intimacy." Almost 150 years ago, the great social reformer Henry Brown Blackwell, married to the equally feminist Lucy Stone, said, "The interests of the sexes are inseparably connected and in the elevation of one lies the salvation of the other."

When a woman feeling more independent than she realized comes home to a man feeling more dependent than he realized, both return to better balance in the relationship.

When Sarah returned to her dynamic husband after having earned the highest score on her computer test, higher than all the young men in her program, the balance of power shifted. The reversal unsettled him, strengthened her. During their marriage, Steve had continued his pattern (from thirty-five years of bachelorhood) of taking trips alone or with friends. Sarah's sabbatical was the first time she took the adventure and he stayed at home. Like many women, Sarah always felt obligated to her husband when she was with him. For four months and for the first time, she felt obligated only to herself, and she enjoyed the feeling. "Since I've returned," she said, "I still have that feeling of obligation to him, but it doesn't run as deep."

For twelve years, Steve's concerns dominated their marriage. He invested more energy in his interests, and she invested more energy in his interests. Her concerns became an afterthought, and he shrugged off what she submerged. Since Sarah's return, he's been trying to attend to her needs, and she's trying to attend to her needs. The result is a healthier marriage and a happier Sarah. "Before I left, I felt off center," she said, "as though I were blindfolded—always falling down and stumbling into furniture. Now I feel the blindfold's off and I'm choosing my steps."

Her first step is to look for contract work in her new career as a "network nanny," which will mean more separations like her sabbatical. Steve wasn't thrilled the first time she left and probably won't be thrilled the next, but he agrees with her that this new lifestyle can work for them.

"We're on a different path now," she said. "It would not have happened if I hadn't left."

It would not have happened if I hadn't left was a frequent refrain in conversations with women returning with stronger identities to dominant men. *I no longer live in my husband's shadow. . . . I became more assertive, a leader in spite of a natural inclination to work behind the scenes. . . . I'm more outspoken and confident now, more trusting of my instincts. . . . I feel like I'm bringing a stronger, more equal person to the marriage. My husband feels I've outgrown him, but I feel I'm just catching up.*

Jessie Bernard called this the Pygmalion effect. The self-image of wives, she wrote in *The Future of Marriage*, becomes more negative with age. It's not due to a husband's clenched fists or sculptor's hands but to the structure of the institution. In marriage, women lose ground in personal development.

Toward the end of his life, Mark Twain explored this subject with his trademark wit and imagination. He wrote "The Diary of Adam and Eve" after the death of Olivia, his wife of thirty-four years, undoubtedly an homage to her. Structured as journal entries, the short story portrays the first couple before and after the Fall. In Eden, Eve proves herself the superior creation. Adam retreats to his hut whenever it rains or fogs and finds Sundays trying since he already rests the other six days of the week. Eve, meanwhile, delights in riding the tigers and leopards and elephants in all weather to explore the grounds. She names every creature she encounters, learns from the animals, plays with them, cares for them. She enjoys improving the estate, weaves flowers into garlands. Gazing at the skies, she meditates on the mysteries of the universe and searches for her purpose. Twain's Eve is intuitive, verbal, curious, compassionate, adventuresome, soulful, passionate about beauty and relationship. Adam is a lug. As ardently as he tries to avoid Eve, she tries to connect, pursuing him and studying his habits "to be useful to him in every way I can, so as to increase his regard." To save him embarrassment, she tries not to flaunt her verbal superiority. To bring him pleasure, she picks the forbidden apple. "So I come to harm through pleasing him," she writes, "why shall I care for that harm?" After the Fall, Adam decides that since he's lost his property, he'll probably become depressed and lonesome without Eve, so he may as well live with her, especially now that they must work for their living. "She will be useful," he writes. "I will superintend." Eve writes, "The Garden is lost, but I have found *him*, and am content."

Twain concludes his story forty years later. In Eve's last entry, she prays that she dies before her husband, "for he is strong, I am weak, I am not so necessary to him as he is to me—life without him would not be life; how could I endure it?" At her graveside, Adam writes, "Wheresoever she was, *there* was Eden."

Women who take solo journeys disrupt this age-old pattern, gain ground in personal development, come home realizing their powers come from their own strengths, not from their relationships with their partners. When they come home more connected to their inner selves, they also come home knowing that authenticity cannot coexist with submission.

Time away and alone realigns the imbalance that can begin in a marriage—as Twain's story illustrates—when a woman expects that the relationship will meet all her needs but a man harbors no such illusion. Solo journeys illuminate sources of meaning outside the relationship so that when women return home, they don't demand so much gratification from their partners and can live more peacefully with their partners' shortcomings. And when women live more peacefully, their partners can live more peacefully with them. *She came back so much easier on herself and on me. . . . There's less tension now in our marriage. . . . She's more willing to accommodate my desires. . . . I don't feel so responsible for her happiness now, so the pressure's off a little.*

It's human nature to blame our unhappiness on those closest to us. Most of us think that if we're not happy within ourselves, then there's something wrong with our marriages. The truth is just the opposite: There's something wrong with our marriages because we are not happy within ourselves. The Jewish theologian Martin Buber expressed this insight. All conflict between two people, he said, is the result of a conflict within a person. The solution to marital conflict, Buber believed, is investment in the self.

Judith Sills, is one of many contemporary psychologists who would agree with this philosophy. The premise of her book *Biting the Apple* is that when women nurture their single souls, they have more to put into their marriages and they take less out—making the marriage richer for both partners. Loving yourself more and needing him less, she writes, changes the experience of love. Sills calls it "not a change in strategy, but a change in spirit."

By nurturing their single souls, women can find that what they once perceived to be a problem in the marriage loses its intensity. The problem is not solved at all, but its significance diminishes as a new and stronger life force develops. That's what happened with Georgia O'Keeffe and the landscape of her husband's life. At the Stieglitz family compound at Lake George, New York, where more than twenty people typically gathered at dinner, where in-laws and children and chaos were constant, the very private O'Keeffe said she often felt "like a hobbled horse." When she arrived at Lake George after her first summer in New Mexico, she exulted, "It is wonderful to be here and be with my funny little Stieglitz—He is grand—so grand that I don't seem to be able to see family about or anything else."

Just as the Stieglitz compound didn't miraculously become quiet, the Arctic Circle doesn't grow warmer and sunnier in a woman's absence. The Bible Belt doesn't become more liberal. A landscape or a city doesn't change, but a woman's perspective on it can. As Sinclair Lewis writes at the end of *Main Street*, Carol Kennicott returned to provincial Gopher Prairie "no longer one-half of a marriage but the whole of a human being." "At last, I've come to a fairer attitude toward the town," she says. "I can love it now."

Lewis wrote award-winning fiction. In real life, a woman's change in perspective tends to be less dramatic. No matter how many summers she spends in the Far East, Debra will probably never say, "I can love the Ozarks now." After each return home, she doesn't chafe less with her environment but she has more energy to battle it, a battle that today has led her to law school for the legal clout to support her activism.

Sally won't say she loves Alaska, either, "but I've made a truce with it."

From having invested time in their own passions, women like Debra and Sally return not with an affinity for their environment but with an acceptance of their connection to it and the insight to make adjustments. After Sally's return to Alaska, she and Peter moved to a new home with more windows so that her environment would at least feel brighter and sunnier. The stronger a woman's identity—her home within—the easier she can live with her surroundings.

The ability to live with the unchangeable is considered one of the defining characteristics of a happy, long-term marriage, because in marriage the unchangeable predominates. From twenty-five years of studies, researcher John Gottman has concluded that 69 percent of problems in marriage are unsolvable because they grow out of a person's personality or character, which isn't going to change. "What's important is not solving the problem," he said, "but the emotions around which you don't solve it." In other words, you can choose to live with your differences with grudging resentment or bemused toleration. Successful, long-married couples view their problems with bemused toleration, as idiosyncracies rather than sins. In *After the Honeymoon,* Daniel Wile, a clinical psychologist in Oakland, California, expresses the same idea, taking it one step further. When we marry, he writes, we are choosing our set of unresolvable problems.

That leaves, according to Gottman's research, 31 percent of marital problems that are resolvable. And sometimes a sabbatical can bring a solution.

It did for Rebecca.

Rebecca is the New Englander who left to paint, live a city life, and join a metaphysical church. In spite of a series of mishaps, including a harrowing first week, during which her car died in the middle of a four-lane highway and she had to spend half her sabbatical money on repairs, she achieved her goals. For the first time in her life, her adult mind was alone. She immersed herself in her painting and exhibited forty canvases in a successful ten-day show.

Rebecca came home with the knowledge she'd sought: For the second half of her life, she would paint full time.

Knowing this made her feel joyful about her experience and strong and centered in herself, but it also crystallized the impasse she and her husband had reached on a long-standing issue. She wanted to sell their house so they could get out of debt and she could paint full time; he didn't want to sell the house he loved and had labored to build.

The day Rebecca returned home (after seven months), her husband initiated the conversation, agreed to sell their house, pay off their debts, and start fresh. "He seemed not only sincere and positive about conceding," she said, "but it was clear that he had done a lot of thinking, which I had hoped would happen. I didn't expect it, but I hoped. I wanted a life of integrity, and now I have it, and my husband and I can live with each other in an adult and creative way. Life isn't perfect, we're not starry-eyed reunited, but he's more thoughtful and cheerful than I've seen him in years, maybe ever. I am not the easiest person to live with, but I have a new gratitude for my life. I won't dishonor it with domestic squabbles—he likes that."

Rebecca's problem was practical where Sarah's was psychological, but both involved long-standing issues their husbands ignored until their wives left home. While most women intuitively know what it takes to pay attention to a marriage, men may need a jolt, and a wife's leaving for four months or seven definitely jolts.

Marion Woodman and Elinor Dickson describe this phenomenon in their interpretation of the myth of Hera and Zeus, the Greek gods representing long-term married love. As the authors write in *Dancing in the Flames*, Hera is the goddess married women turn to for guidance. For years, Hera's life is totally bound up in what her husband does. When Zeus is faithful and attentive, she's warm and nurturing; when Zeus is promiscuous, she turns angry and vindictive. She projects on her husband her own un-lived potential, which means she's always in conflict, not only with him but also within herself. The turning point in their marriage comes when she leaves Zeus to go to her birthplace in Euboea, where she had spent a happy child-hood. There, alone in the mountains, she confronts her inner self. With Hera's absence, Zeus discovers how im-portant she is to him, and, for the first time, he tells her. She returns to Olympus, now ready for the marriage that she's always wanted (which, by the way, lasted 300 years).

When both partners grow, become more separate and autonomous, the relationship becomes interdependent rather than codependent, based on want rather than need. When couples know they can survive alone and en-joy being alone, they also know when they reunite that they are together because they choose to be. "You don't need him," Ruby says to her friend Ada in Charles Fra-zier's best-selling Civil War novel, *Cold Mountain*. "I know I don't need him," Ada says. "But I think I want him." And Ruby responds, "Well that's a whole different thing."

"The normal basis for a lot of marriages is 'fill me up, make me feel better,' because that's what every adolescent is like," said clinical psychologist Bill Bumberry. "When people marry young, that's how the marriage starts out. And a lot of people don't get over that, even in their sec-ond and third marriages. The internal mechanism stays the same. That's partially why the divorce rate is higher for the second marriage than it is for the first."

A relationship of interdependence means: I can get along without you, and I know you can get along without me. We're together not because we're incomplete, but because we want the synergy we have when we're together. With interdependence, marriage enlarges rather than confines. Two do not become one; two become three. Growing as individuals, they can then grow as a couple. Sometimes the result is a whole new marriage.

Before Karen left her husband in Hawaii, both were frustrated in their work. She wanted to move to a big city for a big job; he wanted to move to a more rural area to start a new business. Each went toward the challenge each wanted.

When Karen returned to her husband in Hawaii, she came back a different woman. She'd always relied on him to provide her fun; she learned to entertain herself. She'd always looked to him for home maintenance; she learned to husband her resources on her own. She left with a Ph.D.; she returned "feeling smart for the first time."

"If I hadn't left, I never would have become a vice president," she said. "It felt like a really great accomplishment, and now I never have to do it again. There's a lot more to life than a position, but I can say that now because I've had it." Because she attained what she wanted, she also came home willing to work with her husband on his new business until she found another job. She enjoyed the opportunity, and he enjoyed her help.

When Karen returned, she wasn't the only one who had changed. Her husband had experienced an evolution and revolution of his own. "At first, after Karen left," he said, "I thought, 'What have we done?' Then I felt relief, because suddenly I had freedom, too." He bought a little hut in the woods, which he'd long wanted but Karen had long vetoed. For eight months, he lived in the middle of the rain forest, in a twelve-by-sixteen-foot shack without electricity or running water. To rinse his clothes and dishes, he collected rainwater in large cans. When he wanted a bath, he jumped into a stream. "I'd always made my life so complicated," he said. "Living simply like that made me feel rich for the first time."

And living independently made him feel needy for the first time. "I was your typical macho guy," he said. "I never wanted to admit I needed anyone or anything. For the first time in my life, I could admit that I needed Karen and that it was okay to need her."

When Karen returned home feeling independent and "smart for the first time" to a man feeling dependent and "rich for the first time," each found a new partner, a more whole person with a sense of inner maturity, which first enriched their lives as individuals, then their lives as a couple.

Transformation never comes easily, and the greater the changes, the greater the difficulties achieving them. Leaving her husband was hard, and living apart for two years was hard. At each visit, Karen was more corporate and sophisticated, her husband more entrepreneurial and native. Each visit began or ended in tears. Reuniting was hard, too. But today, the gains outweigh the struggles. "Our marriage is better than it was before," said Karen, "maybe better than it ever was." Her husband agrees. "Karen's leaving did something powerful," he said. "We got ourselves back. Now she appreciates my need to be alone, in fact she encourages it. I kept my hut in the rain forest and spend the night there by myself once every week or two. It's my church, my place of meditation. Letting her go was the smartest thing I ever did."

Like the alchemy that transforms dross into gold, sabbaticals can transform a marriage into a remarriage. What begins as a personal experience, with deep internal changes, can radiate to a new partnership, both freer and more committed. Rilke illuminated the problem of relationship in his *Letters to a Young Poet*: Are you willing to stand guardian over someone else's solitude? He described the reward when the answer is yes: "Once the realization is accepted that even between the closest human beings, infinite distances continue to exist, a wonderful living side by side can grow up, if they succeed in loving the distance between them which makes it possible for each to see the other whole and against a wide sky."

Learning to "love the distance between them" is harder for some couples than for others. Just as sabbaticals illuminate the strengths of a relationship, they reveal weaknesses. One way or another, they will put a relationship in sharper focus, even if a man wasn't looking for it, even if a woman liked the status quo.

When Ann returned after two months working at the summer camp she'd attended as a child, she was dismayed to discover that her husband hadn't missed her as she had missed him. Keith had enjoyed bachelorhood, liked deciding what he'd do in his leisure time. He discovered he didn't want to go back to where he was before, home at six because she wanted him there, submissive when it came to their lives together. "I decided I wanted more control over my life," he said. His decision and her dismay made re-entry difficult, necessitating several sessions of marriage counseling. What Ann learned in therapy was that Keith's not missing her didn't mean he didn't love her; it meant he knew she was coming back. "I had to learn not to take it personally," she said.

Before Ann left, Keith ceded control over their social life either because he didn't know he cared or he couldn't express his feelings. In his wife's absence, he learned that he definitely did care; in marriage counseling, he learned to communicate it. By leaving, Ann pushed their relationship, first to an uncomfortable place, then to a better one.

In sturdy marriages, like Keith and Ann's, couples address their issues and work on remedies. In not-so-sturdy relationships, the illumination of differences can lead one or both partners to want to end the marriage. It would be naive to imply that every sabbatical leads to a better relationship. What is strengthening for a woman does not always turn out to be strengthening for the marriage.

A concert pianist was twenty-eight and had been with her husband for six years (married for three) when she left to fulfill a lifelong dream to study piano in Vienna. A pianist since childhood, she had spent much time alone and had come to enjoy solitude as much as to need it. With her husband's support, she stayed three months. The time away was not motivated by her marriage, but through the lens of distance, she saw the truth of her marriage. Her husband had not given up any of his activities or routines for her, but she had been conditioned to give up hers for him. She saw that she'd been trying so hard to please him that she had given up a lot of herself in the marriage. That summer in Vienna, she said, "I claimed back who I was." To retain her sense of self, she returned to Vienna for a month each summer for the next five years. Each trip she came home rejuvenated; each return, her husband surprised her with spontaneous gestures of thoughtfulness.

She came home with more confidence to talk about what was bothering her in the relationship, so the trips helped temporarily improve her marriage. She came home with a greater ability to live with the problems, so the trips helped lengthen her marriage (their young children made this important to her). And she came home with the knowledge she could live alone and the strength to eventually break away, so the trips helped end her marriage. They also helped ease her divorce. "Distance enabled me to look at the relationship more objectively, without anger and blame," she said. "Though the divorce was painful, we were very civil about it, and today we're good friends."

What makes a sabbatical a success? If a woman's experience makes her stronger, lessens anger and blame, if it enables her to create a more authentic life and model it to her children, yet she and her husband one day divorce, the dissolution of the relationship does not negate her individual gains. Growing, by definition, means change, and people perceive and adapt to change in different ways. One person's positive is another's negative. A sabbatical can highlight a problem and accelerate a decision, but a sabbatical alone doesn't precipitate a divorce. A shift was already stirring. What determines the success of a sabbatical is not whether a woman returns to a happily-ever-after marriage. What determines success is whether she gains the clarity to know what she wants and the strength to act on her desires. The determinant of success is growth.

Three years after Chris's return from the Peace Corps, she and David aren't making long-term predictions. His fear—that Chris would not return—didn't come to pass. Her fear—that their values would be further apart—did. The realization saddens her, but she holds on to the gratitude she feels that on two occasions after her homecoming and "totally out of character for him," David encircled her in his arms and expressed his admiration for what she'd accomplished. He had certainly thrown rocks in her way, he said, and she stood strong and stayed with her assignment to the end. On her part, Chris appreciates David's struggle to stay the course, too. Today, Chris is pursuing a new dream, a degree in psychology so that she can work with children. David is the one traveling again in his work. They're taking their marriage one day at a time—some would say, the only way any of us can take it.

Impact on Children

Some women's fears materialize, and some women's don't.

"My greatest fear in leaving," said Libby, "was that I was deserting my daughters, when, in fact, I gave them a great gift. I gave them the space and time to be with their father. The day I came home, I could immediately see a difference, a closeness in their relationship. I always wanted my husband to be more involved in their lives, but coming home I could see that he wasn't the problem. I never got out of the way."

The real source of inequity on the home front is that women are overinvolved with their children. In the last two years, I have asked every married mother I've encountered, "Did you ever leave? Would you ever leave?" And almost every woman answered, automatically, firmly, sometimes fiercely, "I would never leave my children." Yet what happens when women do leave? When Chris was in the Peace Corps, David said, "I saw my kids more those two years than I ever did before or have since, and I miss it." Of the first time Debra left the Ozarks, where her husband was a professor (with the summer off), he said, "I didn't look forward to being the sole caretaker for three small children, all preschool age. But I learned I liked having total freedom to decide what we'd do each day. I really enjoyed those summers. They were some of the best times of my life."

Were they the best times for the kids, too? Maybe not, but it's hard to say. The effect of a mother's temporary absence is a book in itself, and most of the women I interviewed didn't leave children. But if men enjoyed spending time with their children, as Debra's husband did, as David did, their children certainly profited from that joy. Looking back, children remember the difficulties, but with dads who were good caretakers, life went on, challenging but not traumatizing. Years soften memories, and children, like husbands, tend to focus on the gains.

Darcy's son is sixteen today. The second time his mother left for two months, he was eleven, about to enter the sixth grade at a new school. "I was really upset, and I didn't want her to go," he said. "I felt I'd have a hard time adjusting without her. My dad asked me if I was worried and said he'd help me get through it. I might have cried the night she left, and the first week I thought about her all the time." By the second week, he was discovering the rewards of a more lenient lifestyle with his dad: a later bedtime, a quick "yes" when he wanted to go to a friend's house, fun in the kitchen making desserts. "It ended up that I hardly noticed my mom was gone," he said. "It's not that I didn't miss her, but I knew she'd be back."

"It turned out to be a big turning point in my life," he continued. "In fifth grade I depended on her so much to help me with my homework, to get projects done at the last minute. My dad isn't as big a help with schoolwork, and I had to do it on my own for the first time. That was more meaningful than I thought, realizing that I didn't need her as much as I thought I did."

A child's memories of his mother's absence tend to be memories of his father's presence, but not all women can foresee that. When a woman from the Midwest was offered a six-month consulting opportunity on the California coast, she hung up the phone and screamed with joy. Then she told her fourteen-year-old son the news. Ten years later, they remember the time very differently.

SHE: He looked at me with this sad, little face and said, "Can't you just tell them you have a kid?" My heart stopped.

HE: I wasn't happy she was going away. I'm sure I made some snide remarks.

SHE: He became surly and sullen and distant. Every time I looked at him, he had this martyred look on his face, like he was so put upon. I had figured that everyone could come visit me because I'd be in such a beautiful place on the water, but he made me feel so guilty, I came home every month for a weekend just to do his laundry, grocery shop, and cook and freeze meals.

HE: She says she came home every month, but I don't remember that. What I remember is that it was just my dad and me, and we had a lot of fun. We went out to eat a lot.

SHE: The day I came home, I turned on my computer and he'd programmed it to start up with his voice wailing, "Mom! Help! I'm lost in the computer!" I was startled. He was such a little devil, but the wailing sounded so horrible and his voice was so anguished I wondered if I'd done psychic damage.

HE: Her being away just didn't have much of an impact on my life. A much bigger deal was when she went back to work when I was ten. She wasn't there after school anymore. That's when everything changed, when I had to redefine the role of Mom.

SHE (audibly relieved after I relay this information): All these years I thought I ruined his life. Thank goodness I didn't.

Whether or not women feel guilty, they return with a degree of separation from their children, and their children from them—a healthy sense of detachment. No matter how close or enmeshed the family, women return with the realization that they can extricate themselves from everyone and nothing falls apart. Every mother I interviewed made the same discovery, and every mother was surprised by it: "I realized they got along fine without me." When a woman replaces a narcissistic illusion with a humble reality, everyone benefits.

Extended Effects

Charlotte Overby begins her essay "Sweeping Up": "For forty-nine years, my mother bit her fingernails to red, chapped nothings. When she came home from her first solo trip to Portugal at the age of fifty-three, they were milky, firm and long. She didn't like me to look, but I marveled."

The transformation of Barbara Overby's hands inspired her daughter to write an essay that was published in an anthology of stories by Missouri women. "I became obsessed with the fact that my mother stopped biting her fingernails," said Charlotte, who was twenty the summer her mother began her trips. "I had to know why they grew." What she discovered was that by going to Portugal and doing something she loved, her mother's whole life changed. Her nails symbolized that transformation.

Movement creates a ripple effect, and one transformation led to others. Charlotte worked on her mother's dig as an excavator one summer, and when Overby decided to walk the Camino de Santiago, Charlotte joined her there for two weeks. Her twelfth summer overseas, Overby returned to the Camino with her daughter and fourteen-year-old granddaughter, who felt so proud of walking the 500 miles that she plans to do it again. She'll take her brother and a male cousin, she said, and, next time, *she'll* lead the trek. While the three generations of Overby women walked the pilgrimage, their local coffee shop tacked up a map of their route and, on their return, hosted a show-and-tell gathering. For a decade, Overby's husband enjoyed her experiences vicariously, visited her site several times, read most of her books on Portugal. Her eleventh summer there, he decided to make her experience his own. When she volunteered at a *refugio* after her two-month pilgrimage, he labored alongside her. "Barbara is a far more interesting person than she'd be if she had felt she needed to stay home with me," he said. "When her life became more interesting, so did mine."

Charlotte Perkins Gilman said it a century ago: "The woman is narrowed by the home, and the man is narrowed by the woman."

Women who leave home broaden their homes and the lives of those within. To husbands, friends, children, and grandchildren, they exemplify risk and relay the message that we can create life anew. Joan Mister hoped her 30,000-mile road trip would serve as a legacy for her seven-year-old granddaughter "to see the potential in the long stretch of years." When Mister's story appeared in the *New York Times*, she received e-mail from all over the country, indicating that her journey inspired far more people than one small girl in Brooklyn.

In the end, paradox defines the homecoming, too, for arrival signifies an ending, and an ending signifies a beginning. In leaving home, women arrive at a new meaning of home. Not just a protected physical space and a familial heart place, but a dwelling within, where they feel more comfortable with change, more at home in unfamiliar places, more at home within themselves.

8

REFLECTIONS

Good idea that going West!
—GEORGIA O'KEEFFE,
LETTER TO REBECCA STRAND,
NOVEMBER 5, 1929

I wish I had stayed longer."

"I wish I'd gone farther from home."

"I wish I'd gone to a city where I knew absolutely no one, where no one would have intruded on my time."

"I wish I had gone years earlier."

"If I had gone earlier, I would have grown up sooner, been more self-assured. But I wasn't ready. I wish I'd been ready sooner."

"I didn't leave because our marriage was in trouble, but it could have been in trouble if I hadn't gone."

"If I hadn't gone, the resentment would have been so great that we probably would have divorced."

"I wish I had stayed longer."

Whether women left for one month or two years, took one solo trip or several, many described their experiences in superlatives: *influences to this day how I live . . . invaluable . . . pivotal . . . transformative . . . the best gift I've ever given myself . . . the key to who I am today.* Ellen, who has worked as a media advisor on a presidential campaign, hosted a cable-TV show, starred in regional theater productions, and acted in national television commercials—whose life has been filled with dramatic highlights—said of her teaching assignment overseas, "Going away for those two and a half months was a high point of my life. It's been five years now and it has stayed with me."

If a Disneyesque glow seems to permeate women's stories, it's because the characteristics of their sabbaticals mirror those of a "peak experience." Psychologist Abraham Maslow introduced this concept in one of his best-known works, *Toward a Psychology of Being*. A peak experience, Maslow said, comes from bursts of creativity, moments of insight and discovery, from fusion with nature. He described its characteristics: a sharp contrast with the ordinary experiences of life, a disorientation in time and space, simplicity, aliveness, independence, an emotional reaction of wonder and gratitude. In a peak experience, a person is more spontaneous, expressive, self-determined, strong, "most his or her own identity." Maslow believed that our most fulfilling, happiest, and healthiest moments in life are our moments of greatest individuality.

In the story of a woman's marriage, a sabbatical can reveal character or voice, lend structure or texture. It can set a scene or permeate the landscape, open a chapter or close a volume. It can be epic poem or light verse, subtext or context, monologue or dialogue, focal point or turning point, dominant theme or recurring thread. For some women one sabbatical in a marriage of fifty-five years is enough; for others, it's sporadic, whenever they feel a need or an opportunity beckons; and for others, the first journey away starts a new pattern of living.

Eda LeShan is the author of twenty-five books and a long-time columnist for *Newsday* and *Woman's Day*. On her seventy-third birthday, in 1995, her first play opened off Broadway to a wonderful review in the *New York Times*. The day I spoke with her, the retired family counselor and educational consultant was working on two books and another play. Her regular appearance as a crossword-puzzle answer manifests her status as an icon of popular culture. In her early forties, however, she was not the confident woman she grew to become.

My husband, Larry, was working very hard on a difficult project. He was experiencing burnout and knew he needed time alone. He couldn't explain it very well, and when he left on a six-week pilgrimage—he walked from Athens to Delphi—I felt terribly rejected. I cried every day he was gone, wondered where I went wrong. I was a raving maniac.

My parents had never been apart except for the times my mother was in the hospital having a baby. I married a man who had been alone much of his childhood, who was completely different from me. I was so upset when he left that my therapist encouraged me to go away alone to understand my husband's motivation.

I was terrified, but the next year I left to spend a week at Long Island Beach in New Jersey. Today that isn't a long time to be away, but it was then. The first three days were just about the worst days of my life. I thought I'd die of loneliness. I grew up a protected, middle-class, Jewish girl. I had little experience being on my own, even though I had many good jobs. By the fourth day, I began to appreciate my own company for the first time. I began to search out what would give me pleasure. I came home strengthened, with a better sense of my worth and possibilities. It was a turning point in my life and in our marriage.

After that time, I bought a cottage on Cape Cod, where I went to write and garden. My husband is happiest in the Fordham Library doing his research and I enjoy living with nature, so in the last thirty years we have spent a good part of our lives separate. People thought we were strange and worried about us, but our marriage is as good as it's ever been. We are so free to be ourselves. Psychological understanding is a central force in both our lives, and we have never stopped growing and learning. You don't have to be alone for growth to occur, but for creative development, being alone is terribly important.

When a lobster needs to grow, it has to go out to the ocean and shed its hard shell. It's a dangerous time for the lobster—it has to take a real risk that it won't be eaten. But within forty-eight hours, it casts off its hard shell and a soft shell emerges. Well, we're like the lobster. If we're going to keep growing, we must go out on a reef and take our chances.

In relationships, there is always tension, always a struggle between the desire for intimacy and the yearning for independence, between what Thomas Moore calls "the soul of attachment and the spirit of detachment." A sabbatical is not a universal panacea, but it is one way to embrace both sides of life.

The advantages of a sabbatical in academia and business are widely understood: a time to develop one's mind, focus one's creativity, renew physically and spiritually. The value in leaving one's ordinary world for an extraordinary one is not only in what we discover but also in what we return with: a renewed self, with a dedication to engage in work on a higher level—more conscious, deliberate, and open. The assumption behind sabbaticals is that employees return stronger individuals, with greater insight and broader perspective—resources that will enhance the environment to which they return. Where a sabbatical is valued in the workplace, the benefits can be dramatic and far-reaching.

Where there is a foundation of trust and commitment, a sabbatical in relationships can be equally powerful. I am not suggesting, however, that every married woman—and man—take off alone for distant shores. While it's easy to fall into the trap of evangelical thinking, that if something transformed your life, it will transform everyone's, the reality is we are all vastly different individuals, trailing different histories, harboring different dreams. And with these differences we form marriages radically diverse in expectations and needs. Some women's dreams can be fulfilled in their hometowns; some women's, right at home. Some men hate to travel, aren't adventuresome. Not everyone craves solitude. Some couples are so burdened with financial expenses and caretaking that the problems a sabbatical would entail seem far greater than potential gains. Others with growing children don't want to be anywhere but involved daily with those children's lives. Some women have spent many years alone or in unsatisfying first marriages, and now that they've found their soul mates have no desire to be apart. In relationships where infidelity has proven to be the marital issue, a sabbatical is probably not a wise choice. Some couples already know that continual togetherness works best for them. Marriage is not a one-size-fits-all concept.

And I'm not advocating a one-size-fits-all solution. I'm advocating a broadening of our ideas about what's possible in the marriage of the future. What's universal about marriage is not the answer we find but the question we ask: How do we stay married to one person for a long time when the only constant in life is change? Today's messages promoting stricter divorce laws and a return to the traditional model for marriage focus on making it more difficult to divorce. Why not make it easier to stay married?

The place to begin is with a new definition. We need to view marriage as something other than an institution with all that word's constrictive connotations—public in character, traditional in practice, committed to the status quo. The goals of an institution invariably work against the needs of the individual.

We could view marriage as a laboratory, for example, with all that word's positive implications for breakthroughs and progress. With this definition, marriage becomes a safe place to challenge assumptions, remedy problems, risk new forms of relationship, legitimize experimentation. With this definition, marriage becomes a dynamic state of consciousness, a partnership in progress. Sabbaticals symbolize forward movement.

We could view marriage as an energy system, requiring individual solutions for individual landscapes. With this definition, couples attend to neglected resources, look for new and renewable sources of power, link the conventional with the unconventional, and sometimes reverse paths. When marriage becomes an energy system, the goal is a steady exchange of fresh air—comfort, warmth, and electricity year-round. Sabbaticals bring energy to a relationship.

We could view marriage as an artistic creation, where we invest as much time into composing a partnership as we invest in designing a home, where we're less concerned with adapting to an older model than in innovating a new one. With this definition, marriage becomes a canvas we approach with an open mind, a creative spirit, and a feeling the possibilities are inexhaustible. To bring the canvas to life with color and texture and emotional impact, we need to stay inspired, continually see the world anew. A long-term marriage then becomes an artistic evolution, an unfolding of the multiple selves that exist in us all. With each unfolding we can come to our marriage as a new individual—same body, changed spirit. During times we wish our partners were different people, instead of looking for someone else, first we should see if *we* can become someone else. Sabbaticals provide space to recreate ourselves, time to see the world anew.

We could view marriage as a mutual personal-growth contract, a launching pad to self-discovery rather than a utility ride to the grocery store. Just as corporations founder when they don't pay attention to the psychic needs of their employees, so do marriages. The increasing number of women in midlife filing for divorce, citing as a reason "self-development," should be a wake-up call to view independent acts in marriage not as threats but as the self-development women obviously need. When we see marriage as a personal-growth contract, we commit ourselves to nurturing our own development just as we nurture our partner's. Marriage then becomes an incubator not just for raising families but for realizing dreams, for seeking defining experiences that connect us to who we are at our core. As we age, these defining experiences become increasingly important if we are to continue to be engaged in life. One of the advantages of a sabbatical is that it is a defining experience focused on self-development.

Finally, we can view marriage as a journey of the spirit. My sister-in-law, who is a minister, says that in the 1970s when she helped couples write their wedding vows, many of them wanted to leave out the phrase "for worse." But as any long-married couple knows, it's holding on through the "for worse" that makes a marriage endure. Marriage can be great fun when the jobs are good, the kids are thriving, and the money is rolling in. The real test comes when life blindsides us at four in the morning, when our partners lose their jobs, their health, their hope, when we become depressed or grief-stricken, when the relationship ebbs, as it inevitably will. When we have to put our needs on hold because someone we love has a greater need, the challenge is not just staying the course but doing so with a modicum of grace. Since marriage sabbaticals can be a "for worse" for the partner left behind, they can also be one aspect of a couple's spiritual journey together.

Whatever definition resonates, we need to be more concerned with the essence of relationship and less concerned with form. We need to let go of outdated ideas about how marriage *ought* to be and, instead, look for new ideas about how marriage *might* be.

A marriage sabbatical sounds like a discordant idea to many couples, maybe most, in their early years together. It never occurred to me when I was twenty-one to ask the man with whom I planned to spend the rest of my life how much time alone he needed. It didn't occur to me to wonder about my needs for solitude, either. But as I've learned, the togetherness/separateness dynamic is critical in a relationship, so critical that when couples in love talk about where they want to live and whether they want children, they should add to the conversation: How much time alone do you need? How important is it to you to have solo adventures? How will you feel if I want to go off by myself for a while? In her 1972 treatise *The Future of Marriage*, researcher Jessie Bernard wrote that in the past, the goal for committed relationships was stability. In committed relationships of the future, she predicted, "the emphasis, among both men and women, may well be on freedom."

Sabbaticals are one way to build freedom into marriage, to give it softer edges and wider spaces—to transform it from within.

Looking back, some days I feel my experience was as surreal as a Remedios Varo painting. Did I really go away like that, I wonder, or did I just dream it? I who have been fear-ridden, guilt-laden most of my life, who have stayed married to one man for twenty-nine years, who pulled out of the workforce to stay home with my children when they were little—how is it I came to do something that others see as radical? Other days, I ask myself what all the fuss was about. Why was it such a big deal that I had to sit down to write a book on the subject?

At times like these, I think nothing changed. I still have arguments in my head, just new ones. My routines are the same: I write most days, teach one or two classes a semester. When there's a phone message from one of our sons, Jim returns the call when it's convenient for him to return it, whereas—even if a deadline is looming—I still respond to the call so quickly, so automatically, that the wires feel like an electronic umbilical cord.

Then there are days I think everything changed. We're moving from our home in the suburbs to a co-op in the city—shedding a shell. Jim leaves the house now as much as I do. The boys call him more often. A book on writers' retreats around the world is by my bed. I know I'll be going to them again, maybe every year for a month or so. The time will be mine to nurture myself, revalue my work, a time, also, to miss my husband, sharpen the chemical edge, remember not to take him or his love for granted. Next time, I hope I can go without guilt.

Everything changed and nothing changed. As I finish this book, one year later, these thoughts linger.

I left for three months, the same length of time as one summer vacation when I was a child—just a pixel, really, on the computer screen of a marriage. But during those months I fulfilled three dreams. Not long ago, Jim said, "I just want you to know it's fine with me if you want to do that nine-month master's program in New York. I know we'll be okay." The most important thing I learned by leaving was that it wasn't marriage that held me back. All the barriers to the life I wanted were within myself. And when I realized that, I fell in love with my husband all over again.

I never imagined that I could leave for three months yet stay married. When I discovered that I could, life began to feel wide again, expansive with time, rich with possibility, stretched out before me like the sage-scented fields of Montana.

BIBLIOGRAPHY

Memoirs

Bender, Sue. *Plain and Simple: A Woman's Journey to the Amish*. San Francisco: HarperSanFrancisco, 1989.

Fejes, Claire. *Cold Starry Night: An Alaska Memoir*. Fairbanks/Seattle: Epicenter Press, 1996.

_____. *People of the Noatak*. New York: Alfred A. Knopf, 1966.

Grumbach, Doris. *Fifty Days of Solitude*. Boston: Beacon Press, 1994.

Jaynes, Gregory. *Come Hell on High Water: A Really Sullen Memoir*. New York: North Point Press, 1997.

Katz, Jon. *Running to the Mountain: A Journey of Faith and Change*. New York: Villard, 1999.

Kempe, Margery. *The Book of Margery Kempe*. Translated by John Skinner. New York: Doubleday, 1998.

Lindbergh, Anne Morrow. *Gift from the Sea*. New York: Pantheon Books, 1955.

Sarton, May. *Journal of a Solitude*. New York: Norton, 1973.

_____. *Mrs. Stevens Hears a Mermaid Singing*. New York: Norton, 1965.

Shalom, Sabina. *A Marriage Sabbatical*. New York: Dodd, Mead, 1984.

Steinbeck, John. *Travels with Charley: In Search of America*. New York: Penguin Books, Viking, 1962.

West, Jessamyn. *Hide and Seek: A Continuing Journey*. New York: Harcourt Brace Jovanovich, 1973.

Biographies

Banner, Lois W. *Elizabeth Cady Stanton: A Radical for Woman's Rights*. Boston: Little, Brown and Company, 1980.

Berg, A. Scott. *Lindbergh*. New York: G. P. Putnam's Sons, 1998.

Blanch, Lesley. *The Wilder Shores of Love*. New York: Simon and Schuster, 1954.

Butler, Susan. *East to the Dawn: The Life of Amelia Earhart*. Reading, Mass.: Addison-Wesley, 1997.

Cowart, Jack, and Juan Hamilton, eds. *Georgia O'Keeffe: Art and Letters*. Boston: Little, Brown, 1987.

Eisler, Benita. *O'Keeffe and Stieglitz: An American Romance*. New York: Doubleday, 1991.

Goldstein, Donald M., and Katherine V. Dillon. *Amelia: The Centennial Biography of an Aviation Pioneer*. Washington, D.C.: Brasseys, 1997.

Griffith, Elisabeth. *In Her Own Right: The Life of Elizabeth Cady Stanton*. New York: Oxford University Press, 1984.

Hedrick, Joan D. *Harriet Beecher Stowe: A Life*. New York: Oxford University Press, 1994.

Johnston, Johanna. *Runaway to Heaven: The Story of Harriet Beecher Stowe*. New York: Doubleday and Co., 1963.

Lader, Lawrence, and Milton Meltzer. *Margaret Sanger: Pioneer of Birth Control*. New York: Thomas Y. Crowell Co., 1969.

Lane, Ann J. *To Herland and Beyond: The Life and Work of Charlotte Perkins Gilman*. New York: Pantheon Books, 1990.

Lisle, Laurie. *Portrait of an Artist: A Biography of Georgia O'Keeffe*. New York: Seaview Books, 1980.

Lovell, Mary S. *A Rage to Live: A Biography of Richard and Isabel Burton*. New York: W. W. Norton, 1998.

Milton, Joyce. *Loss of Eden: A Biography of Charles and Anne Morrow Lindbergh*. New York: HarperCollins, 1993.

Robinson, Roxana. *Georgia O'Keeffe: A Life*. New York: Harper and Row, 1989.

Whelan, Richard. *Alfred Stieglitz: A Biography*. Boston: Little, Brown, 1995.

Cultural History

Arios, Philippe, and Georges Duby, eds. *A History of Private Life.* Vols. 1–3. Cambridge: Harvard University Press, 1988.

Cahill, Thomas. *How the Irish Saved Civilization: The Untold Story of Ireland's Heroic Role from the Fall of Rome to the Rise of Medieval Europe.* New York: Doubleday, 1995.

Degler, Carl N. *At Odds: Women and the Family in America from the Revolution to the Present.* New York: Oxford University Press, 1980.

Gilman, Charlotte Perkins. *The Home: Its Work and Influence.* New York: McClure, Phillips, and Co., 1903.

Goodsell, Willystine. *A History of Marriage and the Family.* New York: The Macmillan Company, 1934.

Green, Harvey. *The Light of the Home: An Intimate View of the Lives of Women in Victorian America.* New York: Pantheon Books, 1983.

Hite, Shere. *Women and Love: A Cultural Revolution in Progress.* New York: Alfred A. Knopf, 1987.

Hochschild, Arlie, with Anne Machung. *The Second Shift: Working Parents and the Revolution at Home.* New York: Viking, 1989.

Labarge, Margaret Wad. *A Small Sound of the Trumpet: Women in Medieval Life.* Boston: Beacon Press, 1986.

Marsh, Margaret. "From Separation to Togetherness: The Social Construction of Domestic Space in American Suburbs, 1840–1915." *Journal of American History* 76 (2) (September 1989).

Murdock, George P. "World Ethnographic Sample." *American Anthropologist* 59 (1957).

Psychology and Mythology

Baruch, Grace, and Jeanne Brooks-Gunn, eds. *Women in Mid-Life.* New York: Plenum Press, 1984.

Bernard, Jessie. *The Future of Marriage.* New York: World Publishing, 1972.

Bettelheim, Bruno. *The Uses of Enchantment: The Meaning and Importance of Fairy Tales.* New York: Alfred A. Knopf, 1985.

Borysenko, Joan. *Guilt Is the Teacher, Love Is the Lesson.* New York: Warner Books, 1990.

Buchholz, Ester Schaler. *The Call of Solitude: Alonetime in a World of Attachment*. New York: Simon and Schuster, 1997.

Campbell, Joseph. *The Hero's Journey: The World of Joseph Campbell*. San Francisco: Harper and Row, 1990.

_____. *The Hero with a Thousand Faces*. Princeton: Princeton University Press, 1949.

_____. *Myths to Live By*. New York: Viking, 1972.

Carter, Betty, and Monica McGoldrick, eds. *The Changing Family Life Cycle*. 2d ed. New York: Gardner Press, 1988.

Chinen, Allan B. *Once upon a Midlife: Classic Stories and Mythic Tales to Illuminate the Middle Years*. Los Angeles: Jeremy P. Tarcher, 1992.

Csikszentmihalyi, Mihaly. *Creativity: Flow and the Psychology of Discovery and Invention*. New York: HarperCollins, 1996.

Drebing, Charles, et al. "The Dream in Midlife Women: Its Impact on Mental Health." *International Journal of Aging and Human Development* 40 (1) (1995).

Earle, John R., et al. "Women, Marital Status, and Symptoms of Depression in a Midlife National Sample." *Journal of Women and Aging* 10 (Winter 1998).

Erikson, Erik H. *Childhood and Society*. 2d ed. New York: W. W. Norton, 1963.

_____. *Dimensions of a New Identity: The 1973 Jefferson Lectures in the Humanities*. New York: W. W. Norton, 1974.

Gallagher, Winifred. *The Power of Place: How Our Surroundings Shape Our Thoughts, Emotions, and Actions*. New York: Poseidon Press, 1993.

Gilligan, Carol. *In a Different Voice: Psychological Theory and Women's Development*. Cambridge: Harvard University Press, 1982.

Gilligan, Carol, and Lyn Mikel Brown. *Meeting at the Crossroads: Women's Psychology and Girls' Development*. Cambridge: Harvard University Press, 1992.

Gottman, John M., and Nan Silver. *The Seven Principles for Making Marriage Work: A Practical Guide from the Country's Foremost Relationship Expert*. New York: Crown Publishers, 1999.

_____. *Why Marriages Succeed or Fail: What You Can Learn from the Breakthrough Research to Make Your Marriage Last.* New York: Simon and Schuster, 1994.

Heyn, Dalma. *Marriage Shock: The Transformation of Women into Wives.* New York: Villard, 1997.

Ingersoll-Dayton, Berit, et al. "Separateness and Togetherness: Interdependence over the Life Course in Japanese and American Marriages." *Journal of Social and Personal Relationships* 13 (3) (August 1996).

Johnson, Robert A. *She: Understanding Feminine Psychology.* New York: Harper, 1976.

Jung, C. G. *The Structure and Dynamics of the Psyche.* Vol. 8 of *The Collected Works.* New York: Pantheon Books, 1960.

Lowenthal, Marjorie Fiske, Majda Thurnher, and David Chiriboga. *Four Stages of Life: A Comparative Study of Women and Men Facing Transitions.* San Francisco: Jossey-Bass, 1975.

Maslow, Abraham H. *Toward a Psychology of Being.* 3d ed. New York: John Wiley and Sons, 1999.

McGoldrick, Monica. "Women and the Family Life Cycle." In Betty Carter and Monica McGoldrick, eds., *The Changing Family Life Cycle: A Framework for Family Therapy.* 2nd ed. New York: Gardner Press, 1988.

Miller, Jean Baker. *Toward a New Psychology of Women.* Boston: Beacon Press, 1976.

Pearson, Carol S. *The Hero Within: Six Archetypes We Live By.* San Francisco: Harper and Row, 1989.

Phelps, Ethel Johnston. *The Maid of the North: Feminist Folk Tales from Around the World.* New York: Holt, Rinehart and Winston, 1981.

Segaller, Stephen, and Merrill Berger. *The Wisdom of the Dream: The World of C. G. Jung.* Boston: Shambhala, 1989.

Sheehy, Gail. *New Passages: Mapping Your Life Across Time.* New York: Random House, 1995.

_____. *Passages: Predictable Crises of Adult Life.* New York: Dutton, 1976.

Sills, Judith. *Biting the Apple: Women Getting Wise About Love.* New York: Viking, 1996.

Stein, Murray. *In MidLife: A Jungian Perspective.* Dallas, Tex.: Spring Publications, 1983.

Wile, Daniel B. *After the Honeymoon: How Conflict Can Improve Your Relationship.* New York: John Wiley and Sons, 1988.

Woodman, Marion, and Elinor Dickson. *Dancing in the Flames: The Dark Goddess in the Transformation of Consciousness.* Boston: Shambhala Publications, 1996.

Philosophy and Religion

Ariel, David S. *Spiritual Judaism: Restoring Heart and Soul to Jewish Life.* New York: Hyperion, 1998.

Buber, Martin. *I and Thou.* New York: Macmillan, 1970.

Heschel, Abraham Joshua. *The Sabbath: Its Meaning for Modern Man.* New York: Farrar, Straus and Giroux, 1951.

Kierkegaard, Søren. *The Sickness unto Death: A Christian Psychological Exposition for Edification and Awakening.* London: Penguin Books, 1989.

Miles, Sian, ed. *Simone Weil: An Anthology.* New York: Weidenfeld and Nicolson, 1986.

Montaigne. *The Complete Essays of Montaigne.* Translated by Donald M. Frame. Stanford: Stanford University Press, 1943.

Moore, Thomas. *SoulMates: Honoring the Mysteries of Love and Relationship.* New York: HarperCollins, 1994.

Nouwen, Henri J. M. *Clowning in Rome: Reflections on Solitude, Celibacy, Prayer, and Contemplation.* Garden City, N.Y.: Image Books, 1979.

Rilke, Rainer Maria. *Letters to a Young Poet.* Rev. ed. Translated by M. D. Herter Norton. New York: W. W. Norton, 1954.

Russell, Bertrand. *Marriage and Morals.* New York: Horace Liveright, 1929.

Saiving, Valerie. "The Human Situation: A Feminine View." In Carol Christ and Judith Plaskow, eds., *Womanspirit Rising: A Feminist Reader in Religion.* San Francisco: Harper & Row, 1979; reprinted from the *Journal of Religion* (Chicago: University of Chicago Press, April 1960).

Thoreau, Henry David. *Walden or, Life in the Woods.* New York: New American Library, 1980.

Fiction

Berg, Elizabeth. *The Pull of the Moon.* New York: Random House, 1996.

Colwin, Laurie. *Happy All the Time.* New York: HarperPerennial, 1978.

Lessing, Doris. "To Room Nineteen." In *Doris Lessing Stories.* New York: Alfred A. Knopf, 1978.

Lewis, Sinclair. *Main Street.* New York: New American Library, 1961.

Tyler, Anne. *Ladder of Years.* New York: Alfred A. Knopf, 1995.

ACKNOWLEDGMENTS

Writing a book is a journey, too, filled with fear and hope and paradox. It's a solo journey for which one needs others. At the same time, it's a self-absorbed isolation that means neglecting those you need. For their help—and in some cases, forgiveness—deepest thanks go to:

Karen Koman, for convincing me the subject was a book and coming up with the title;

My agent Lisa Bankoff and my editor Marnie Cochran, for being dream allies—dedicated publishing pros and delightful women;

The Ucross Foundation of Wyoming, Hedgebrook of Washington State, and Arin Waddell for providing the glorious space to write, for giving me my sabbatical;

The women—and men—whose stories fill these pages, for inspiring me and keeping me inspired;

The many professionals who shared their time and insights, and particularly the four who shared them over and over again: Alice Brand-Bartlett, psychoanalyst and Edward Greenwood Professor at the Karl Menninger School of Psychiatry in Topeka, Kansas; Bill Bumberry, Ph.D., clinical psychologist in St. Louis, Missouri; John Gottman, Ph.D., professor of psychology at the University of Washington and co-director of The Gottman Institute in Seattle; and Patricia Vesey-McGrew, Jungian analyst in Boston, Massachusetts;

Friends and colleagues Jane Ferry, Sally Howald, Kit Jenkins, Joan Johnson, Jane Peters, Roberta Brown Root, and Karen Scheeter, for their careful readings, honest feedback, and joyful company;

Martha Baker, for editing two drafts in their entirety with a sharp eye and a warm heart;

ASJA members Murray Bloom, Dan Carlinksy, Florence Isaacs, Sallie Randolph, and Victoria Secunda; and Rosemary Danielle and Doris Helmering, for veteran advice along the way;

Bill Olbricht at Washington University's Olin Library and Ellen Eliceiri and her staff at the Eden-Webster Library for invaluable research assistance;

Marco Pavia, the production editor at Perseus, for his kindness and patience with my continual and last-minute changes;

Melissa Griggs, Donna Shatz, Ann Wald, and my sisters-in-law Patricia, Beckie, and Mia for support when I most needed it;

My brother Chris, for being a wonderful editor, advisor, and friend;

My parents, for honoring the solitude I needed and taking pride in what I needed it for;

My sons Eric and Brian, whose candid critiques of an early draft pushed me to write a better one, whose exasperated refrains of "aren't you finished *yet?*" prodded me to the last page, whose laughter and love calmed me down, lifted me up, and kept me sane;

And to Jim, for believing the book could make a difference and for acting on that belief, reading countless pages, listening countless hours, offering ideas, walks, meals, time-management plans, for not once complaining that in exposing my life I was exposing his, for actually coming up with embarrassing moments from his life to include, for helping me stay focused so I could finish, for helping me live with insecurity so I could let it go.